WICHITA

VISIONS FROM THE HEARTLAND

AD ASTRA PER ASPERA

EATON

BY HOWARD INGLISH

BOARD OF TRADE CENTER

WICHITA

VISIONS FROM THE HEARTLAND

by
Howard Inglish

Corporate Profiles by
Eric Allison

Art Direction by
Brian Groppe

Produced in Cooperation
with the Wichita Area
Chamber of Commerce

TOWERY PUBLISHING, INC.

page 1 & 2 photo credits:

BACKGROUND PHOTO:
WALTER DEPTULA

PAGE 1 INSET PHOTOS:
TOP:
HENRY NELSON

BOTTOM:
DAVID DINELL

PAGE 2 INSET PHOTOS:
TOP ROW, LEFT TO RIGHT:
DAVID DINELL
PAUL BOWEN
VIC BILSON
Courtesy WICHITA RIVER FESTIVAL / LARRY FLEMING

SECOND ROW, LEFT TO RIGHT:
Courtesy WICHITA SYMPHONY SOCIETY
PAUL BOWEN
PAUL BOWEN
DAVID DINELL

THIRD ROW, LEFT TO RIGHT:
KEVIN FOX /STUDIO 151
RICARDO REITMEYER
KEVIN FOX / STUDIO 151
PAUL BOWEN

BOTTOM ROW, LEFT TO RIGHT:
Courtesy WICHITA RIVER FESTIVAL / LARRY FLEMING
Courtesy WICHITA RIVER FESTIVAL / LARRY FLEMING
Courtesy THE BOEING COMPANY
VIC BILSON

ACKNOWLEDGMENTS

MY PARTICIPATION IN THE PROJECT, *Wichita: Visions from the Heartland*, HAS BEEN ONE OF THE most intriguing and challenging in my career. As the photography editor, I looked at more than 36,000 slides and prints over a six-month period. From the group of companies, organizations, and outstanding photographers who participated, approximately 1,900 photographs were selected for consideration, and more than 400 of those appear in the book.

In writing the essay, there were a number of key people who gave their advice and assistance. First and foremost, I would like to thank Kimberly Cott, who somehow found the time during her senior year at Bethel College to assist me in collecting information for the essay and in organizing the photographs. I also want to thank Patty Towery, my editor on this project, for her guidance, direction, and patience. And I would like to thank my parents for their understanding of the time commitments involved.

Others I would like to thank for their important advice and assistance are Stacey Boothe, Randy Brown, Gene Dickinson, Bill Ellington, Cindy Mines, Henry Nelson, Tammy Steinert, and Connie White.

This book, more than any I have seen, best reflects the true spirit of Wichita, and I am proud to have been a part of its creation.

—HOWARD INGLISH

LIBRARY OF CONGRESS CATALOGING-IN-PUBLICATION DATA

Inglish, Howard.
  Wichita: Visions from the Heartland / by Howard Inglish;
corporate profiles by Eric Allison; art director, Brian Groppe.
    p.   cm. — (Urban tapestry series)
Includes index.
ISBN 1-881096-05-X
1. Wichita (Kan.)—Pictorial works.   2. Wichita (Kan.)—Industries.
3. Wichita (Kan.)—Civilization.   I. Allison, Eric James, 1953-   .   II. Title.   III. Series.
F689.W6I54   1993
978.1'86—dc20   93-40266
                                                                                                         CIP

TOWERY Publishing, Inc.
1835 Union Avenue
Suite 142
Memphis, TN 38104

URBAN
TAPESTRY
SERIES
TOWERY
PUBLISHING, INC.

PUBLISHER: J. Robert Towery
EDITORIAL DIRECTORS: Patricia M. Towery
                                  David Dawson
SENIOR EDITORS: Michael C. James
                                  Ken Woodmansee
ARTICLES EDITOR: Allison Jones Simonton
ASSISTANT ART DIRECTOR: Anne Castrodale
TECHNICAL DIRECTOR: William H. Towery
COPY EDITOR: Stinson Liles
CONTRIBUTING EDITORS: Janis Friesen
                                  Frank Garofalo

Contents

"There is a special place in every city that people are drawn to—a place that helps define a city's character and captivates all who experience its sights and sounds. In Wichita, that magical spot is found downtown, where the winding Arkansas and Little Arkansas rivers gracefully converge to form a beautiful backdrop beneath the rising skyline. Indeed, the rivers are the true lifeblood of our city and a constant reminder of Wichita's innate allure."

A look at the corporations, businesses, professional groups, and community service organizations that have made this book possible.

HOWARD INGLISH

The "W" on the north side of the West Bank Stage amphitheater beckons Wichitans to climb the hill and enjoy open-air concerts each spring.

FOREWORD

WICHITA IS AN "ALL-AMERICA CITY." YOU WOULD EXPECT a comment like that from the Chairman of the Chamber of Commerce, but we are proud of the national recognition our city has received for its spirit of entrepreneurship and volunteerism. To illustrate the recognition our city has received, you hold in your hands solid proof that we are fortunate to live in an area that offers a high quality of life.

This book, *Visions from the Heartland*, is sponsored by The Chamber in the belief that it will serve as a graphic reminder of what a great city Wichita really is. In addition to outstanding photography, *Visions from the Heartland* profiles some of America's finest corporate citizens and outlines the spirit and philosophy many of these citizens have demonstrated in serving our community so well.

We of The Chamber sincerely hope you enjoy owning and giving *Visions from the Heartland* so that it will serve as a reminder of our fine city for many years to come.

Brian E. Barents
1993 CHAIRMAN OF THE BOARD
WICHITA AREA CHAMBER OF COMMERCE

A City of Celebrations

THERE IS A SPECIAL PLACE IN EVERY CITY THAT people are drawn to—a place that helps define a city's character and captivates all who experience its sights and sounds. In Wichita, that magical spot is found downtown, where the winding Arkansas and Little Arkansas rivers gracefully converge to form a beautiful backdrop beneath the rising skyline. Indeed, the rivers are the true lifeblood of our city and a constant reminder of Wichita's innate allure.

Every May we celebrate our rich heritage at the high-spirited Wichita River Festival. The community-wide event, with its block-party feel, is an exhilarating time for all of us to reunite, relax, laugh, and let off a little steam. More importantly, it's a time when Wichitans from every walk of life become "family."

Hot air balloons dot the blue, cloudless sky with a smattering of vivid colors, ice cream socials delight children and adults alike, and sand castle and tug-of-war contests inspire a bit of friendly competition between neighbors. There is also a Treasure Island hunt that brings out the pirate in everyone and a "Walk With Dorothy," featuring Gino Salerno's hand-carved *Wizard of Oz* characters in O.J. Watson Park.

The final Saturday is capped off by a flyover of B1-Bs and F-16s from McConnell Air Force Base, followed with an open-air concert by the Wichita Symphony and a spectacular fireworks show courtesy of Wichita-based Austin Fireworks, one of the world's best recognized pyrotechnics companies. This brilliant, thundering display over the Arkansas River is viewed by an estimated 100,000 spectators. And each year, all of us sitting on the riverbanks—our senses overloaded with 10 days worth of wonderful sights, smells, and sounds—are delighted once again to feel a surge of excitement as the bursting colors paint multiple, abstract images in the clear Kansas sky.

The River Festival is a perfect prelude to summer, when the sunsets over golden wheat fields are picture-postcard perfect, and

COURTESY WSU MEDIA RESOURCE CENTER / JIM MEYER

the seemingly endless variety of outdoor activities makes our weekends fly by. One of the real treats of the season is the annual Jazz Festival at the Century II complex. Such greats as Count Basie, Dizzy Gillespie, Ray Charles, Wynton Marsalis, Pat Metheny, B.B King, and Dr. John have graced the stage with their infinite talents, filling the night with the scintillating strains of their music.

Yet for many of us, going out on the town during the warmer months translates to, "Let's go to the game."

For a sports fan, there is hardly a better experience than watching baseball on warm summer nights at Lawrence-Dumont Stadium, with the downtown skyline in the background. The stadium is home to the Wichita Wranglers, a AA team that won the 1992 Texas League championship, and to the National Baseball Congress, founded in the 1930s by Raymond "Hap" Dumont. The NBC is the premier amateur baseball tournament in the nation and has seen such major leaguers as Satchel Paige, Tom Seaver, Roger Clemens, Barry Bonds, and dozens of other stars join in the annual August event.

Indeed, this is a big baseball town, and has become even more so since Wichita State coach Gene Stephenson revived the school's baseball program in 1978. The crusty Stephenson is a master recruiter and superb game coach who is known for calling the unorthodox pitch, hit, or run signal that leaves players on the other team standing in their tracks. He came to WSU from Oklahoma in the spring of 1977 to start a baseball program with no players or field to play on. Yet from his leaky office beneath the west stands of the football stadium, and with one of the smallest budgets in college baseball, Stephenson embarked on what many would view as an impossible dream.

The team played at different facilities around town the first two seasons, then began playing on its own field in 1979, with seating limited to small bleachers atop a flat-bed truck. But, oh how things have changed over the past decade.

Today, the team draws sell-out crowds to Eck Stadium-Tyler Field—one of the nation's top college baseball facilities. And the

WICHITA'S SKYLINE SHINES ACROSS THE BIG ARKANSAS RIVER DURING THE RIVER FESTIVAL. THE FINAL NIGHT OF THE 10-DAY FESTIVAL ATTRACTS A ROLLICKING CROWD OF MORE THAN 100,000 PEOPLE.

Shockers now lay claim to being one of the country's leading college baseball programs; in the past six years, they have been to the NCAA College World Series five times, and have played for the collegiate championship in three of those five appearances, winning the trophy in 1989.

However, there's more to summer than watching the games; Wichitans like to join in the action. You'll find us lining up for the exhilarating rides at Joyland Amusement Park, catching the waves at Barnacle Bill's FantaSea Park, or practicing our golf and baseball swings at Sports World. Some of us take leisurely strolls in one of the wildlife parks or along the rivers. Others ride the paddle boats at O.J. Watson Park, bicycle on some of the city's 100 miles of bike paths, or play tennis at the

Ralph Wulz Riverside Tennis Center. Then again, we might be headed for a Ballet in the Park production, or simply admiring some of the 120 outdoor sculptures that dot the city's landscape.

And we can't forget the summertime weather—an attraction in its own right—which produces an abundance of awesome sights: spectacular thunder and lightning storms, sensational and loud in their fury as they roll across the prairie; and breathtaking, radiant sunsets that light up the open plains as if an artist had tossed a dozen hues of orange, red, yellow, pink, and purple onto a wide blue canvas.

As cooler weather rolls around we move at a brisk pace trying to keep up with the hectic lineup of

festivals and events, including the Old Town Chili Cookoff, the Black Arts Festival, Pow Wows at the Mid-America All-Indian Center, Oktoberfest, the Night of the Living Zoo Halloween gala, the Wichita Winter Fest, and the annual Christmas Parade.

Sports enthusiasts enjoy the thrills of Wichita State's tension-packed basketball games at Henry Levitt Arena—or "The Round House" as it is affectionately known. The Shockers have gone to the NCAA tournament seven times, and the 1965 team—led by All-American Dave Stallworth—played in The Final Four. Teams of the 1980s produced pro stars Antoine Carr, Cliff Levingston,

and Xavier McDaniel. Another famous Wichita roundballer is Lynette Woodard, who gained national fame in the Olympics and as the first female member of the world-famous Harlem Globetrotters.

Also during the fall and winter months, more than 8,000 fans consistently pack the Kansas Coliseum to cheer for the Wichita Wings, the most successful and oldest indoor professional soccer team in the country. Minor league hockey, with the Wichita Thunder, and professional tennis, with the Wichita Advantage, also keep sports fans enthralled.

And year-round, the ever-expanding Sedgwick County

Zoo—honored with a number of national awards over the past decade for its exhibits and breeding programs—delights old and young alike. Animals are grouped by geographic regions in natural habitats, such as the African Veldt, Asian Steppes, and a tropical rain forest. The zoo's newest attraction—the recently opened, 11-acre, North American Prairie Exhibit—also places emphasis on natural settings, allowing unobstructed viewing for the more than 400,000 patrons who visit the zoo each year.

But we don't have to go to the zoo to see wildlife. In the spring, when the flowers of the prairie add

hues reflecting almost every color of the rainbow, animals of all kinds—deer, raccoons, rabbits, bobcats—dash across backyards and through the city's 330-acre park system anchored in the Riverside area. And thanks to the multitude of green trees and open, grassy playgrounds dotting neighborhoods throughout town, Wichita retains the lush, pastoral appearance that attracted the city's earliest settlers over 125 years ago.

"One of the important things our forefathers did was to preserve the parks and open spaces along the river and in the middle of town," says Frank Smith, city parks director. "This achievement remains today a major landmark in the city." ▶

"THE PEERLESS PRINCESS OF THE PLAINS"

WHEN J.R. MEAD FIRST ESTABLISHED A trading post here on the banks of the Arkansas River in 1868, this sleepy frontier area was inhabited mainly by traders and roaming bands of Native Americans. At that time, only a few campfires dotted the landscape where, yes, the buffalo too did roam.

The topography of the area was marked by the rivers, which drained a sloping valley in the center of the territory that would later become Kansas. There were rolling hills to the east, while to the west and north vast plains stretched as far as the eye could see. But despite the formidable challenges before them, Mead and a handful of other pioneers rolled up their sleeves, and within a year, the first church and school were organized. By 1870, Wichita—named after the Wichita Indian Tribe—was incorporated as a city. Two years later, Col. Marsh Murdock founded *The Wichita Eagle*, the state's largest newspaper.

Spurred by the influx of cowboys driving hundreds of thousands of cattle out of Texas north along the Chisholm Trail, early Wichita was indeed a rough and tumble cowtown. It was a city where Wyatt Earp, William "Buffalo Bill" Cody, and Bat Masterson walked the dusty streets, enforcing their own brand of law and order on the untamed Western frontier.

Just west of the river, the area known as Delano was especially wild and wooly, and all manner of vice could be found in the town's boisterous taverns, dance halls, and houses of ill-repute.

Saloon owner Rowdy Joe Lowe was one of Delano's most infamous characters, and his establishment was known throughout the West for its rip-roaring good times. Though Delano wasn't considered a gunfighter's town, Rowdy Joe and rival saloon owner Red Beard once dueled in the middle of town beneath the hot

August sun. Red later died from his wounds, and Rowdy Joe had to leave Delano under the cover of night.

But by the 1880s, the rambunctious cowtown elements were fading, and Wichita was fast becoming the commerce center of Kansas. The decade brought electricity to the homes in the Riverside neighborhood and the first electric trolleys to the bustling downtown streets. Successful businessmen built expensive two- and three-story homes in the Riverside and Midtown neighborhoods, and later throughout the rolling pastures in College Hill.

East of the river near the Santa Fe tracks, the grand Eaton Hotel was built in 1887. Thirteen years later it became part of the city's folklore when fervent temperance crusader Carry Nation—armed with a steel hatchet and an iron will—made her famous saloon raid, smashing the hotel's bar, furniture, mirrors, liquor bottles, and, for good measure, a nude painting entitled *Cleopatra at the Roman Bath* by Wichitan John Noble. Her campaign against demon rum, tobacco, scantily clad women, and most other kinds of sin gained her fame from coast to coast.

During the 1880s, speculators from as far away as England were buying land in Wichita based on reports of the city's explosive growth, and it was not long before Wichita trailed only New York and Kansas City in its number of real estate transactions. But as the decade came to a close, overbuilding and rampant land speculation caused Wichita's economy to crash. It would prove to be the first of many boom and bust cycles that the city would endure. However, as the new century approached, Wichitans once again set about building their city, their dreams, and their futures.

One indicator of the city's resurgence was the establishment of the area's first institutions of higher education. Wichita State University—originally Fairmont College when it was founded in 1895—was the first municipal college west of the Mississippi River. Friends University, founded by Quakers in 1895, also provided the area's residents with quality educational opportunities. And after the turn of the century, Kansas Newman College added its name to the impressive list of academic institutions in the city.

As if to give its blessing to the peaceful merging of the waters, the 44-foot sculpture, *Keeper of the Plains*, stands in front of the Mid-America All-Indian Center at the confluence of the Big Arkansas and Little Arkansas rivers.

For centuries, Native American tribes raced across the Kansas plains hunting the hundreds of thousands of buffalo that once roamed the West. After a hunt, many tribes rested in the area where the two rivers meet, and some set up temporary camps for the summer. This Charles M. Russell painting, *Indian Buffalo Hunt*, (left) is in the permanent collection of the Wichita Art Museum.

A lot has changed in the past century. Today, Wichita State is the third largest university in Kansas with an enrollment of over 15,000. The school is recognized nationally for its aviation and engineering programs, as well as its beautiful, 330-acre campus featuring an 18-hole golf course and one of the country's most extensive outdoor sculpture collections. And both Friends University and Kansas Newman—each with an enrollment of 1,600 students—have achieved a nationwide reputation for their high academic standards.

But even more importantly, the entrepreneurial path laid by Frank and Dan Carney of Pizza Hut, Tom Devlin and Frank Barton of Rent-A-Center, and Jack DeBoer of Residence Inns has dramatically transformed the city's business climate. Today, thousands of small and medium-sized companies have sprouted throughout town, adding new diversity to our growing list of successful businesspeople. Indeed, not since the post-World War II years has downtown Wichita seen so many new endeavors—showing what can happen when Wichita spirit is mixed with commitment and elbow-grease.

Old Town is a perfect example. Comprised of a dozen square blocks of turn-of-the-century warehouses on the eastern edge of downtown, this area of the city has seen dozens of small, independent retail operations, arts and crafts stores, and restaurants and clubs open their doors in the past few years. The relocation of the downtown transit center to the edge of Old Town, and the reintroduction of restored trolleys to downtown Wichita after a 60-year absence, also have brought more accessibility and excitement to the area.

Mary Wright and her family have owned the Old Mill Tasty Shop on East Douglas since 1982. It's the oldest restaurant in the Old Town area, dating back to 1932, when Otto and Erna Woermke first opened the diner's doors. Now that Old Town is thriving, Wright has extended business hours and is thrilled that new storefronts are opening up so fast it seems "just like a boomtown."

"I think our generation remembers what downtown used to be—when coming here as a child was exciting," Wright says. "I remember being fascinated at seeing my reflection in the blue glass of the old Russell Stover candy store and by all the windows decorated magically for Christmas. These are experiences that my generation shares—memories that are in our hearts and our minds—and we want our grandchildren to have similar experiences."

Rich Vliet, one of the newest developers opening businesses in Old Town, also has an interesting perspective of this burgeoning entertainment district. "The vision I and others have is that this area is rich in history and color and needs preservation. It requires tenacity and a willingness to take risks, but it's gratifying that we're attracting so many people with the variety and quality of the new businesses opening in Old Town."

Along with Wichita's ever-growing economy, the city's cultural amenities have blossomed as well. Only a few blocks away from the river at the edge of downtown are many of our most popular museums, collectively known as the Museums on the River. They consist of Botanica–The Wichita Gardens, the Wichita Art Museum, the Old Cowtown Museum, and the Mid-America All-Indian Center. Other popular cultural sites include the First

National Black Historical Society of Kansas, the Children's Museum of Wichita, the Wichita Omnisphere and Science Center, and the Wichita-Sedgwick County Historical Museum, housed in the original city hall building completed in 1892.

The Mid-America All-Indian Center is site of the unofficial Wichita symbol, Blackbear Bosin's breathtaking, 44-foot *Keeper of the Plains* statue.

Each year, people from all 50 states and dozens of foreign countries visit Wichita's nationally praised Old Cowtown Museum. You won't find gunfights here, but you will find Wichitans dressed in 1870s outfits, reenacting the lives of the city's settlers. The small prairie town is so authentic that it has been used as a movie set for *Sarah, Plain and Tall—Skylark*, starring Glenn Close.

Near the city's center, the Wichita Art Museum is known for its Murdock Collection of American art, as well as its permanent collection of Western art, featuring works by Charles M. Russell and Frederic Remington. One can sit on the museum's patio next to the outdoor sculptures and watch couples take relaxed canoe rides on the Little Arkansas.

Wichita has a long tradition in the performing arts, as well. The city's stage and theatre community has produced stars such as Hattie McDaniel, a blues singer who gained fame in the 1940s with her Oscar-winning role as Mammy in *Gone With the Wind*, and Carla Burns, a winner of the Laurence Olivier Award in London for her role as Queenie in *Showboat.* Others include television and movie actor Don Johnson and Kirstie Alley of *Cheers* fame.

But no one has contributed more to the promotion of Wichita's performing arts than Mary Jane Teall, who started the Experimental Theatre in 1946 and the Wichita Community Theatre in the 1950s. "I learned to never underestimate Wichita audiences," Teall states. "Right after World War II, there wasn't much here in terms of theatre. But Wichitans have consistently demonstrated they appreciate quality entertainment."

Today, there are year-round theatre groups such as the Wichita Community Theatre, the University Theatre at WSU, and the Wichita Center for the Arts, which is the city's oldest arts organization, offering instruction in the visual and performing arts. And every summer we are treated to productions by half-a-dozen community and professional theatre groups. This menu is headed up by Music Theatre of Wichita summer performances.

The Wichita Symphony Orchestra, founded in 1944, is one of the most successful orchestras in the country. Able to draw on its national reputation and a unique alliance with Wichita State University, the symphony has consistently been able to attract world-class permanent conductors, such as Zuohuang Chen, the symphony's current maestro.

Truly, Wichita's strength as a cultural center is evident in its wide range of amenities. Add to that a heritage of volunteerism and entrepreneurship, a strong, diverse economy, and tradition of religious faith anchored by more than 500 churches, and you get a city with the steadiest growth of any mid-sized metropolis in the south central plains. ▶

A WINDOW IN A BUILDING OF THE OLD COWTOWN MUSEUM FURNISHES A KEYHOLE VIEW OF LIFE IN 1880S WICHITA.

A Spirit of Vision and Dreams

WICHITA HAS AT VARIOUS TIMES LAID CLAIM to being the tractor and broomcorn capitals of the world, and for several decades leaders promoted the name, "The Peerless Princess of The Plains." But it is as "Air Capital of the World" that the city's claim to fame is now solidly attached.

Wichita's long aviation heritage began in earnest in the 1920s when air industry pioneers Clyde Cessna, Lloyd Stearman, and Walter Beech got their fledgling manufacturing operations off the ground. Just before the Great Depression, Wichita had 16 companies producing one-fourth of all the nation's commercial airplanes.

World War II brought a huge expansion to Wichita's aircraft manufacturing industry. Today, leading aviation employers in the Wichita area include Boeing Wichita, Learjet, Cessna Aircraft, and Beech Aircraft Company.

Boeing Wichita (the successor to Lloyd Stearman's venture) has been the largest employer in a six-state region for the past decade. With its 1,100 acres, 11 million square feet of facilities, and 15,000 employees, the Wichita plant is the largest single-site aerospace manufacturing center in the world. Boeing Wichita produces most of the frames and structural work for the Boeing 727s and 757s, as well as three-fourths of the components for the popular 737s.

But it was not only aviation that established Wichita as a center of industry; many other Wichita businesses have made their mark too. The Coleman Company name has become known worldwide since W. C. Coleman produced his first lantern in 1914. More than 50 million lanterns and millions of pieces of camping and outdoor recreational equipment have been manufactured by the Wichita company for shipment around the globe. In the early 1900s, innova-tive business leader A.A. Hyde invented a soothing product that during flu season was to become a household word—Mentholatum. And in 1921, two enterprising Wichitans established the prototype for quick-service restaurants when they launched the White Castle hamburger chain in the city.

Nearly 40 years later, in 1958,

THE ORIGINAL PIZZA HUT

Frank and Dan Carney borrowed $600 and established their first Pizza Hut in a small red-bricked building that has since been moved to the campus of Wichita State University. Pizza Hut, Inc., owned by PepsiCo, still maintains its international headquarters in Wichita.

The favorable business climate in Wichita has seen the rise of many other important homegrown companies, such as Chance Manufacturing, the nation's largest designer and manufacturer of amusement rides; Koch Industries, the nation's second largest privately held company, with oil and gas holdings throughout the world; and Sheplers, the world's largest Western wear store. In recent years the services of Brite Voice Systems, Lone Star Steakhouse, and Beauty Warehouse have also been promoted nationally from their Wichita base.

And in the area of financial services, Wichita's Fourth Financial Corp., with large holdings in Kansas and Oklahoma and assets in excess of $5.8 billion, is one of the Midwest's largest bank holding companies.

But there's also the matter of the city's link to the land. Except for an occasional off-year, Kansas consistently has been the leading wheat producing state, and the 1993 harvest was once again first in the nation. There is a good deal of farming within the Wichita city limits, and it's still front page headlines when wind, rain, hail, or drought threaten the area's wheat crop. ▶

IT WAS LAND THAT ENTICED THOUSANDS OF IMMIGRANTS ACROSS AN OCEAN AND HALF A CONTINENT TO THE PRAIRIES OF CENTRAL KANSAS. THE SETTLERS OF THE 1800S BROUGHT THEIR OWN VARIETY OF WHEAT WITH THEM, AND TODAY KANSAS IS CONSISTENTLY THE LEADING WHEAT-PRODUCER IN THE NATION.

IN 1958 THE CARNEY BROTHERS OF WICHITA BORROWED $600 FROM THEIR MOTHER TO START A SMALL PIZZERIA CALLED PIZZA HUT IN THIS RED BRICK BUILDING, NOW LOCATED ON THE CAMPUS OF WICHITA STATE UNIVERSITY. TODAY, THE RED-ROOFED PIZZA HUTS ARE POPPING UP ALL OVER THE WORLD, BUT THE COMPANY STILL MAINTAINS ITS HEADQUARTERS IN WICHITA.

PRODUCTS MADE IN WICHITA ARE known worldwide, but none more than those made by the city's four major aircraft manufacturing firms. A Learjet (TOP) soars over rugged terrain, while Air Force One (MIDDLE), which has all its special modifications and remodeling completed in Boeing Wichita facilities, climbs above Mount Rushmore. A Cessna Citation X business jet (BOTTOM) speeds to its destination, and a Beechjet 400A (OPPOSITE) is captured over the downtown Wichita skyline.

▶ COURTESY LEARJET INC.

▶ COURTESY BOEING WICHITA

▶ COURTESY CESSNA AIRCRAFT

▶ PAUL BOWEN

"An All-America City"

DESPITE OUR HISTORY AS A PROGRESSIVE, visionary city, Wichita has, throughout the years, battled an inferiority complex. Perhaps that's because some unenlightened folks from other parts of the country still think of the city as a "cowtown," complete with tumbleweeds, cowboys, and streets paved with dust.

Consider the recent experience of Larry Hatteberg, a nationally recognized photojournalist and news anchor with Wichita's KAKE-TV. Hatteberg recalled a conversation with a New York television producer.

PRODUCER: "Do you have an airport out there we can fly into?"

HATTEBERG: "Well as a matter of fact, we do. But you know, I'm glad you asked. You see you have to call ahead of time to let them know you're coming. That's because sometimes the ponies get loose from the reservation nearby and we have to go out and round 'em up so the planes can land."

The producer, who swallowed Hatteberg's tale hook, line, and sinker, responded: "Well, OK. I'm glad you told me. Do they have a phone out there so I can call them?"

Fortunately, the unenlightened quickly change their perception about Wichita after spending just a short time here. In fact, it doesn't take long for those new to Wichita to be taken in by the city's unmistakable magic.

That "magic" was acknowledged in 1993 when the National Civic League named Wichita an "All-America City" in recognition of its community-wide approach to combatting urban problems with unique solutions. The judges for the award were especially impressed with Wichita's spirit of volunteerism, citing recent programs by neighborhood associations and government agencies that helped provide new housing for many of the city's low-income families.

But the spirit of helping those in need has always been important

▶ HENRY NELSON

in Wichita. Whether that notion is handed down from the strong religious traditions of Kansas pioneers or is a part of the farming tradition of helping a neighbor rebuild a barn blown down by a spring storm, it is one of the shining attributes of this city built along the rivers.

In 1934, that spirit was demonstrated by Dr. Martin F. Palmer, who founded the Institute of Logopedics—now known as Heartspring—to treat children with multiple disabilities. Rainbows United, founded in the early 1970s by Wichitan Linda Weir-Energen, is also known for its work with developmentally handicapped children.

And the Wichita spirit has made the local Big Brothers and Sisters organization one of the most successful in the nation. Nick Mork, who has directed the Wichita chapter since 1971, attributes the city's fund-raising success to a "small-town heart with big-city resources. Even people who come here from other cities find themselves helping make life a little better for those who are less fortunate."

But the tradition of helping others was most evident on April 26, 1991, when a devastating tornado—with wind speeds of more than 200 miles an hour—carved a path through the edge of town, roared across McConnell Air Force Base narrowly missing the B-1B planes stationed there, and

WICHITA'S OLD TOWN GETS INTO THE HOLIDAY SPIRIT WITH A DISPLAY OF YULETIDE FINERY. THE EATON HOTEL (LEFT), BUILT IN THE CITY'S FIRST MAJOR BOOM DAYS OF 1887, IS EXPECTED TO BE RENOVATED INTO A RETAIL AND OFFICE COMPLEX, RETURNING THE STRUCTURE TO THE GRANDEUR IT HAD MORE THAN A CENTURY AGO.

IN THE 1990 CENSUS, THE POPULATION OF WICHITA SURPASSED THE 300,000 MARK, WHILE THE POPULATION FOR THE METROPOLITAN AREA REACHED HALF A MILLION. WICHITA IS NOW THE LARGEST CITY BETWEEN KANSAS CITY AND DENVER.

then went on to destroy several hundred homes in suburban areas and tragically left 17 dead.

Most of us wondered how those hardest hit would recover from the disaster. But businesses and individuals pitched in to house and feed several thousand Wichitans left temporarily homeless. Countless other volunteers

helped methodically comb over hundreds of acres hoping to find a treasured photo, a family Bible, or any other special personal item that might boost morale.

Thankfully, such a storm has been a rarity during the city's history. Today, you can drive the path of the tornado, and except for a few broken trees, these neighbor-

hoods look like those half-a-mile away that were spared. And there i a snap to the step and a gleam in the eye of these rugged individuals who recovered and prevailed.

That's why city-wide events like the annual Wichita River Festival are celebrated with such vigor. It's a chance to reflect on all of the things the community has accomplished in the past as well as

opportunity to look with xcitement towards all that is yet store for the city.

Perhaps Elma Broadfoot—Wichita's first elected woman ayor—said it best about this ver-changing heartland city: Wichita is blessed with a truly nique and wonderful blend of ntrepreneurial and volunteer pirit. I think it goes back to our early history. We have a base of community values here—hard work, determination, a strong sense of family, and a dedication to the quality of life we want. This is a value system all Wichitans share."

Truly, we Wichitans have learned that if we continue to apply our abundant energies to giving, building, and celebrating, anything is possible. The lessons of the past few decades are simply this: If we are willing to experiment with new ideas and act on our own unique, bold vision, this city of the heartland will grow in new and dynamic ways yet to be imagined. Stay tuned for the next 125 years.

DURING WICHITA'S FIRST YEAR AS A trading post community, industrious settlers established a school and church. The painting *Wichita in 1869* (permanent collection of the Wichita-Sedgwick County Historical Museum) depicts the settlement, based on interviews conducted by the artist, C.A. Seward, in the 1930s.

GOLF COURSE COMMUNITIES HAVE been growing on the city's edges at a healthy pace over the past 15 years. Today, neighborhoods like Tall Grass, Willow Bend, Reflection Ridge, Lakepoint, and Terradyne have become some of Wichita's most popular places to live.

26

HIGHWAYS STRETCHING TO THE horizon form the foundation for a comprehensive expressway system that allows Wichitans to motor from almost any part of the city to another in a maximum of 25 minutes. PICTURED: the Canal Route-Kellogg Overpass Interchange.

THE BIG ARKANSAS WINDS ITS WAY south through Wichita on a long journey to the Mississippi River. In the downtown area, the Lincoln Street dam maintains a year-round water level that makes the river perfect for canoeing and boating.

THE DAZZLING INTERACTION OF SUN
and shape makes the Riverview
Building one of downtown's most
striking and photographed buildings.

THE STATE'S TALLEST BUILDING,
Epic Center, contains more than
300,000 square feet in its 22-story
structure.

DOWNTOWN'S OTHER LEADING OFFICE building, Fourth Financial Center, is noted for the openness of its design. The atrium's windows reflect Wichita's skyline and bring sunlight and warmth to its spacious interior.

KANSAS NEWMAN COLLEGE IS A four-year college that has seen rapid enrollment growth in the past decade. The 60-year-old college changed its name from Sacred Heart in 1973 to honor John Henry Cardinal Newman, a leading Catholic theologian. His gentle spirit is depicted in a sculpture in front of the Administration Building.

DAVIS HALL TOWERS OVER FRIENDS University and west Wichita. The massive structure, completed in 1898, was designed by architects Proudfoot and Bird, who are responsible for some of Wichita's largest and most important turn-of-the-century buildings. The Romanesque hall is one of several Proudfoot and Bird designs on the National Register of Historic Places.

THE CAMPUS OF WICHITA STATE University has one of the most extensive outdoor sculpture collections of any university in the nation. A contemplative Thomas Jefferson is caught mid-stride in this statue by Donald De Lue. During Jefferson's presidency, the government acquired through the Louisiana Purchase much of the land that later made up the state of Kansas.

THE ENTRYWAY TO THE EATON HOTEL has seen many famous political figures grace its doors over the past century, from temperance leader Carry Nation to 1932 presidential candidate Alf Landon to his daughter, U.S. Senator Nancy L. Kassebaum.

The Hotel Eaton Barbershop was one of the first new businesses to open as part of the revitalization of the Carey House Square Block in Old Town. The $7 haircuts have proven popular with a wide range of customers.

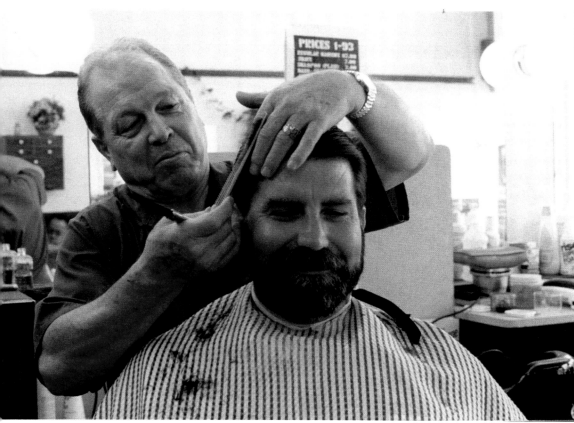

VICTORIAN, GINGERBREAD-STYLE DETAILS are on display in older neighborhoods throughout Wichita. The Bestor Brown Masonic Lodge (BOTTOM LEFT) and the restored Sternberg House (BOTTOM RIGHT) are representative of the many elegant homes in the College Hill and Midtown areas.

THE OPULENT LIFESTYLE OF WICHITA'S early business leaders can be seen in the authentically re-created Wichita Cottage room at the Wichita-Sedgwick County Historical Museum.

If you look up in any direction, you're likely to see a variety of architectural styles. Wichita's diverse heritage presents itself in the form of a decorative scroll, escutcheon, or arched window gracing one of the city's many unique buildings.

FRANK LLOYD WRIGHT DESIGNED THIS Prairie School style home (TOP) in 1919 for Henry J. Allen, a renowned journalist and former Kansas governor. The home has been restored in recent years and is now open to the public.

The sweeping curves of Century II (BOTTOM LEFT), the city's convention and theatrical center, contrast with the strong rectangular forms of the Wichita Public Main Library (BOTTOM RIGHT)

on South Main. Both structures were completed in the late 1960s as part of a major urban renewal project.

WHEN SPRING IS IN BLOOM, THE entire city feels the effects. A stroll among the thousands of plants and flowers at Botanica-The Wichita Gardens (TOP) is the perfect antidote for the hectic pace of urban life. On the edge of the city, sunflowers can be found in abundance as they re-stake their claim as the state's favorite flower. Along the river, purple wildflowers help paint a canvas of brilliant colors. And the beauty of well-kept, open spaces is evident in Central Riverside Park (BOTTOM CENTER), the anchor of the city's park system.

THE OLD SEDGWICK COUNTY Courthouse (TOP LEFT) has served the city well over the past century. Even since a new courthouse was built in 1958, the original sandstone building has continued to function in support of the court system and a number of county agencies.

The Hillcrest Apartments (BOTTOM LEFT), which tower above College Hill and much of east Wichita, provide a unique and luxurious home for residents.

The Occidental Hotel (BOTTOM RIGHT), constructed in 1874 when Wichita was growing from a sleepy village to a bustling city, was restored to stately elegance more than a decade ago. The building, which now houses modern offices, is one of the oldest hotel structures west of the Mississippi.

The Wichita-Sedgwick County Historical Museum (TOP RIGHT)—originally built as Wichita's City Hall in 1892—has seen numerous political debates conducted within its historic walls, including even a few fisticuffs at city commission meetings, which were commonly referred to as the "Tuesday night fights."

The Board of Trade Building (OPPOSITE), in the heart of downtown stands in solemn and stately repose a it has since it was constructed in 1919 For more than four decades the building was the headquarters for the Association of Grain Dealers, the nation's leading buyer and seller of wheat. The huge windows on the top floor enabled dealers to judge the gra with the aid of the natural Kansas sunlight.

WITH MORE THAN 500 CHURCHES, synagogues, mosques, and temples serving more than 70 denominations, Wichita is blessed with an abundance of places to worship. St. John's Episcopal Church (BOTTOM RIGHT), organized in 1869, is Wichita's oldest church. St. Anthony's Catholic Church (BOTTOM CENTER), was constructed in 1902 and still serves an active parish. The building, with its unique architectural features, has been carefully preserved and is listed on the National Register of Historic Places. St. Mary's Cathedral (LEFT), the largest church in the city, is the most prominent church building in the downtown area. The First Mennonite Brethren Church (TOP CENTER) and the Central Community Church (TOP RIGHT) are two of the largest churches on the city's west side.

ONE OF THE CITY'S MOST STRIKING places of worship is the St. George Orthodox Christian Cathedral (TOP LEFT), erected in the early 1990s in northeast Wichita. The Harvey D. Grace Memorial Chapel (TOP CENTER) on the campus of Wichita State University has provided thousands of students a place for quiet reflection.

The modern architecture of two churches on the city's east side, seen in the Eastminster Presbyterian Church (BOTTOM LEFT) and in the Hillside Christian Church (BOTTOM CENTER), stand in contrast to the venerable and more traditional architectural style of the Plymouth Congregational Church (RIGHT) in the College Hill neighborhood.

THE BEAUTIFUL, UPLIFTING SOUNDS OF a choir singing in unison are always inspirational, while the spoken word and religious symbols offer another dimension. The Reverend Tyrone Gordon (BOTTOM) of St. Mark United Methodist Church is also on the Wichita School Board. A menorah sculpture (OPPOSITE) stands on the grounds of the Temple Emanu-El in east Wichita.

▲ HENRY NELSON

THE CITY IS FORTUNATE THAT ITS cultural makeup includes a variety of ethnic heritages. Martial arts are taught in the city parks every spring and summer (OPPOSITE). Grace Wu Monnat (LEFT) teaches Tai Chi in Central Riverside Park during one of her Saturday morning classes. The Buddhist Temple (RIGHT) in nearby Haysville provides a beautiful setting for quiet meditation.

NATIVE AMERICANS WERE THE FIRST residents to stake their claim to the slice of land between the Big and Little Arkansas rivers. Today, in remembrance of the Wichita tribe that once lived here, the Mid-America All-Indian Center honors the city's Indian heritage with a museum and a host of special events, including the annual Pow Wow, which in 1993 drew 30,000 spectators. The friendship totem pole by Norman Jackson (OPPOSITE, TOP RIGHT) of the Haida-Tlingit tribe has been a dramatic presence inside the Indian Center since 1978.

KEVIN C. FOX / STUDIO 151

48

NORTH HIGH SCHOOL, THE CITY'S
second oldest public school, displays
remarkable sculpture and relief murals
by Bruce Moore. The architectural
details of the school's exterior
highlight the Native American and
pioneer traditions of the 19th century.

The wings of eagles and airplanes
are prominent motifs on the Kansas
Aviation Museum (BOTTOM), erected
in 1936. The handsome building is the
work of architect Glen Thomas, who
also designed North High School. It
was the first home of the Wichita
Municipal Airport; but when the
airport moved in the 1950s to allow for
the construction of McConnell Air
Force Base, the building became a
storage facility. In the 1980s a private
group decided it would best serve the
community as a museum honoring
Wichita's colorful aviation heritage.

AD ASTRA PER ASPERA

BRITE VOICE SYSTEMS (TOP), headquartered in Wichita, is a world leader
in providing electronic classified ads
and audio text information.

The brightly lit carousel (BOTTOM)
is one of the many painstakingly
crafted products of another Wichita-
based company, Chance Industries,
which produces amusement rides for
parks around the world.

A Coleman Company worker
(OPPOSITE) at the firm's large facility
in northeast Wichita is one of 1,500
employed in the city by the international manufacturer of camping,
outdoor, and recreational equipment.

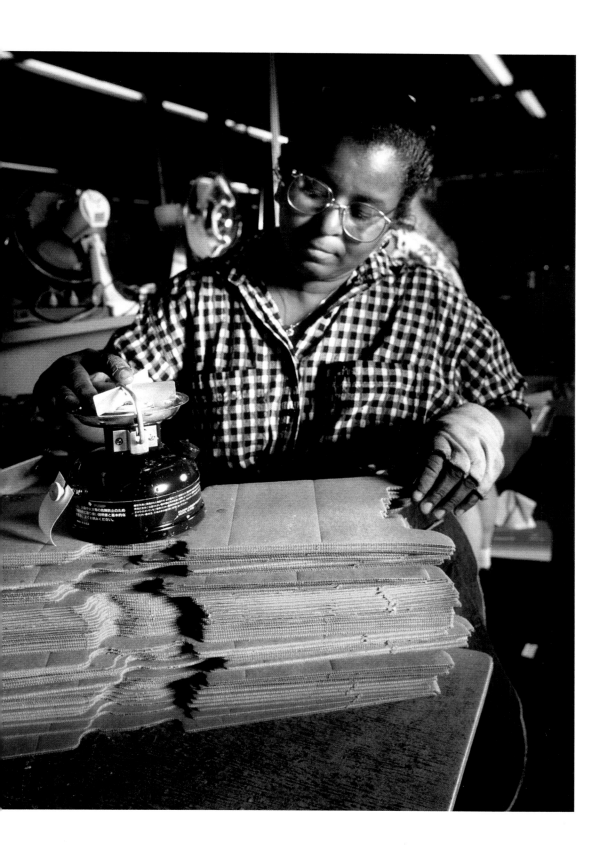

Wᴵᴄʜɪᴛᴀ's ʀᴇᴍᴀʀᴋᴀʙʟᴇ ᴀᴠɪᴀᴛɪᴏɴ history stretches back to the 1920s, and the city proudly claims to be the "Air Capital of the World."

Pride in craftsmanship is reflected in the face of this worker at Boeing Wichita (ᴛᴏᴘ), which builds about 75 percent of the airframes of the Boeing 737, the most popular commercial jetliner in the world.

Boeing workers rewire cabling (ᴏᴘᴘᴏsɪᴛᴇ ᴛᴏᴘ) and install an engine (ᴏᴘᴘᴏsɪᴛᴇ ʙᴏᴛᴛᴏᴍ) at the Boeing Wichita facility, the state's largest employer and the largest single-site private aerospace manufacturing complex in the world.

The crowded assembly line at Beech Aircraft (ʙᴏᴛᴛᴏᴍ) stays busy producing one of the country's most popular small business jets, the Beechjet 400ᴀ.

CONSTRUCTION ON THE WEST SIDE OF Wichita (LEFT) has taken off at a feverish pace in the past decade, with thousands of new homes built.

Another center of construction activity is the Old Town area (RIGHT), where renovation of turn-of-the-century warehouses has resulted in the opening of more than a dozen new restaurants.

Commercial construction is also booming throughout the city (OPPOSITE), as foundations are poured, frames are erected, and earth is moved.

THE CANAL ROUTE, OR I-135, IS THE primary transportation artery for the city's north-south traffic and for travelers with Nebraska or Oklahoma destinations.

▲ HENRY NELSON

Many of the older bridges in the Wichita area have stood the test of time with grace and character.

New development on the city's edge brings more efficient, though less architecturally decorative overpasses and bridges, like those under construction for the new Northeast Expressway.

HARKENING TO DAYS GONE BY, WHEN travel on two-lane roads and a one-night stay in a small roadside motel were the norm, these bright neon signs light the way for red-eyed, weary travelers.

60

MURALS BRIGHTEN UP OLDER BUILD-ings throughout Wichita's core area, providing sometimes startling scenic relief for motorists and a creative outlet for commercial artists. Murals with perhaps a more serious artistic purpose can also be found. *Personnages Oiseaux* by Joan Miro (OPPOSITE BOTTOM LEFT) at Wichita State University is a must-see for visitors to the campus.

▲ RON JONES

NEAR DOWNTOWN, A HODGE PODGE of businesses adds color to the central city. There's traditional manufacturing, represented by the unique sign of Wichita Ponca Canvas Products (which recently moved to west Wichita), and new retail activity in Delano Square, the site of most of the action during Wichita's wild and wooly frontier days.

Other well-known, longtime businesses, such as the West Side Flower Shop or the Nu-Way Cafe, are thriving. The special pressurized cooking of ground beef at Nu-Way, the original location of one of Wichita's oldest restaurant chains, has kept generations of devotees coming back to the west Douglas site.

▲ HOWARD INGLISH

A SAMPLING OF EYE-CATCHING BUSI-
ness signs from the west side of
Wichita illustrates the city's ethnic
and cultural diversity.

Located in the northwest section of
the city, Connie's Mexico Cafe is a
favorite stop for Wichitans with a
craving for authentic south-of-the-
border cuisine.

The colorful tiles of the Wichita
Hotel mosaic, reminiscent of artwork
in Southwestern locales, advertise the
city's ties to the cultures of Spain and
Mexico.

The Thai Binh Super Market and
99 Egg Roll are two of many ethnic
markets and restaurants that offer a
taste of the Far East.

▲ DAVID DINELL

HENRY NELSON

Many of Wichita's most recognized businesses were established around the last turn of the century. Steffen's Dairy has provided Wichitans a steady source of wholesome milk and ice cream since the 1900s, and today still produces dairy foods at its East Central Avenue facility.

From the days when buffalo herds roamed free to the bygone era of the Chisholm Trail, Wichita's history is intricately linked to cattle. The "Peerless Princess of the Plains" pays homage to the bovine genus in myriad ways. A relief on the wall of North High School (LEFT) depicts the North American bison. Buffalo once grazed the plains in such numbers that it seemed impossible the shaggy beasts could be brought to the brink of extinction.

This mural of a bullfight (RIGHT) is one example of the many Spanish influences that recur throughout the city, including many homes and businesses that employ Spanish-American and Southwestern architectural designs and motifs.

Borden's famous "Elsie the Cow" has nothing on Steffen's Dairy. The Holstein (OPPOSITE LEFT) stands proudly above the Wichita company's main entrance.

A stainless steel sculpture of a bull (OPPOSITE RIGHT) stands guard in front of the Kansas Coliseum, a regional venue for scores of sports and entertainment events.

▶ PAUL BOWEN

ESTABLISHED AS A HARNESS, TACK, AND saddlery vendor, Sheplers has grown from its original location in Wichita into a company of 20 stores throughout the Mid- and Southwest. In the 1960s Sheplers added western-wear jeans, boots, and ladies apparel to its stock, a business move that undoubtedly propelled the company to its prominence as the largest retail chain of western stores in the world.

THE COTILLION BALLROOM hosts local dances and events, as well as a wide range of national entertainers. Recent headliners have included native Wichitan Joe Walsh, a veteran of the rock group Eagles, country and western star Waylon Jennings, and stand-up comedians Paula Poundstone and George Wallace.

And every Wednesday night, the Cotillion sponsors its "over 28" Club Dance, a popular gathering at which ballroom aficionados dance the night away.

Dancing *al fresco* (OPPOSITE) is a western-attired couple stepping to the sounds of the River Festival.

▲ HENRY NELSON

For 10 glorious days in May, hundreds of thousands of Wichitans and out-of-town guests are treated to hot-air balloon rides, bathtub races, fireworks, flyovers, a parade, fishing contests, music of every kind, ethnic foods, arts and crafts, talent shows— and nearly every other type of fun under the sun. The occasion is the annual Wichita River Festival, which celebrates the coming of spring and life along the river.

THOUSANDS OF SPECTATORS LINE THE banks of the Arkansas River and watch from vantage points on bridges during River Festival events. Each year the slate of activities grows, yet admission for all 10 days worth of events is an unbelievable bargain—a $2 "festival button."

Individuals and civic groups build rivercraft of all shapes and sizes to compete in festival contests. One popular event is the Antique Bathtub Race, which, despite its name, rarely features old bathtubs. Participants in one of the river races (BOTTOM LEFT) pass by Wichita's Century II, located in the very heart of the city.

NOT ALL WICHITA RIVER FESTIVAL events take place on the river. The festival's 10-Kilometer Run attracts competitors from across the country and fills downtown streets to capacity.

Runners jockey for the best positions (TOP, OPPOSITE) as the race gets under way.

Another festival contest caters to bicycle enthusiasts.

EACH YEAR, THE WICHITA RIVER Festival opens with a parade that features scores of fantastic floats and special personalities. Its route snakes through downtown and passes in front of the historic City Hall, now the Wichita-Sedgwick County Historical Museum (BOTTOM). Completed in 1892, the stone building with its central clock tower was designed by architects Proudfoot and Bird. The tower was restored in the 1980s after being destroyed by fire.

A perennial parade favorite, a unicycle rider, thrills the younger crowd (TOP).

THE SOUNDS OF MUSIC CREATE A delightful background to the River Festival—country-western, pop, rock 'n' roll, gospel, jazz—you name it, and it's probably being played on a stage somewhere in the city. This young banjo player is enjoying his day in the limelight.

WICHITANS NEVER TIRE OF THE ceremonial "piping up" of Admiral Windwagon Smith's mythical prairie schooner that sailed across the plains. Resurrected from an old folklore tradition, the Admiral and his schooner are integral facets of the River Festival experience.

ALTHOUGH ATTENDANCE FLUCTUATES with the weather, the Wichita River Festival draws hundreds of thousands of people to town each spring. In 1993 rains forced the cancellation of a number of festival events. Yet the soggy conditions didn't dampen the spirits of those who attended the remaining contests, races, dances, ceremonies, and concerts. When the festival is in full swing, Wichita's mounted police and their regular-officer compatriots put in long hours of crowd and traffic control.

ONE NEVER KNOWS WHAT MIGHT BE just around the corner during the Wichita River Festival. A bevy of ballerinas graces the scene in front of the Wichita-Sedgwick County Historical Museum on Main Street.

Six days a week, from sunup to sundown, the Wichita Metropolitan Transit Authority runs 23 regular bus routes in the metropolitan area.

A harmonica player shares a melody with a friend in front of the *Kansas Daydream* mural that graces the newly constructed Metropolitan Transit Authority building.

AGRICULTURAL ENTERPRISES REMAIN A staple of the city's economic health, as illustrated by these huge grain elevators that tower above the trains waiting to carry Kansas wheat to the world. In 1993 Kansas farmers once again led the nation in wheat production.

THE COUNTRYSIDE AROUND WICHITA is dotted with oil rigs, reminding travelers and natives alike that the oil industry also plays an important role in the Kansas economy.

The Wichita Mid-Continent Airport, which features nine airlines providing direct service to most of the nation's largest cities, serves more than 1 million passengers annually. The Leonardo Nierman sculpture, *Magic Flight* (BOTTOM), was unveiled inside the airport's main entrance in 1990 as a memorial to civic leader Barry Staub.

The Farm Credit Bank Building (top) is one of the most popular office locations in the city, offering tenants a magnificent view of the Big Arkansas River. In nearby Riverside Park, Park Villa (bottom) is a favorite place for friends and family to come together for rest and relaxation.

A LONE BICYCLER FOLLOWS THE PATH along the river as it winds its way towards downtown. The gently rolling Little Arkansas provides a magnificent setting for hundreds of residents living in the Riverside area.

Mayor Elma Broadfoot (top), Wichita's first woman mayor elected at large, takes special pride in the spirit of volunteerism that helped Wichita win the "All-America City" award.

Sheriff Mike Hill (bottom left) oversees a law enforcement agency that serves all of 1,008-square-mile Sedgwick County.

When Boris Yeltsin (bottom right) visited the city in 1993, he spoke openly to students and media during his address at Wichita State University. Later in the day, Yeltsin spent time on a local farm and even operated a combine.

HENRY NELSON

The skywalk to the Fourth Financial Center (TOP) provides warmth and comfort for Wichitans during wintertime, as does the skywalk linking Main Street to the Epic Center (BOTTOM LEFT), the state's tallest building. The atrium of Fourth Financial (BOTTOM RIGHT) is also a welcome sight for pedestrians seeking relief from the unpredictable Kansas weather.

▲ DAVID DINELL

PERSONAL CARE AND STATE-OF-THE-ART technology are hallmarks of Riverside Hospital (TOP), which serves the city's west side. At the University of Kansas School of Medicine-Wichita (BOTTOM), students practice with "Harvey," a very cooperative cardiac simulator.

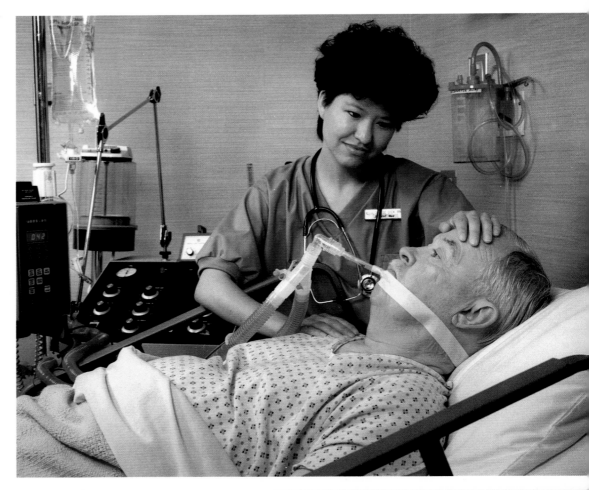

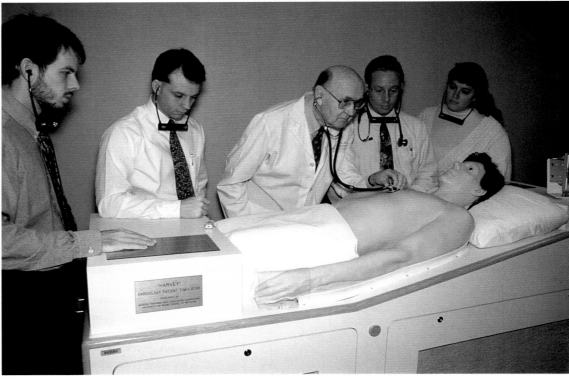

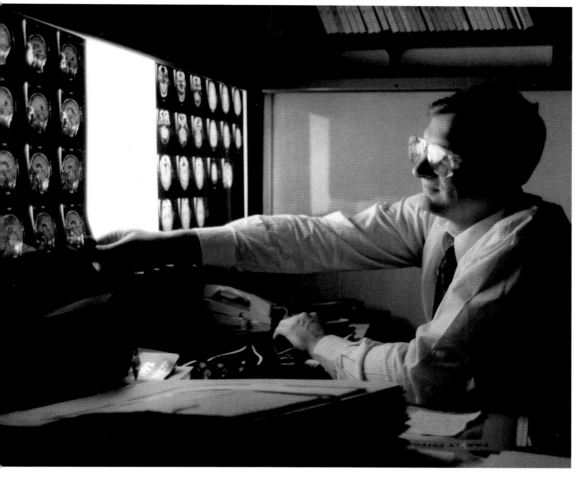

St. Joseph Medical Center, which is the city's oldest health care provider, features the most advanced and sophisticated diagnostic equipment. A patient receives a 100 percent oxygen treatment in a hyperbaric oxygen chamber at HCA Wesley Medical Center (BOTTOM), which celebrated its 80TH anniversary in 1992.

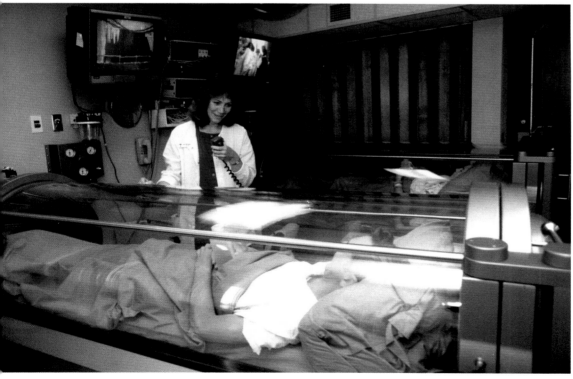

It's natural for Wichitans to look to the sky, considering the city's rich aviation history. In 1993 Pizza Hut's infamous Big Foot blimp made its debut, soaring east over Kansas toward New York, where it unceremoniously crashed onto the top of a Manhattan apartment building.

Jets soar high during the McConnell Air Force Base annual air show and open house (TOP RIGHT), while on the ground, spectators check out a historic Stearman biplane (BOTTOM LEFT) at the Kansas Aviation Museum's air show. A veteran pilot of the Vietnam War (BOTTOM RIGHT) shows a visitor around the cockpit of a B-52.

▲ COURTESY McCONNELL AIR FORCE BASE

▲ COURTESY McCONNELL AIR FORCE BASE

MASTERING THE SOPHISTICATED avionics of the B-1B (TOP) requires years of training for the highly skilled pilots, and the same can be said of the KC-135 tanker (BOTTOM LEFT). Back on the ground, a technician (BOTTOM RIGHT) tests the control panel for a B1-B weapon systems trainer.

An unusual visitor to McConnell Air Force Base in 1993 was the NASA Space Shuttle, riding on the back of a Boeing 747 while making a refueling stop.

A BRILLIANTLY COLORED HOT-AIR balloon makes its gentle rise into the clear, blue Kansas sky during the annual River Festival. Prior to lift off, balloonists must first spread out the hundreds of square yards of canopy, while at the end of the day, chase cars provide logistical support once the balloon has landed.

BEFORE SPRING ROLLS OVER THE KANSAS prairie, the grand Irish tradition of a St. Patrick's Day parade brings special vitality—and lots of green—to downtown Wichita (TOP). Green is also the color of choice on Earth Day (BOTTOM), which is celebrated with a series of educational events that inspire curious students to protect the environment.

WHILE "ROYALTY" LOOKS ON, performers break into 16th-century song and dance for the thousands of Wichitans attending the annual Kansas Newman Renaissance Faire.

The authentic costumes, songs, drama, and food provided by the Society for Creative Anachronism help make this a favorite springtime event.

IN THE SUMMER, WICHITANS EXPLORE the many ethnic traditions that add flavor to the city at the Multicultural Festival (TOP RIGHT). The festival is a whirlwind of dance, song, food, and companionship.

WITH THEIR OWN UNIQUE STYLE OF verve and spice, the Zydeco band, Terrance Simien and the Mallet Playboys (TOP LEFT) delights the crowd at the annual Chili Cook-off. At the Cinco de Mayo Festival, (BOTTOM), a wide variety of colorful performers entertain throughout the week.

WICHI

ANOTHER IMPORTANT WARM-WEATHER gathering is the Black Arts Festival, which draws thousands of people from around the state to the campus of Wichita State University for a celebration of African-American culture (TOP LEFT).

This heritage is also celebrated in Project Freedom's mural on East 13th (TOP RIGHT). The organization promotes ethnic pride and stresses the values of education and a drug-free lifestyle.

A VARIETY OF TREATMENT OPTIONS are available at Wichita's four acute-care hospitals and the city's many clinics and health care facilities. Two generations unite as a premature baby reaches for a nurturing touch (TOP) in the neonatal intensive care unit at St. Joseph Medical Center. A harpist provides soothing sounds at the hospital's Neonatal Intensive Care Unit (BOTTOM). An RN cradles an infant in the neonatal intensive care unit at St. Francis Regional Medical Center (OPPOSITE), acknowledging the importance of human contact for healthy development.

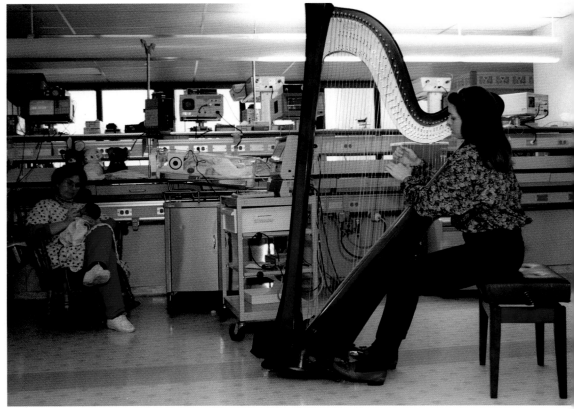

THE UNIVERSAL APPEAL OF THE maternal image is seen throughout the city in a number of artworks, such as *Mother and Daughter* by Charles Grafley (LEFT), located on the Wichita State University campus.

Mary Cassatt's *Mother and Child* (RIGHT) is one of more than 7,000 pieces that make up the Wichita Art Museum's permanent collection of American art.

Art reflects life in Bruno Luchessi's popular sculpture, *After Shopping* (OPPOSITE, LEFT), located in the Farm and Art Market plaza in Old Town.

A mother shelters her child from the wind—and the world—in *Mut und Kind* by German sculptor Gerhard Marcks (OPPOSITE, RIGHT) on the Wichita State University campus.

ALTHOUGH IT IS KANSAS' LARGEST city, Wichita continues to be a community of close-knit neighborhoods where families gather together on warm summer nights. On a sweltering August evening, a pool party offers a chance to relax and forget life's daily hassles. And weekends often find friends coming out for a block party, children playing together in the front yard, and neighbors up and down the street mowing their lawns.

KEEPING COOL IN THE SUMMER CAN be a challenge, but the absence of a coastline does not keep Wichitans from relaxing in a refreshing pool or catching a wave at Barnacle Bill's FantaSea Water Park, a 28-acre theme park that features a wave pool and challenging water slides. For those who take their water sports more seriously, Wichita State University's Heskett Center offers an Olympic-sized swimming pool (BOTTOM LEFT).

A LONG-TERM EFFORT TO BEAUTIFY the area around the Arkansas River has led to the development of a park and museum district. Art and recreation blend well here, as shown by these rowers gliding past the Wichita Art Museum.

CHENEY RESERVOIR, LOCATED HALF AN hour from Wichita, offers a quiet getaway from the hustle and bustle of city life.

IN 1992 WICHITA NATIVE BILL KOCH set the yachting world on its ear when his *America3* crew captured the coveted America's Cup. To show his appreciation for the support and encouragement he received from Wichitans, Koch donated the *Jayhawk*—one of three boats he used in the winning effort—to his hometown. It is shown near the site where a new boathouse—financed by Koch—is being built along the river on the edge of downtown.

VOLLEYBALL CONTESTANTS DO BATTLE on the banks of the Big Arkansas River during one of more than 80 events held each year as part of the Wichita River Festival.

COURTESY WICHITA PUBLIC SCHOOLS / ROBERT BROOKS

PARENTS WHO SEEK ACCESS TO THE resources and diversity of urban life, but do not like the isolating big-city feel, find that Wichita public schools offer a perfect balance.

Computers in the classroom enable the city's students to explore many different career paths.

But video games and electronic toys aside, sometimes a piece of chalk is all a child really needs to have a good time.

The Wichita Public School System has developed an extensive magnet/ alternative school program in an effort to meet the needs of all the city's children.

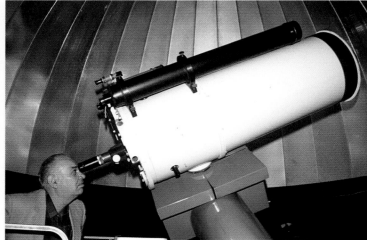

THE MOON HANGS IN SILENT STILL-
ness on a clear Kansas night as seen
through one of the telescopes at
Lake Afton Public Observatory.

Visitors to the Wichita Omnisphere often find the static electricity
exhibit a shocking experience, while
the planetarium provides a quiet
look at the nighttime sky.

At the Omnisphere's annual magic
bubble show, one of the center's
biggest attractions, a young student is
both enraptured and encaptured by
the giant soap bubble.

NOTHING IS QUITE AS DELIGHTFUL AS climbing to the top of the jungle gym on a bright sunny day...or pretending to be a firefighter at the Children's Museum...or sliding down the twisted chute of a tornado slide at one of the city's many parks.

SINCE ITS INSTALLATION OUTSIDE Century II in 1972, the *Tripodal* sculpture (TOP) by American James Rosati has been a popular perch for children attending community events at the downtown convention center.

In 1993 the National Civic League named Wichita an "All-America City" in recognition of its community-wide approach to solving big-city problems with unique solutions.

Community leader Matt Greene (TOP LEFT), who works at Iqraa African-American Books and Gifts, also heads up the Coalition Against Gun Violence in Wichita.

The Children's Miracle Network, an agency sponsored by St. Francis Regional Medical Center and the University of Kansas School of Medicine-Wichita, raises more than $300,000 during its annual telethon (TOP RIGHT) to help sick and injured children throughout the state of Kansas.

Actress Susan Dey (BOTTOM), of "LA Law" television fame, visits a little girl at Heartspring, a local, nonprofit organization that provides educational, physical, medical, and behavioral support to children with multiple disabilities.

HOWARD INGLISH

THE KANSAS FOOD BANK (TOP) provides food for thousands of Wichitans each year. While some of the food comes from government agencies, much of it is still donated by citizens and private businesses.

Hundreds of Wichitans serve as Big Brothers and Big Sisters to children who need love and support from an adult friend. The agency, one of the five largest and most successful in the national organization, raises funds through a wide range of efforts, including the annual pumpkin sale.

▲ COURTESY BIG BROTHERS AND SISTERS OF SEDGWICK COUNTY

A trip to Wichita's Joyland Amusement Park promises a little bit of everything, from a spin on one of the many exhilarating rides to colorful clowns and plenty of merry music.

WICHITA COMMUNITY THEATRE (TOP) features lots of homegrown talent each season, including this hilarious production of *Run for Your Wife.* The nonprofessional theatre holds open auditions for its eight annual productions, allowing members of the community to try their hand at acting.

DAVID DINELL

The annual River Festival's activities continue throughout the heat of the day, sometimes making even the youngest of participants exhausted, while others wisely find relief under an umbrella.

The cooler, more hospitable evening breezes of a clear Kansas night attract thousands of Wichitans to the popular outdoor movies in Central Riverside Park (OPPOSITE, BOTTOM RIGHT).

Critical tasters (BOTTOM RIGHT) sample more than 100 varieties of chili each September at the Old Town Chili Cook-off, an event which draws more than 10,000 hungry Wichitans to the popular district.

CURIOSITY MAY HAVE KILLED THE CAT, but that's not enough to keep this dog from poking his nose where it doesn't belong.

AT WICHITA GREYHOUND PARK, IT'S the dog who stays focused who usually wins the race. The three-level complex, one of the finest racing facilities in the nation, features a restaurant and sports lounge along with general seating. The park is also one of the premier entertainment and tourist attractions in the state.

In Wichita, the phrase "Take me out to the ballgame" has become a familiar theme. Larry Davis (TOP) is the longtime director of the National Baseball Congress, held in Lawrence-Dumont Stadium each August. Considered the nation's preeminent amateur baseball tournament, the event has seen hundreds of major leaguers step up to the plate.

Under the leadership and direction of Steve Shaad (BOTTOM LEFT), the Wichita Wranglers have become one of the most successful minor league baseball organizations in the nation, with new attendance records set almost every year. The AA franchise is affiliated with the San Diego Padres.

At Wichita State University, record-setting crowds have helped the baseball program become one of the leaders in attendance, number of wins, and trips to the College World Series. Coach Gene Stephenson (BOTTOM RIGHT) has guided the team's fortunes since 1977, when the sport was reintroduced at WSU.

Lawrence-Dumont Stadium (OPPOSITE, TOP) was built in the 1930s and remodeled in the 1980s. Its location next to the river and just across from downtown makes it a favorite place for Wichita sports fans.

In the first year, a crowd of 100 was considered a good turnout. But today it is not unusual for more than 5,000 fans to pack the Tyler Field/Eck Stadium complex (OPPOSITE, BOTTOM LEFT), home of the Wichita State Shockers. In 1989 WSU won the College World Series, an event it has qualified for five times in the past six years.

▼ MADELINE McCULLOUGH

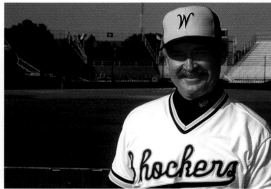

PROFESSIONAL SPORTS IN WICHITA
have grown in popularity over the past
15 years, as perhaps best seen by the
fortunes of the Wichita Wings soccer
team (TOP, BOTTOM LEFT), which
often packs sell-out crowds into the
Kansas Coliseum. A member of the
National Professional Soccer League,
the Wings are the oldest professional
soccer franchise in the country and are
known for their fierce competitiveness.

A relative newcomer to Wichita
sports, the Wichita Thunder professional hockey team (TOP, BOTTOM
RIGHT) has proven to be a big favorite
with folks who like a more bone-
jarring brand of action.

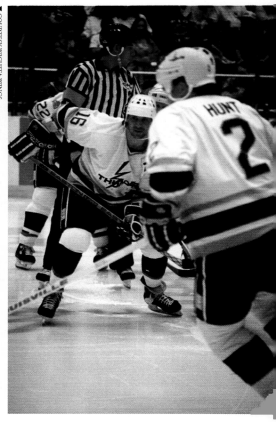

FOR THOSE WHO WOULD RATHER JOIN in the competition, Wichita offers a wide variety of recreational opportunities. Tennis is popular year-round in the city, and thanks to facilities such as the Wichita Racquet Club, competitors can volley away without worrying about the fickle Kansas winds. And on every weekend, you'll find people of all ages participating in everything from golf at Reflection Ridge Country Club to boxing during the River Festival to youth hockey leagues.

▶ HENRY NELSON

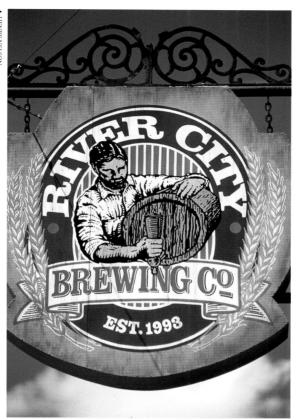

The city's refurbished Old Town area is booming, and the center of much of the action is the Wichita Farm and Art Market, a three-story facility housing two-dozen retail stores and eateries. The historic ambience of Old Town's buildings, brick streets, parking facilities, and street lights adds to the charm of this turn-of-the-century district that was deteriorating until renovations began in the late 1980s.

▶ HENRY NELSON

DAVID DINELL

HENRY NELSON

VADA SNIDER

RICH VLIET (ABOVE LEFT), DEVELOPER of the Larkspur Restaurant and several other Old Town properties, and Mary Wright (ABOVE RIGHT), owner of the Old Mill Tasty Shop, are two of the visionaries whose commitment to Old Town has stretched over a decade.

Both were members of the original group which formed the Old Town Association, sponsor of the Chili Cook-off and a number of popular events in the historic area.

OTHER PROMINENT ELEMENTS ADDING to Old Town's success are the trolley system, which was reintroduced to Wichita after a 60-year absence, thanks to a group of private citizens led by Wichitan Phil Miller (BELOW CENTER), and the River City Brewing Co., where owner Monte Griffin

(BELOW RIGHT) brews up his uniqu beer with ingredients imported fro as far away as Europe. In the Dela retail area west of downtown, Wic Hat Works owner Jack Kellogg (BELOW LEFT) creates just the right hat for fashionable men and wome of all ages.

▲ HENRY NELSON

▲ DAVID DINELL

ERY PART OF TOWN, THE GROWING
f entertainment and dining
ings has increased dramatically
the past decade. In the northeast
on of the city, Antoine Toubia
VE LEFT) is the culinary force
nd a variety of establishments,
ding the Piccadilly Market and

Back in Old Town, there is plenty to do both before and after dining and shopping. For six months out of the year, the Wichita Farm and Art Market (ABOVE RIGHT) offers entertainment on the plaza to complement the outdoor market's activities.

Wichitan Rick Meyer (BELOW LEFT) lets loose on his saxophone as the sweet sounds of jazz fill the River City Brewing Co., one of more than a dozen restaurants and clubs participating in the Jazz Walk held every other

month in Old Town. More up-tempo action can be found at The Aviator Live! (BELOW RIGHT), where they serve up a mixture of music and spirits to suit every passenger's taste.

THE EXCITEMENT OF OLD TOWN involves more than its setting of newly refurbished, historic buildings. Annual events such as the Chili Cook-off bring out the spicy side of everyone, including Jan Miller (BOTTOM LEFT), Miss Chili Pepper 1989. Diana Fanning (BOTTOM RIGHT), Farm and Art Market manager, enthusiastically conquers the daily challenge of juggling the indoor retail shopping complex with the outdoor market activities. Her eclectic workday may include everything from working with the fruit and vegetable vendors to coordinating the appearance of a rather large circus star to providing the sweet and tasty pleasures for a watermelon-eating contest.

MADELINE McCULLOUGH

▲ HOWARD INGLISH

In an age of electronics and computers, many Wichita craftspeople still prefer to work patiently by hand. A sampling of these diverse crafts and designs can be seen in one-of-a-kind pottery pieces made by an aspiring art student; carefully repaired shoes by Spencer Tolbert, who has given new life to the tired feet of Wichitans for more than four decades; uniquely painted fabric clothing by Sharon Jesik; and intricate, vivid Ukrainian eggs created by Wichitan Marilyn Cain.

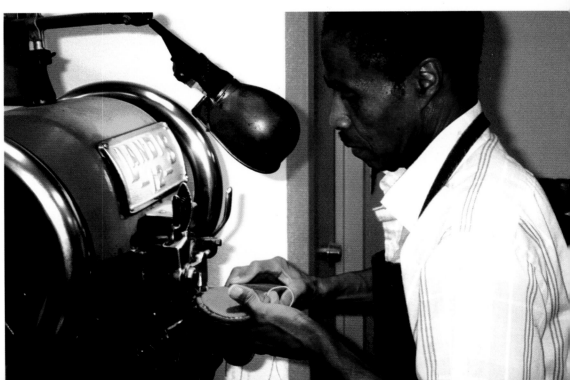

ART LOVERS IN WICHITA CAN FIND AN abundance of exhibits to feast their eyes on. One of the favorite places to view collections is the prestigious Litwin Gallery, where owner Harry Litwin (OPPOSITE, TOP) proudly shares his latest artistic finds. Or there is an endless variety of art to observe in the city's public museums, including the Ulrich Museum of Art on the campus of Wichita State University (OPPOSITE, BOTTOM). In this exhibit, many visitors try to discern the difference between the works of art and the spectators themselves. Wichitans also enjoy the art of music, such as the jazzy sounds from a lone saxophone player sliding from table to table at the Larkspur Restaurant.

THE WICHITA ART MUSEUM (TOP) is nationally recognized for its extensive collection of Western art. The facility also features a treasure of American masterpieces from colonial days through the 20TH century.

Summa Cum Laude #2 (OPPOSITE) by Daniel Ben-Schmuel, and *Three Women Walking* (BOTTOM) by Francisco Zuniga are two of the more than 50 pieces included in the Outdoor Sculpture Collection at the Edwin A. Ulrich Museum of Art on the WSU campus.

THREE WOMEN WALKING, 1981.
Francisco Zuniga, Mexican,
(b. Costa Rica, 1912).
Bronze, 76 3/8 inches high.
Cast number one of an edition of four.
Gift of George and Virginia Ablah.

DURING THE 1993-1994 SEASON, THE Wichita Symphony Orchestra marked its 50TH anniversary. The orchestra, which has won national praise and has attracted outstanding conductors over the past several decades, is now led by Maestro Zuohuang Chen (OPPOSITE LEFT). The symphony performs from October through April at the Century II Concert Hall, and in May puts on an additional Pops Concert in the Convention Hall (ABOVE).

EACH YEAR JAZZ LOVERS FROM KANSAS and throughout the Midwest converge on Wichita for the week-long series of events that make up the Wichita Jazz Festival. Concerts, classroom instruction, and contests for high school and college bands lead up to the big finale—an all-day entertain- ment marathon at Wichita's Century II. Well-known jazz musician Branford Marsalis (BOTTOM RIGHT), band leader for "The Tonight Show," discusses the finer points of jazz with students during one of the seminar sessions held at Wichita State University.

THE MAGIC OF THE FOOTLIGHTS enables actors and audiences alike to escape to imaginary worlds. Wichita Children's Theater & Dance Center encourages children as young as age four to sing, dance, and express themselves through acting. The Center is the home base for the Tales for Tots players, who are featured in major stage productions such as *Yankee Doodle* (TOP LEFT) and *Alice in Wonderland* (BOTTOM LEFT).

FOR MORE THAN 20 YEARS, MUSIC Theatre of Wichita has offered a taste of Broadway during its summer presentations. World-class performers from throughout the country work with a talented regional crew and c to bring the curtain up on old favorites, such as *Singing in the Rai* (TOP RIGHT), and current hits like *the Woods* (BOTTOM RIGHT).

TER THEATRE AT THE WICHITA ter for the Arts combines fessional actors and directors with l nonprofessionals to create a que approach to community theater. *The Murders: A Greek Trilogy* (TOP LEFT) and *Amadeus* (BOTTOM LEFT) were two of Center Theatre's most popular productions.

WICHITA STATE UNIVERSITY'S FINE Arts Department also hosts a multitude of performances (TOP AND BOTTOM RIGHT) by student and professional artists, showcasing a broad array of dance, theatre, and musical talent.

You can take a step back in time in a visit to Old Cowtown Museum, where cowboys, saloon girls, blacksmiths, and local townspeople re-create life in Wichita during the rough and tumble days of the late 1800s. Old Cowtown is so authentic, Hollywood used the "town" for the filming of *Sarah, Plain and Tall—Skylark*, starring Glenn Close (TOP).

Just as in the days of old, the local showplace in Old Cowtown is still the saloon. The Empire House Restaurant and Theater (BOTTOM) presents melodrama in a dinner theater setting, serving up good food, laughter, dancing, and fun.

DAVID DINELL

Sculptor Gino Salerno has delighted Wichitans with his whimsical and lifelike tree-trunk carvings found throughout the city. A favorite is the Wizard of Oz Exhibit in O.J. Watson Park, where a walk down the Yellow Brick Road can be taken with the Scarecrow, the Lion, the Tin Man, Dorothy, and aspiring Dorothys, too.

THROUGHOUT THE YEAR THE SUBTLE brilliance of nature adds its magical touch to the city. A delicate lily floating in a pond at Botanica or a ray of sunshine bursting through a canopy of leaves offers evidence that Wichita is truly a beautiful place.

THE SEDGWICK COUNTY ZOO, WHICH combines the power of imagination with the beauty of nature, is a nationally recognized facility that provides enjoyment and education for some 400,000 patrons each year. Featuring hundreds of different species living in environments that mimic natural habitats, the zoo takes special pride in its breeding program.

Gino strikes again! Sculptor Gino Salerno adds another tree-trunk masterpiece to one of the 80 parks that grace the city's landscape. The Lima, Peru, native works full-time for the city library system, yet finds time to carve more than a dozen sculptures each year.

THE BIG AND LITTLE ARKANSAS RIVERS aren't the only spots in town for water recreation. When the weather is warm, Wichitans of all shapes and sizes take to the area's lakes and streams for swimming, fishing, or a quiet read along the banks.

Though the term "cowtown" no longer applies to Wichita, the city's frontier heritage is remembered at rodeos, state fairs, and family gatherings throughout the year.

Fall signals much more than just a seasonal change; it introduces the time of year when Mother Nature reinvents the color scheme all over town.

WICHITA THRIVES AS THE METROPOLITAN hub of Kansas, offering urban sophistication found in few other areas of the state. Yet it remains indebted—and forever linked—to its agricultural roots.

THERE IS NO GETTING AROUND THE FACT
that Wichita weather can be fierce,
with high winds, intense rain and hail
storms, freezing winter storms, and
summer days hot enough to fry eggs
on a sidewalk.

Unlike many other metropolitan areas in the country, Wichita offers all of the sights and sounds of the big city with the beauty of the country just a short drive away.

WICHITANS LOVE TO CELEBRATE LIFE at many of the city's entertainment and dining establishments, whether it's eating a plate of mouth-watering ribs at Adams Barbecue (OPPOSITE), dancing to downhome blues at the recently closed Coyote Club (TOP AND BOTTOM LEFT), or losing out in a "Kiss the Pig" contest at the Cattleman's Ball benefit.

THOUGH THE AMOUNT OF OPEN SPACE within the city limits has dwindled significantly since Wichita was incorporated in 1870, there are still plenty of places to enjoy the pristine beauty that greeted the area's first settlers.

As the city has grown, the number of farms in Wichita has declined considerably, but the sun has far from set on area farmers, whose character is still deeply rooted in the strong work ethic and determination first exhibited by those who plowed this land more than 125 years ago.

WINTERS IN KANSAS ALMOST ALWAYS bring heavy snows, often providing picture-postcard scenes reminiscent of days gone by. But just when you thought you'd entered a Norman Rockwell painting, water-skiers on the frigid river (BOTTOM LEFT) prove that Wichitans thrive on creating new traditions.

WICHITA

PROFILES IN EXCELLENCE

A LOOK AT THE CORPORATIONS,

BUSINESSES,

PROFESSIONAL GROUPS,

AND

COMMUNITY SERVICE

ORGANIZATIONS

THAT HAVE MADE

THIS BOOK POSSIBLE.

BY ERIC ALLISON

WICHITA
1870 - 1927

1870	City of Wichita
1876	INTRUST Bank, N.A.
1879	St. Joseph Medical Center
1886	Fleeson, Gooing, Coulson & Kitch, L.L.C.
1887	BANK IV
1889	St. Francis Regional Medical Center
1895	Wichita State University
1902	The Coleman Company, Inc.
1902	Kansas Newman College
1905	Fidelity Savings Association of Kansas
1909	KG&E, a Western Resources Company
1910	Emprise Bank
1912	HCA Wesley Medical Center
1913	Broadway Mortuary
1917	Wichita Area Chamber of Commerce
1920	JCPenney
1925	Dondlinger & Sons Construction Co., Inc.
1927	Cessna Aircraft Company

A BLACKSMITH PERFORMS HIS SKILLED CRAFT AT THE OLD COWTOWN MUSEUM, WHERE VISITORS CAN FIND AN 1870S RE-CREATION OF WICHITA THAT INCLUDES A SCHOOLHOUSE, GENERAL STORE, SALOON, ONE-ROOM JAIL, AND THE FAMOUS MUNGER HOUSE.

CITY OF WICHITA

WICHITA IS A DYNAMIC, PROGRESSIVE city that honors its heritage of positive community values. It has twice been recognized as an "All-America City"— a place where spirit and leadership have combined to overcome community challenges and where families, businesses,

FROM ITS INCORPORATION IN 1870, WICHITA HAS GROWN INTO A THRIVING URBAN COMMUNITY.

schools, churches, and cultural activities thrive.

Incorporated in 1870, the City of Wichita is today divided into six area districts, each of which elects a representative to the city council. The council and mayor work in conjunction with the city manager to develop and execute policies that ensure Wichitans affordable and attainable housing, safe streets, excellent schools, cultural and recreational attractions, and opportunities for expanding commerce and industry.

centers. But, through innovative partnerships with developers and business coalitions, Wichita's city council has reversed the exodus and has helped create a new spirit of enthusiasm for downtown revitalization and retail development.

Since 1991 more than $75 million has been committed toward revitalization efforts, ranging from development of the Arkansas River as a natural resource and cultural center to expansion of Wichita's historic Old Town district, which now thrives with outdoor markets,

ness district. As a result, Wichita was faced with two options: either work together to clean up the area or have the site placed on the Environmental Protection Agency's federal Superfund list.

The city council determined the public interest would best be served by taking an active leadership role and forming partnerships with the private sector and other units of government to find a solution. Thus, Wichita initiated a comprehensive environmental cleanup plan in cooperation with a major local corporation that agreed to fund a substantial portion of the project. The City of Wichita also created a tax increment finance district and convinced the state legislature to allow a portion of property tax revenues generated within the district to help pay for the cost of cleanup.

As a result of these efforts, the area was spared from designation

FACING ADVERSITY

As with any community, progress and growth do not occur without occasional adversity. But Wichita is a city whose residents respect one another, a place where ordinary citizens feel they can make a difference. By tapping this can-do spirit, council members and city staff have found innovative ways to meet local challenges.

For example, as retail and commercial growth expanded toward Wichita's east and west borders, retailers in the downtown business district eventually followed their customers to the new shopping

shops, restaurants, and a new Transit Center with trolley service.

ENVIRONMENTAL RESPONSIBILITY

Successfully managing adversity has also led to national recognition of the City of Wichita's environmental efforts. While the manufacturing industry has always been a vital component of the area's economic health, it has also created environmental hazards in the form of groundwater pollution.

This contamination, which went unrecognized until 1990, affected a major portion of the central busi-

a Superfund site and the associated decline in property values. Economic activity has increased, and lending institutions continue to make substantial loans in the area to spur further economic growth.

The City of Wichita has received both national and international recognition for its innovative approach to solving the contamination problem, and in 1992 was awarded a $100,000 grant from Ford Foundation, in conjunction with Harvard University, which selected the project for its "Innovations in State and Local Government Award."

[K]ANSAS NEWMAN COLLEGE

[A] FOUR-YEAR PRIVATE LIBERAL ARTS COLLEGE steeped in the tradition of educating the whole person, Kansas Newman College offers outstanding academic programs that prepare students to meet their personal and professional goals. ◆ The institution began in 1902 as a boarding school for girls and

[beca]me Sacred Heart Junior Col[lege] in 1933 to prepare women for [the t]eaching profession. Sacred [Hea]rt gave itself new direction in [196]2 and became a four-year liberal [arts] college. A coeducational insti[tutio]n since 1965, the school was [rena]med Kansas Newman College [in 1]973 in honor of John Henry [Car]dinal Newman, a 19th century [theo]logian and educator. Affiliated [with] the Catholic church, the [colle]ge is a mission of the Adorers [of th]e Blood of Christ.

[DIV]ERSE PROGRAMS

[On] a 50-acre main campus in [sout]hwest Wichita, Kansas New[man] has continually expanded its [acad]emic program, adding new [areas] of study to meet the needs of [its st]udents, the community, and [the s]tate. Associate, bachelor's, and [mast]er's degrees are offered in busi[ness,] education, humanities/social [scien]ces, nursing, and science/ [math]/allied health. Kansas New[man] offers the state's only bache[lor's] degree in medical sonography [and i]s one of only two colleges in [the s]tate with a degree program in [occu]pational therapy.

[O]ff-campus programs include a [bach]elor's degree in nursing with [class]es at six central and western [Kan]sas locations, accelerated de[gree]s in business and education [at] central and western Kansas [camp]uses, and a bachelor's degree [in to]tal quality management [thro]ugh classes at The Boeing Com[pany], Cessna Aircraft Company, [and] Butler County Community [Coll]ege. In addition, Kansas New[man] has partnered with McConnell [Air F]orce Base in Wichita since [199]1 to offer a business degree.

RECENT GROWTH

Since Sister Tarcisia Roths, Ph.D. became Kansas Newman's ninth president in 1991, the school's average annual enrollment has risen dramatically from 800 students to more than 1,800 in 1993. Students hail from all over the United States, as well as from numerous foreign countries.

"Students choose Kansas Newman because of our commitment to the individual and our flexibility," says Sister Tarcisia, noting that the college offers nontraditional programs, such as accelerated degree completion programs for mid-career students. "Students appreciate our approach of educating the whole individual. They also appreciate the fact that we build a solid academic foundation by demonstrating the interconnectedness of knowledge, which helps them learn to think clearly and logically."

Kansas Newman's low student/ teacher ratio of 13 to 1 is another reason the college is an attractive choice. The majority of classes are taught by full-time faculty, most of whom are easily accessible to students after class periods. "We believe accessibility helps students succeed," says Sister Tarcisia. "Consider our nursing and pre-med programs. Ninety-six percent of our nursing students pass their certification exams the first time, while 90 percent of our pre-med students are accepted by their first choice of medical schools."

Accredited by several national, regional, and state agencies, including the North Central Association of Colleges and Secondary Schools, Kansas Newman has one of the lowest annual tuitions among the

A QUALITY, VALUE-CENTERED EDUCATION FOCUSED ON THE STUDENT IS THE HALLMARK OF KANSAS NEWMAN COLLEGE. IN JUST SIX YEARS, ENROLLMENT HAS INCREASED ALMOST 200 PERCENT.

KANSAS NEWMAN'S RENAISSANCE FAIRE, WHICH CELEBRATES ITS 16TH YEAR IN 1994, IS ONE OF WICHITA'S MOST UNUSUAL SPECIAL EVENTS.

state's independent colleges. On-campus housing is available, as well as multiple sources of financial aid.

"While we stress Christian values in everyday life, students here represent every religious denomination," says Sister Tarcisia. "The result is an education that respects and empowers individuals, and gives them the self-confidence to succeed intellectually, spiritually, and socially."

INTRUST BANK, N.A.

FOR MORE THAN 100 YEARS, WHEN FINANcial analysts such as Sheshunoff and Veribanc, Inc. have rated the nation's top banks for financial safety and soundness, INTRUST Bank, N.A. has consistently ranked near the top. INTRUST has long been considered by industry analysts to be one of the most secure banks in the United States.

Through the years, sound, responsible lending policies have positioned INTRUST to achieve continued profitability and a strong capital position. Due to its excellent fiscal management, many major out-of-state financial institutions and investors choose the bank's certificates of deposit and other savings instruments for their investments.

But INTRUST is far more than a commercial bank. It is a community institution that six generations of Wichitans have trusted and used. In fact, Wichita and INTRUST have literally grown up together.

INTRUST began in 1876 as Farmers and Merchants Bank in a rented room at the corner of St. Francis and Douglas in the fledgling cattle town of Wichita. Its assets were $50,000 in cash and an 8,000-pound safe. From those mest beginnings INTRUST Financial Corp. has grown to become one of the state's largest financial organizations, with more than $1.5 billion in assets, 28 offices throughout Kansas and Oklahor and customers in all 50 states.

In 1993 the organization underwent a name change. The holding company and the Wichita bank, which had been known as First Bancorp of Kansas and First National Bank in Wichita for m years, changed their respective names to INTRUST Financial C and INTRUST Bank, N.A. Oth Kansas banks within the holding company also were renamed with the INTRUST Bank signature.

"It is important to have a unif corporate image in order to build name awareness on a regional basis," explains C.Q. "Chuck"

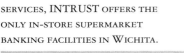

AS A LEADER IN INNOVATIVE BANKING SERVICES, INTRUST OFFERS THE ONLY IN-STORE SUPERMARKET BANKING FACILITIES IN WICHITA.

andler III, chairman of the holding company and the Wichita TRUST Bank. "A corporate ne change is never easy— ecially for an organization that ore than 125 years old."

He continues, "We were pleased ome up with the name of TRUST, which is not only a word but is relevant to our iness. It uniquely fits the way do business. A tradition of trust been our legacy to customers over 100 years."

indeed, the Chandler family, in its fourth generation of own- ip of the bank, has been synony- us with banking throughout the dwest since the turn of the cen- . C.Q. Chandler, grandfather Chuck Chandler, purchased trolling interest in the bank in 0. The tradition continues with . "Charlie" Chandler IV,

ident of INTRUST Financial p., Wichita, and vice chairman he board of INTRUST Bank, .

During the 1920s and 1930s— icult times for the banking ustry—the eldest Chandler was uently called upon by banking cials in Kansas, Oklahoma, as, and Colorado to help estab- community banks. He started e than 75 banks throughout Midwest, helping to stabilize l economies and then returning ership of the banks to local ens.

uch commitment to maintain- the financial security of the re- is an asset that does not appear

on a balance sheet, but it serves to support the foundation on which INTRUST was established.

INTRUST's success is attribut- able not only to sound financial management and commitment to the good of the community, but also to savvy recognition of changes in the Wichita populace and gen- eral consumer attitudes. As Chuck Chandler is fond of saying, "If you're standing still, you're going backwards." And that is a direction INTRUST has never taken.

Anticipating a trend toward consumer convenience and the emergence of consumer credit, INTRUST pioneered the local introduction of MasterCard in 1968. Since that time, INTRUST Card Center has grown to become the largest credit card issuer in Kansas with cardholders nation- wide. Continued growth is pro- jected through the bank's successful national marketing and affinity programs, which include credit cards associated with leading Mid- western universities and other organizations.

In 1973 INTRUST was the first bank in Wichita to introduce auto- mated teller machines, and in 1993 it was the first local bank to adapt some of its machines for both English and Spanish languages to better serve the community's grow- ing Hispanic population.

In 1990 INTRUST introduced an unprecedented convenience to local customers with the installa- tion of banking branches inside the superstores of the area's largest grocery chain. These branches offer deposit and loan services with extended evening, weekend, and occasional holiday hours.

"We introduced Kansas to the concept of supermarket banking, and these branches have become extremely successful," says Charlie Chandler. "With more and more two-income families, time is always at a premium, and getting to the bank by 6:00 p.m. isn't always possible. Opening these in-store branches is probably the best cus- tomer service and public relations

move we have ever made."

While INTRUST has created a loyal customer base in retail bank- ing, it has continued to provide a broad range of commercial and trust banking services. "We don't see ourselves as a niche banker cater- ing to any one group," says Chuck Chandler. "Rather, we have devel- oped depth in services that meet the needs of the community, includ- ing mid-size to large businesses in Wichita and around the country."

He adds, "We feel an even greater sense of responsibility to Wichita as more and more home- grown companies are purchased by national and international conglom- erates. We intend to be here—and be family owned—well into our second century of banking."

FOUR GENERATIONS OF CHANDLERS HAVE PROVIDED SOUND FINANCIAL LEADERSHIP TO THE WICHITA COMMUNITY.

THE ANNUAL FIRST CITIZEN'S AWARD, GIVEN IN RECOGNITION OF OUTSTAND- ING VOLUNTEERISM, IS ONLY ONE EXAMPLE OF INTRUST BANK'S CONTINUED SUPPORT OF COMMUNITY SERVICE (LEFT).

ST. JOSEPH MEDICAL CENTER

NO DISCUSSION OF ST. JOSEPH MEDICAL Center would be complete without emphasizing the hospital's motivation for pioneering its many and varied programs. Quite simply, the impetus is St. Joseph's perception of people's needs and the practice of medicine in a "patient-friendly"

FROM ITS BEGINNINGS IN WICHITA MORE THAN 100 YEARS AGO, ST. JOSEPH MEDICAL CENTER HAS GROWN INTO A MODERN MEDICAL FACILITY OFFERING A FULL RANGE OF HOLISTIC, FAMILY-CENTERED SERVICES, INCLUDING COMPLETE SURGICAL CARE.

manner. St. Joseph Medical Center's reputation for developing and administering innovative health care dates back more than 100 years. The philosophy took root

Joint Commission on Accreditation of Health Care Organizations. The 600-bed medical center employs nearly 2,500 people and utilizes the services of over 550 phy-

St. Joseph patients benefit from a highly skilled and experienced medical staff backed by the most technologically advanced diagnostic, surgical, and treatment equipment and techniques, including magnetic resonance imagery, laser technology, and a computerized sonography system. The hospital is also the community leader in endoscopic surgery.

Complementing its outstanding reputation for quality care, St. Joseph is an established teaching center affiliated with 40 colleges and universities throughout the United

in 1879 when a small group of Wichita women banded together to help the poor and the homeless, as well as to practice midwifery and attend to injuries and sicknesses.

Today, St. Joseph Medical Center is a not-for-profit, state-of-the-art medical facility handling approximately 18,500 patient admissions and 220,000 outpatient visits a year. It is accredited by The Commission on Accreditation of Rehabilitative Facilities and the

sicians. St. Joseph Medical Center's campus covers 40 acres in southeast Wichita and offers a full range of holistic, family-centered services including trauma services, cardiac/vascular services, diabetes research and treatment, emergency care, gerontological services, home health care, respiratory therapy, rehabilitation, complete surgical care, women's health care, sports medicine, psychiatric care, and addiction treatment.

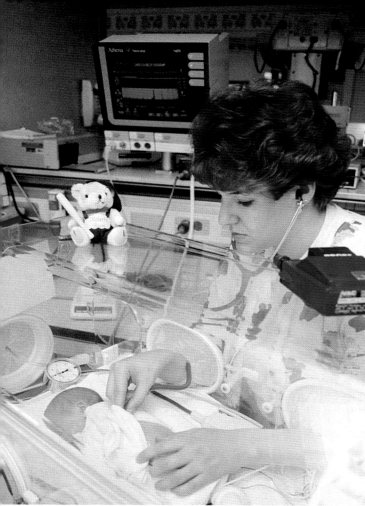

es. These affiliations enable
pital personnel to pursue allied
lth careers in fields ranging from
ological technology and social
k to addictions counseling. A
ety of residency programs are
available, including St. Joseph's
onally recognized Family
ctice Residency program.

**SURING A POSITIVE
RTHING EXPERIENCE**
oseph was the first hospital in
area to allow one-room (also
wn as "birthing room") labor,
very, recovery, and postpartum
. The program is just one aspect
t. Joseph's Family Birthplace
helps ensure happy parents and
thy babies by serving families
re a birth, during delivery, and
at home.
he Family Birthplace begins
ervice by encouraging prenatal
and fitness. Prenatal testing,
cise programs, breathing
niques, diet, and education
prepare women for the birth
erience.
Comfortable and secure, each
hing room is equipped with
-of-the-art medical equipment
constantly monitors mothers

and babies. The atmosphere is also
perfect for visits from family and
friends anxious to welcome the
baby and congratulate the parents.
St. Joseph further demonstrates its
sensitivity and understanding by ad-
mitting fathers during labor, delivery, and postpartum care; allowing
their presence during feeding times;
and permitting them into operating
rooms during caesarean section
delivery. St. Joseph was also one of
the first hospitals to establish procedures for sibling visits.

At-risk newborns grow stronger
and healthier in St. Joseph's Neonatal Intensive Care Unit (NICU).
Premature or ill newborns benefit
from the skill of highly qualified
neonatologists and the most advanced medical equipment available. So respected is St. Joseph's
NICU that at-risk newborns from
hospitals outside the city are often
transferred to St. Joseph for specialized care.

Regardless of a baby's birth
health, it is important to St. Joseph
that all newborns leave for home
with parents who are confident of
providing a loving, nurturing environment. To ensure this—and complete the final stage of the birthing

experience—the Family Birthplace
helps the family get settled at
home. Obstetric nurses call mothers to schedule a home visit and
newborn check-up, and families are
encouraged to contact the Family
Birthplace day or night with ques-
tions on infant care.

FROM THE COMFORT OF THE FAMILY
BIRTHPLACE (BELOW) TO THE STATE-
OF-THE-ART NEONATAL INTENSIVE
CARE UNIT (LEFT), ST. JOSEPH OFFERS
COMPREHENSIVE CARE FOR PREGNANT
WOMEN AND NEWBORNS.

**REHABILITATIVE CARE
ENHANCES QUALITY OF LIFE**
St. Joseph realizes that the successful practice of medicine can only be
measured by how well individuals
live their daily lives once released
from the hospital. For this reason,
rehabilitation, adaptation, education, and motivation are important
parts of patient treatment.

THE HOSPITAL WAS ONE OF THE FIRST
IN THE AREA TO OFFER ERGOS, A WORK
EVALUATOR/SIMULATOR DESIGNED TO
HELP INJURED WORKERS SAFELY
RETURN TO WORK IN THE SHORTEST
POSSIBLE TIME PERIOD.

ST. JOSEPH'S EASY STREET FACILITY IS A REPLICA OF AN AVERAGE NEIGHBORHOOD WHERE PATIENTS IN PHYSICAL, COGNITIVE, AND SPEECH THERAPY RELEARN AND PRACTICE SKILLS VITAL FOR DAY-TO-DAY LIFE.

WITH THE GOAL OF IMPROVING THE QUALITY OF LIFE FOR PATIENTS, THE HOSPITAL'S PSYCHIATRIC THERAPY PROGRAMS FOCUS ON RECOVERY AND ENCOURAGE THE INVOLVEMENT AND SUPPORT OF FAMILY AND FRIENDS.

Nowhere is that more evident than in St. Joseph's advanced physical rehabilitation programs, which employ the most sophisticated technology. The successes of Easy Street, Back To Action, Ergos,™ and Sports Medicine are recognized and lauded across the country. For example, Goodwill Industries' Easter Seals, which provides vocational training for people with disabilities, recently awarded its "National Graduate of the Year" award to a young Wichita woman who suffered severe injuries in a car accident. Through months of rehabilitation at St. Joseph, she recovered from severe brain damage

to obtain a job and become a source of inspiration to others who have suffered a disabling injury.

Easy Street, one of St. Joseph's most successful physical rehabilitation programs, is designed to "Pave the Way to a Smoother Recovery." The Easy Street facility is a replica of an average neighborhood—complete with streets, sidewalks, curbs, stairs, entrances, businesses, and vehicles—where patients in physical, cognitive, and speech therapy relearn and practice skills vital for day-to-day life. Participants come to understand the purpose of their therapies by applying them to real-world situations. St. Joseph was the first health care facility in the region to offer Easy Street.

The Back to Action Center (BAC) Work Therapy program is designed to help injured workers safely return to work in the shortest possible time period. To help achieve that goal, St. Joseph was one of the first hospitals in the area to offer Ergos, a work evaluator/simulator. Ergos combines computerized job descriptions with the U.S. Department of Labor's system for classifying jobs by physical demand. Seven "work" stations duplicate industrial working conditions found on most job sites, providing a clear look at a patient's present abilities and helping him or her set goals for the future. The informa-

tion obtained through Ergos is invaluable to employees, employers, physicians, and insurers in determining the capabilities of injured individuals and at what level they should re-enter the workplace to help prevent further injury.

In order for people to have fun playing sports, St. Joseph believes is important to take health seriously. That's why athletes—from the professional soccer player to the weekend golfer—seek out the services of St. Joseph's Sports Medicine program. Its "three-point-play" plan of education, prevention, and treatment/rehabilitation is the key to the program's success. Athletes are first individually screened to evaluate fitness level, diet, and injury. Computerized exercise equipment is then used for strengthening, rehabilitating, and monitoring athletes.

Since one of the primary goals the Sports Medicine program is to prevent injuries from happening, education is a major emphasis. Players, coaches, trainers, parents, and physicians receive instruction on ways to avoid athletic injuries through proper pre-activity banding, wrapping, taping, and bracing plus pre-season testing, nutrition education, stress management, and cardiovascular fitness.

The next step is to ensure proper implementation of athletic pro-

A "THREE-POINT-PLAY" PLAN OF
EDUCATION, PREVENTION, AND
TREATMENT/REHABILITATION FORMS
THE FOUNDATION OF THE SPORTS
MEDICINE PROGRAM.

ms. To that end, St. Joseph
rts medicine trainers provide
dical services during athletic
nts, maintain ongoing player
ication, conduct pre-season
luations, and monitor team
mbers throughout the season.
The success of this complex
gram depends on St. Joseph's
hly skilled professionals. Teams
specialists include sports medi-
e physicians, orthopedic sur-
ns, physical therapists, athletic
iners, exercise physiologists, and
tritionists. Sports Medicine's
roughness and depth have
mpted professional soccer, ice
key, and baseball teams, as well
rea high schools and colleges, to
ke St. Joseph their official sports
dicine provider.

PROVING LIVES THROUGH
NTAL THERAPY
Joseph Medical Center's Psychi-
c Center and Addiction Services
ist patients in addressing many
the problems that plague society
ay.
The primary goal of St. Joseph's
chiatric therapy is to improve

the quality of life for patients. Programs focus on recovery and encourage the involvement and support of
family and friends. Then, educational and therapeutic programs
help patients confront such problems as chemical dependency,
sexual abuse, grief trauma, and
behavioral disorders. Much of
St. Joseph's success is credited to its
team philosophy that unites the
physician, nurse, social worker, and
case manager. With one voice, they
encourage patients to make choices,
demonstrate accountability, and accept responsibility for their actions.

For patients with severe psychiatric problems, a day-care clinic at
the hospital reinforces therapy and
provides ongoing care.

COMMUNITY MISSION
The benefits of St. Joseph Medical
Center extend beyond patients and
their families. The hospital is also
concerned with administering to
the Wichita community and surrounding counties. As was the case
in the late 1800s, healing and caring for people are still St. Joseph's
primary goals.

Every day, representatives of
the medical center can be found
throughout the area teaching,
training, and giving time to the
populace. It may be through Ask-
A-Nurse, a health information service that averages 3,000 to 5,000
calls per month, or by extending a
helping hand to the elderly through
Care-Link, which offers educational programs and discounted
services to the elderly. St. Joseph
also reaches the public through
presentations to local organizations,
churches, and schools.

The hospital administration and
staff believe that such interaction
leads to a healthier community and
enhances people's lives on every
level. Hence, in addition to being
an outstanding medical facility,
St. Joseph Medical Center has a
positive impact on the home,
workplace, and leisure activities
of thousands of Kansans.

HEALING AND CARING FOR PEOPLE
REMAIN THE PRIMARY GOALS OF
ST. JOSEPH MEDICAL CENTER.

FLEESON, GOOING, COULSON & KITCH, L.L.C.

FLEESON, GOOING, COULSON & KITCH, L.L.C. is among the oldest law firms in Kansas. Founded in 1886 by C.H. Brooks, the firm is widely recognized for its high professional standards and its ability to successfully pursue lengthy and complex legal issues in many fields.

Today, Fleeson, Gooing remains firmly rooted in Kansas while continuing to expand its activities

THE FIRM'S OFFICES ARE LOCATED ON THE 16TH FLOOR AT 125 N. MARKET STREET (RIGHT).

throughout the region.

The firm now includes more than 30 lawyers, collectively holding degrees from 16 law schools including the University of Kansas and Washburn University.

In the early years of the firm's practice, Brooks and his partners provided counsel to the meat packing, banking, lumber, and milling industries around which Wichita's economy developed. Brooks was a prime mover in organizing the Wichita Union Stockyards and served as its first president. He also served as president of Stockyards National Bank, establishing the firm's leadership in banking law which continues today. The firm

FOUNDER C.H. BROOKS HAD BEEN ACTIVE IN THE WICHITA COMMUNITY FOR SEVERAL YEARS WHEN THE CITY HALL BUILDING WAS COMPLETED IN 1892 (ABOVE).

took its present name in 1945.

Throughout its long history, Fleeson, Gooing has maintained a strong interest and an active involvement in community affairs. This philosophy has allowed the firm to develop a special rapport with the city and its residents.

Today Fleeson, Gooing provides a broad range of services through practice groups focusing on civil, commercial, and white collar criminal litigation, including personal injury and product liability; employment law; constitutional and media law; corporate and business law; banking law; taxation; pensions and employee benefits; estate planning, trusts, and probate proceedings; real estate, development, and construction law; energy law; environmental law; and health care law.

FOR THE BENEFIT OF THE CLIENT

The firm's attorneys place great emphasis on gaining a thorough familiarity with the business, soci and economic environment in which their clients operate. Thus, they are able to ensure that the needs of clients are clearly understood and that desired goals in the face of complex legal situations o disputes are accurately identified and aggressively pursued.

While offering a wide range of services as a firm, the individual lawyers tend to concentrate their practice activities in a few areas of the law. This allows each lawyer t develop a high level of expertise i those areas, enabling the firm to better serve unique client interest According to Bill Thompson, cha man of the firm's Executive Com mittee, Fleeson, Gooing best serv its clients through a cooperative a proach designed to bring togethe the various skills of its attorneys. "For example," he points out, "if we are involved in a corporate acq sition, we may bring in lawyers h ing expertise in corporate law, tax law, environmental law, real estat law, employment law, pension la and other areas when appropriate

LITIGATION AND COMMERCIAL LAW

Because the law is shaped and refined through litigation, the firm historically has chosen trial work as one mainstay of its practice. Fleeson, Gooing has an active an sophisticated practice in civil and commercial litigation, placing th firm in the forefront of developin substantive law.

The firm successfully defended America's only manufacturer of

o vaccine in a landmark suit llenging the adequacy of the ning given in connection with ribution of the product. Other s have led to the adoption of doctrine of informed consent in lical malpractice and the rule of ct liability for highly dangerous ducts.

he firm's corporate, business, banking practice addresses the ds of a variety of clients, from proprietors to multinational porations. Services include busi- s formation, acquisition, and gers; business and tax planning; assistance in public and private irities offerings. The firm is a ognized leader in the area of ler liability disputes. Its sophisti- d tax practice handles income, sales, and property taxation at evels—local, state, and federal. leeson, Gooing has long been mportant participant in the vities of the state's oil and gas ustry. For more than 40 years, firm has represented the thwest Kansas Royalty Owner's

Association. This representation has included numerous complex class action cases concerning one of the world's largest natural gas fields, the 1.7 million-acre Hugoton Field in southwest Kansas. The firm's efforts on behalf of the group— including appearances before the United States Supreme Court, the Federal Courts of Appeals, and the Federal Energy Regulatory Com- mission—have led to the successful recovery of more than $100 million

in royalties for clients and have es- tablished a national reputation for the firm in this area of practice.

COMMITMENT TO THE LAW AND THE COMMUNITY

From the start, the attorneys of Fleeson, Gooing have been actively involved in community affairs. Attorneys associated with the firm have served as mayor, state represen- tative, president of the Wichita School Board, and president of the Wichita Area Chamber of Com- merce, and as chairpersons or board members of numerous state and local civic and nonprofit groups. The firm has also been regularly represented in leadership positions in the Wichita and Kansas Bar Associations as board members, committee chairpersons, and officers.

Characterizing the firm, senior partner Tom Kitch comments, "Fleeson, Gooing, Coulson & Kitch has a reputation for taking on tough cases that present points of law that need definition. We stand ready to devote the resources neces- sary to meet the needs of our cli- ents, whatever they may be. This frequently places us on the leading edge of the most complex and chal- lenging issues. While all lawyers work with the law, our firm has consistently been involved in shaping the law."

THE WICHITA STATE UNIVERSITY, ONE OF THE FIRM'S CLIENTS, OVER- LOOKS THE CITY FROM ITS EAST SIDE LOCATION (ABOVE).

THE FIRM USES A COOPERATIVE APPROACH TO BRING TOGETHER THE DIVERSE SKILLS OF ITS LAWYERS IN PURSUING COMPLEX CLIENT ISSUES (ABOVE LEFT).

COMPUTER TECHNOLOGY PLAYS AN IMPORTANT ROLE IN THE PRACTICE OF LAW TODAY (LEFT).

BANK IV

IN 1935, FOLLOWING THE CRASH OF BOEING'S XB-17 experimental bomber, a somber group of bankers gathered in Seattle to decide the fate of The Boeing Company. Representatives of some of the nation's largest financial institutions were there, including a lone delegate from Wichita's Fourth National Bank.

THE BANK IV SIGN IS A FAMILIAR SYMBOL OF THE STRENGTH AND COMMITMENT OF THE STATE'S LEADING BANKING ORGANIZATION.

AN ARCHITECTURAL FOCAL POINT IN DOWNTOWN WICHITA, FOURTH FINANCIAL CORPORATION'S HEADQUARTERS FEATURES A COMMISSIONED CALDER MOBILE IN THE ATRIUM.

To most who had offered financial backing for the speculative project, the crash represented failure. But as each bank pulled its support, the representative from Wichita, Arthur Kincade, demonstrated his faith in Boeing and its Wichita operations by agreeing to assume the entire loan.

Today, Fourth National is known as BANK IV, the flagship of a growing financial services network of community banks in the Midwest. BANK IV and its holding company, Fourth Financial Corporation, help protect the financial strength of the region through technology, personnel, and sound banking practices. "The relationship between a bank and its community is much more than 'deposits in, de-posits out,' " says Darrell Knudson, chairman and CEO of Fourth Financial. "If the communities we serve aren't better off having us as a neighbor, then we're not doing our job."

Adds Gordon Greer, chairman of BANK IV Kansas, "By focusing on services, technology, and quality, along with managing risk and profitability, BANK IV provides a financial resource to meet the myriad needs of consumers and commercial customers throughout our markets."

COMMITTED TO CUSTOMER CONVENIENCE

Since its founding in 1887, BANK IV has maintained a strong commitment to customer conven-

ience. Customers today enjoy around-the-clock banking through VIA automated teller machines and access to more than 100,000 ATMs worldwide. Likewise, customers can get immediate information about accounts or financial services through InIVmation, BANK IV's free 24-hour telephone customer service system. Thanks to these and other efforts, the bank earned a convenience rating of 8.5 (on a scale of one to 10) in a recent BANK IV service quality study.

For even greater convenience, customers enjoy the same array of banking opportunities at all full-service branches. "We always look for ways to make BANK IV easier to use," Knudson says. "In several cities we're testing supermarket branches and drive-through ATMs so no matter where you are, you're never far from BANK IV."

FOCUS ON CONSUMER BANKING

Once known primarily for its emphasis on commercial services, BANK IV today offers consumers new ideas in packaged account products, investment services, debit and credit card services, and home financing. Its personal checking, savings, and installment loan services help individuals or growing families save time and money. Similar programs—like "checkless checking" with cash-debit cards and VISA credit cards—give customers the purchasing power they need at home and across the globe.

Likewise, the bank's personal investment and annuity services make planning for the future easy. Licensed brokers offer a variety of income, growth, and tax-free bond funds. BANK IV also has a highly regarded personal Trust Department.

But this focus on personal banking has not come at the expense of BANK IV's longtime commitment to the success of area businesses.

ether it's deciphering the com-
ties of foreign exchange rates
ooking for new ways to finance
tal investment for the future,
NK IV delivers for diverse com-
cial customers.

ourth Financial's multibillion-
ar assets and its array of special-
services are an important draw
major corporations considering
ove to Kansas. But BANK IV's
mitment to small and mid-size
inesses is equally impressive.
company, regardless of its size,
take advantage of BANK IV's
management, commercial
nce and leasing, and asset
agement services.

or example, through Sweep
ounts, business customers can
idle funds working with con-
ient overnight electronic invest-
t. Companies can also take
antage of Contact IV, which
ws direct access to the bank's
nframe so customers can moni-
and get the most from their
ds.

ANK IV serves businesses in
- to moderate-income areas
ugh its Community Develop-
t Corporation. Headed by an
ependent board of directors, the
C helps businesses and neigh-

borhoods see possibility where before there was despair.

THE PEOPLE BEHIND THE BANK

BANK IV believes that success in
banking, like in any other business,
depends on the quality of the people who work in the industry.
Therefore, the bank strives to recruit the brightest and most dedicated individuals, whether they are
recent college graduates or career
bankers.

BANK IV is equally committed
to keeping its staff motivated and
enthusiastic by providing a work
atmosphere in which individual talents are developed and rewards are
possible. For example, an employee
task force was formed in 1993 to
design, review, and select computerized customer support systems. As a
result, BANK IV customer service
representatives can provide more information, speed up new account
openings, compare pricing options,
and customize documents for every
customer.

Throughout the BANK IV network, associates are encouraged to
do whatever it takes to satisfy their
customers, shareholders, and the
community. Therefore, building an

individual's skills in banking, management, and community responsibility is critical. Recognizing that
each of its associates has leadership
potential for the future, the bank
gives them the authority to solve
problems on the spot without
going through a complicated approval process.

With this combination of service, technology, and quality personnel, BANK IV will continue to
grow as a regional financial institution, serving the needs of individuals and businesses close to home
and around the world.

ONE OF BANK IV WICHITA'S MOST
VISIBLE COMMUNITY PROJECTS IS THE
ANNUAL BANK IV RIVER RUN, EACH
YEAR ATTRACTING OVER 10,000
RUNNERS.

AS WICHITA'S LEADING COMMERCIAL
BANK, BANK IV OFFERS A FULL
RANGE OF SERVICES FOR BUSINESSES
OF ALL SIZES (ABOVE LEFT).

ST. FRANCIS REGIONAL MEDICAL CENTER

ENSURING THE HIGHEST QUALITY HEALTH care while advancing the practice of medicine has been the mission of St. Francis Regional Medical Center since 1889. The state's largest hospital, St. Francis has on staff more than 600 physicians and 3,500 employees who apply the latest in health services knowledge, technology, and techniques in a caring environment.

The institution had its humble beginnings in 1886 when pioneer doctors Andrew Fabrique and J.E. Oldham opened a 12-bed hospital in a dilapidated three-story house in Wichita. Despite the doctors' best efforts, the hospital soon faced financial ruin. Outside help was sought. At the request of the Right Reverend John J. Hennessy, Bishop of the Diocese of Wichita, five German Sisters of the Sorrowful Mother arrived in Wichita in 1889 from Rome to make the hospital their first overseas mission.

Despite countless obstacles, including the fact that the Sisters spoke only German, the hospital re-established itself. The Sisters were guided in their healing ministry by four core values—service, human dignity, wisdom, and vision. The medical center has continued to follow these values for more than 100 years.

Because of its dedication and medical proficiency, St. Francis would be called upon time and again, in the early years as well as today, to help Kansans through emergencies and epidemics and to bring the latest in health services to the area. Out of each crisis would come medical progress and the establishment of new services, such as a nursing school in 1917, the first blood transfusions in the We during the '30s, coronary care in the '40s, cancer treatment during the '50s, joint replacement in the '70s, and organ transplantation ir the '80s.

Today, St. Francis' 55-acre can pus in central Wichita is the hub for some of the most advanced pa tient care, education, and research in the Midwest. Health services a provided through inpatient and o patient programs at the Wichita facility, as well as through outrea programs across the state. In keeping with the Sisters' healing mission, St. Francis also provides millions of dollars in charitable ca annually.

CENTERS OF EXCELLENCE
Mindful of its mission to provide medical services to those in need, St. Francis strives to give care of t highest quality. Medical center st provide general and specialty care through 14 Centers of Excellence multidisciplinary teams of physicians and allied health profession.

FOUNDED IN 1889, ST. FRANCIS REGIONAL MEDICAL CENTER IS TODAY THE LARGEST NOT-FOR-PROFIT MEDICAL CENTER IN KANSAS (BELOW).

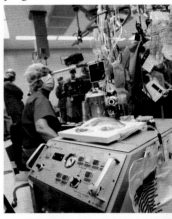

THE SPECIALISTS IN ST. FRANCIS' HEART CENTER (TOP RIGHT) PERFORM MORE THAN 50,000 DIAGNOSTIC AND THERAPEUTIC PROCEDURES ANNUALLY.

AS ONE OF ST. FRANCIS' 14 CENTERS OF EXCELLENCE, THE NEWLIFE CENTER (BOTTOM RIGHT) MAKES NO COMPROMISE IN THE QUALITY OF MEDICAL CARE AND NURSING.

ked by the latest technology. edicine's greatest advances come n teams of professionals work-together," says Sister M. Sylvia n, SSM, president and chief cutive officer of the medical ter.

he centers of excellence range ely from coronary care to pediat-, from trauma services to psychi-c care, and from cancer and epsy treatment to the Burn Cen-the only such facility within a -mile radius of Wichita. Many he centers were the first of their d to be established in Wichita or

has resulted in the founding of St. Francis Research Institute, parent of the area's first and only Orthopaedic Research Institute, which developed the Wichita Frame to help trauma patients recover without traction; the Psychiatric Research Institute; and the Center for Phase I (pharmaceutical) Research.

Complementing the medical center's emphasis on research is a strong commitment to education. St. Francis is a teaching center for medical students and resident physicians, offering many clinical resi-

continues to strive toward ever-higher levels of efficiency and cost-effectiveness. St. Francis has shown strong leadership in creating—and re-creating—an effective health care system that meets regional needs. In an environment that embraces innovation, employees are encouraged to think creatively to determine ways the medical center can improve upon the quality and delivery of its services.

The commitment to quality health care, the advancement of medicine, and the values of the founding Sisters will remain stead-

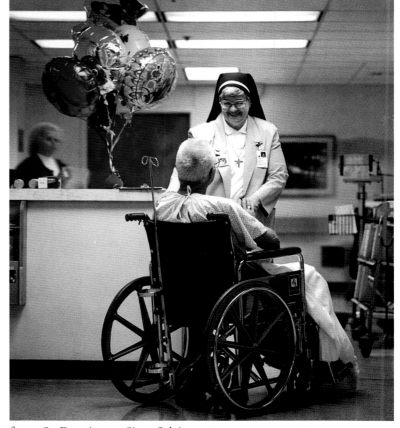

sas. As a result, the city's first ney, heart, pancreas, and bone row transplants occurred at rancis. The Surgery Center the first in Wichita to use -saving equipment that allows ents to have their own blood sfused during surgery.

he centers of excellence not y make possible the sophisti-d care one would normally find much larger city, but also pro-e avenues for medical research. rancis' dedication to research

dency programs. There also are educational programs for nurses and allied health professionals. "Being involved in education calls forth the best from everyone," says Sister Sylvia. "The words 'teaching institution' and 'top quality' often go hand in hand, and we strive to maintain these labels for St. Francis."

LEADERSHIP FOR THE FUTURE

St. Francis, like other medical centers with strong charitable visions,

fast at St. Francis, says Sister Sylvia. It is because of this dedication that the medical center's list of accomplishments is as long as its history, and both are sure to grow.

Summing up St. Francis' philosophy, Sister Sylvia says, "We are committed to making each patient encounter a personal one that demonstrates our mission of healing and caring and provides a distinctive quality that exemplifies our values."

SPONSORED BY THE SISTERS OF THE SORROWFUL MOTHER, ST. FRANCIS FOLLOWS THE MISSION "TO SERVE THE UNSERVED WHO SUFFER."

ST. FRANCIS' 10-BED BURN CENTER (ABOVE LEFT), THE ONLY FACILITY OF ITS KIND WITHIN 180 MILES OF WICHITA, GIVES THE INTENSE, COMPREHENSIVE CARE REQUIRED TO EASE PAIN AND REHABILITATE SERIOUSLY INJURED PATIENTS.

WICHITA STATE UNIVERSITY

WICHITA STATE UNIVERSITY'S CAMPUS encompasses 330 acres in northeast Wichita. Its metropolitan setting makes it unique among Kansas Regents' institutions and fosters extraordinary opportunities to merge teaching, research, and classroom education with

practical partnerships in the community.

"It is important to understand that the core activities of the university—teaching, research, and service—are powerful contributors to campus and community relationships," says university president

Eugene Hughes. "These elements can change individual lives and improve the fabric of the community. Such influences are the essence of what a university should be."

Since its founding in 1895, the university's enrollment has grown to nearly 15,000 students. WSU

offers comprehensive educational opportunities through more than 150 undergraduate, graduate, and doctoral degree programs in six degree-granting colleges—business, education, engineering, fine arts, health professions, and liberal arts and sciences. The university serves a large number of nontraditional students; the average student age is 28, and 80 percent of WSU students work full- or part-time.

"While balancing educational and work commitments, these students—and our faculty—are actively involved in the mission of a metropolitan university, which is to support the educational, economic, and cultural enrichment of the community and the state," Hughes says.

BUILDING PARTNERSHIPS

Over the years, the university has established countless partnerships in health care, business, public schools, government, and the arts. Through these important local alliances, WSU students take a more active role in learning, and the entire community benefits from practical applications of their research and scholarship.

For example, Wichita's position as the major medical and referral center in south-central Kansas has given WSU students numerous opportunities to gain clinical experience in their chosen health care fields. For those pursuing careers in communicative disorders, practicums are available with such local organizations as Heartspring, the world's leading educational center for children with severe hearing and speech disorders. The university offers cultural enrichment through its Connoisseur Series, Opera Theater, and University Theatre. Many successful entrepreneurs, such as Rent-A-Center founders Frank Barton and Tom Devlin and Pizza Hut founders Dan and Frank Carney, have attended or support WSU and the W. Frank Barton School of Business.

Among the university's most

WSU'S METROPOLITAN SETTING FOSTERS EXTRAORDINARY OPPORTUNITIES TO MERGE TEACHING, RESEARCH, AND CLASSROOM EDUCATION WITH PRACTICAL PARTNERSHIPS IN THE COMMUNITY (ABOVE).

SINCE ITS FOUNDING IN 1895, THE UNIVERSITY'S ENROLLMENT HAS GROWN TO NEARLY 15,000 STUDENTS (RIGHT).

DAN MOORE

DAN MOORE

cessful research, technical, and ncial partnerships have been e related to Wichita's aviation stry. The Boeing Company, sna Aircraft Company, Beech raft Corporation, and Learjet have played significant roles in enhancement of research and neering facilities at the univer- In return, students graduating state-of-the-art engineering grams provide an abundant em- ee base for the benefit of local regional companies.

he National Institute for Avia- Research at WSU integrates er education, government, and ness in cooperative efforts to nce the U.S. aviation industry. ted in a $7-million, 74,000- re-foot facility, the institute des research and training labo- ies for aerodynamics, pro- ion, basic materials, cryogenics superconductivity, composite ctures, crash dynamics, icing, puter-aided design and manu- ring, avionics, and flight lation. The institute conducts arch sponsored by industry and ernment under grants from the artment of Defense, the Depart- t of Education, the Federal tion Administration, and the ional Aeronautics and Space inistration.

IPUS EXPANSION

e past 20 years, WSU has e than doubled its instructional e through the addition of state- e-art facilities for art, music, cation, engineering, health essions, biological sciences, ical education, dance, mathe- ics, physics, computer science, tennis. A new building to se the Elliott School of Commu- tion for print and broadcast nalism, public relations, and ertising is scheduled for com- ion in 1994.

omplementing the impressive pus is a nationally renowned, iece outdoor sculpture collec- that accents the university's

more than 60 buildings. Also of note is Wiedemann Hall's Great Marcussen Organ, the first such in- strument installed in North Amer- ica by the 187-year-old Danish firm of Marcussen and Son.

"A university should offer its stu- dents both educational and cultural advantages," Hughes comments.

"Wichita State University provides a unique blend of scholarship, creativity, innovation, cultural awareness, and leadership in every academic field. All of these ele- ments combine to make us a metropolitan university of national stature."

AMONG THE UNIVERSITY'S MOST SUCCESSFUL RESEARCH, TECHNICAL, AND FINANCIAL PARTNERSHIPS HAVE BEEN THOSE RELATED TO WICHITA'S AVIATION INDUSTRY (LEFT).

COMPLEMENTING THE UNIVERSITY'S 60-PLUS BUILDINGS IS A NATIONALLY RENOWNED, 54-PIECE OUTDOOR SCULP- TURE COLLECTION (ABOVE).

WSU OFFERS COMPREHENSIVE EDUCATIONAL OPPORTUNITIES IN SIX DEGREE-GRANTING COLLEGES— BUSINESS, EDUCATION, ENGINEERING, FINE ARTS, HEALTH PROFESSIONS, AND LIBERAL ARTS AND SCIENCES (LEFT).

THE COLEMAN COMPANY, INC.

CONSUMER REPORTER DAVID HOROWITZ didn't believe this story: A Coleman television ad claimed that one of the company's coolers—packed full of shrimp and ice—had survived a devastating car fire. Later, when the car was inspected and the cooler was opened, not only did the shrimp remain

frozen, but there was still ice in the cooler.

Horowitz, host of the nationally syndicated television show "Fight Back," challenged The Coleman Company to prove it. So as millions of Americans watched, the same model cooler, filled with frozen shrimp and ice, was put in a car which was then set ablaze. Sure enough, after the flames died down and the cooler was opened, the shrimp and ice gave America positive proof that Coleman products are "unbelievably tough."

The Coleman Company's longtime and celebrated dedication to quality design and construction has made it the leading manufacturer and marketer of brand-name consumer products for the camping, outdoor recreation, and do-it-yourself markets.

STARTING OUT WITH LAMPS
The company was founded in 1900 when school teacher and part-time salesman W.C. Coleman began selling gas lamps in the Oklahoma Territory. Coleman's flair for promotion, his own unshakable belief in his product, and an opportune loan provided him enough money to move his business to Wichita in 1902. The next year he purchased the patent rights from the lamp's manufacturer. With improvements to the original design, the young company introduced the Coleman Arc Lamp, the first of many items that would build a reputation for reasonably priced, quality products.

In 1940 W.C. Coleman's son, Sheldon, took over the company and led it through decades of

growth. During World War II, the Coleman GI pocket stove was designed and put in production in 60 days at the behest of the Army Quartermaster Corps. GIs picked the pocket stove and the Jeep as the two most important pieces of non-combat equipment they used.

In 1988 Sheldon's son, Sheldon C. Coleman, assumed leadership of the publicly held company that, by then, had produced more than 40 million Coleman lanterns and a vast array of other products.

In 1989 the company went

private after it was purchased by MacAndrews & Forbes. Although no Coleman family member has remained in a management role since the acquisition, the new leadership is dedicated to the tradition of providing exceptional products at superior value to consumers on a

worldwide basis.

Privately held until 1992, whe it returned to the New York Stoc Exchange, The Coleman Compa used that interval to divest itself unrelated businesses. The compa also completed a critical self-examination and has since made

sweeping internal changes and improvements.

Coleman today is sharply focused on the products it knows best: lanterns, camp stoves, coole heaters, jugs, canoes, fishing boa sleeping bags, tents, backpacks, portable electric lights, and acces

FOR DECADES, THE COLEMAN LANTERN HAS BEEN A MAINSTAY OF THE COMPANY'S REPUTATION FOR REASONABLY PRICED, QUALITY PRODUCTS.

A COLEMAN COOLER—PACKED FULL OF SHRIMP AND ICE—NOT ONLY SURVIVED A DEVASTATING CAR FIRE, BUT IT KEPT THE CONTENTS FROZEN, PROVING THAT COLEMAN PRODUCTS ARE "UNBELIEVABLY TOUGH."

Wichita, manufactures and fills disposable propane cylinders and produces precision machined components for the company's other products.

THE CHALLENGE TODAY

Coleman's most difficult task today may be competing against its own high quality, says Lawrence Jones, chairman and CEO of The Coleman Company. "We don't have product obsolescence by design," he says. "There are people still using their grandfathers' lanterns on camping trips. That's a great testimonial for the company, but in order to keep growing and remain profitable we have introduced new and improved products, strengthened marketing, streamlined production methods, and developed foreign markets."

Building an increased presence in major foreign markets—Japan and the Pacific Rim, Europe, and Latin America—is central to the company's long-term strategy. That effort often requires great determination, hard work, and patience,

says Jones. For example, Coleman opened an office in Japan in 1976, but it took almost 12 years to become a viable competitor there. When the company wanted to sell liquid-petroleum gas stoves and lanterns, Japan required that the products be 100 percent defect-free. "We built 10,000 stoves in our Wichita factory," recalls Jones. "A Japanese team inspected 17 percent of the stoves at random, and they all passed." Today the Coleman name is as recognized in Japan as it is in the United States. Overall, the company's products are distributed in more than 100 foreign countries.

Jones says that the process of making Coleman a more efficient, profitable, and market-responsive company has been difficult at times, but it is paying off. He believes the company's commitment to long-term viability, plus its continuing dedication to product quality, will make Coleman's light shine ever brighter in the future.

BUILDING AN INCREASED PRESENCE IN MAJOR FOREIGN MARKETS—JAPAN AND THE PACIFIC RIM, EUROPE, AND LATIN AMERICA—IS CENTRAL TO THE COMPANY'S LONG-TERM STRATEGY.

COLEMAN IS THE LEADING MANUFACTURER AND MARKETER OF BRAND-NAME CONSUMER PRODUCTS FOR THE CAMPING, OUTDOOR RECREATION, AND DO-IT-YOURSELF MARKETS (LEFT).

for the recreation and leisure markets; and for the do-it-yourself market, Powermate portable generators and pressure washers. The company has the leading market share its major product categories. With a worldwide work force of 00, Coleman manufactures products at its Wichita headquarters, as l as plants in Maize, Kansas; w Braunfels, Texas; Lake City, th Carolina; Cedar City, Utah; rney, Nebraska; and Inheiden l Haldensleben, Germany. The 0,000-square-foot Wichita plant kes coolers, jugs, and lighting, king, and heating products. The nt in Maize, just northwest of

FIDELITY SAVINGS ASSOCIATION OF KANSAS

FIDELITY SAVINGS ASSOCIATION OF KANSAS is a locally owned federal savings bank and the largest residential mortgage lender in Wichita. Based on its 1993 asset size of $700 million, Fidelity is also the largest savings institution headquartered in Wichita. ◆ Nine retail banking locations offer local residents convenient access to a full array of financial services. Fidelity presently has three residential loan offices in the Wichita area—Downtown, Northrock, and Northwest Centre—and one in Lawrence, Kansas.

Fidelity is also a significant servicer of mortgage loans. Every month, more than 30,000 customers in 46 states mail their mortgage payments to Fidelity Savings.

In 1993 a mortgage lending subsidiary, American Fidelity Mortgage Corporation, was opened in San Diego, California. Fidelity also has two other subsidiaries: Fidelity Management Corporation, which manages income property in Wichita and Topeka, and Fidelity Insurance Agency, which provides full insurance coverage for home, automobile, and life.

EMPLOYEES OF FIDELITY SAVINGS GATHER IN HERITAGE SQUARE PARK OUTSIDE THE COMPANY'S DOWNTOWN WICHITA OFFICE. IN FRONT (FROM LEFT) ARE CLARK BASTIAN, PRESIDENT; CLAY BASTIAN, EXECUTIVE VICE PRESIDENT; AND MARVIN BASTIAN, CHAIRMAN.

MAKING DREAMS COME TRUE

In 1936 a front page story in the *Wichita Beacon* newspaper extended an invitation to a "Housing Clinic of Interest to All Wichitans." The story urged readers to hear the words of Homer C. Bastian, Kansas' first director of the Federal Housing Administration (FHA), who would explain the new Federal Housing Act designed to make the dream of home ownership a reality for many Americans.

Six years later, in 1942, Bastian's own dream came true. Recognizing Wichita's potential as a trade area and a growing housing market, he left his job with the FHA and purchased a Wichita real estate lending company, The Fidelity Investment Company. In 1947 he was joined by his son, Marvin, who had just returned from World War II service. The Bastians operated the business from a two-room downtown office suite. Using their government loan program experience, the father-and-son team developed a business ideally suited to help meet the postwar demand for housing and loans.

The company quickly made a name for itself in government FHA/VA home lending. Homer and Marvin Bastian created loan correspondent relationships with a number of major life insurance companies that had an appetite for purchasing pools of the Fidelity-originated mortgages.

Fidelity Investment's success as a mortgage banker allowed it to diversify in new, innovative ways. With Marvin Bastian's leadership, the company expanded in the postwar years into home building, real estate development and sales, apartment management, and insurance.

AIR CAPITAL SAVINGS ACQUISITION

In the late 1960s, Marvin Bastian became chief executive officer of the Fidelity companies and found himself at a crossroads. Independent mortgage bankers like Fidelity

estment had entered a decline as insurance companies began ning away from residential mort-es to pursue commercial real ate and other more lucrative estments. Bastian realized he uld have to either sell the family iness or diversify into something v.

n 1975 Bastian successfully ac-red Air Capital Savings, a fledg-; savings and loan in Wichita n $32 million in assets. While it small in size, Air Capital had n innovative. It was the first ft in the area to open branch ces and the first to utilize com-er technology.

Renamed Fidelity Savings Associ-n of Kansas, the thrift became parent of the other Fidelity com-ies. The acquisition provided new sources of funds for mort-e lending: membership in the eral Home Loan Bank system retail deposit relationships ugh the savings customer base. The company's leadership was ex-ded by the addition of Marvin tian's two sons—Clark in 1976 Clay in 1980. Today Clark es as president, and Clay is exec-e vice president.

By 1986 Fidelity had outgrown headquarters. Recognizing the ortance of a vital downtown dis-t, the Bastians were committed emaining in the heart of the . A $6-million, five-story, state-he-art office building was con-cted at the south end of itage Square Park in the same ck as Wichita's first city hall.

ELITY TODAY— NOVATIVE BANKING

he 1980s, the nation's thrift ustry confronted the risks of esting in long-term assets (loans) le funding those assets with rt-term deposits and borrow-s. Fidelity responded by adopt-an innovative asset-liability nagement program designed to w the institution and provide tection from interest rate volatil-As a result, the company has

consistently exceeded all federal tests for capital adequacy.

Since the acquisition of Air Capital Savings in 1975, Fidelity has grown 22 times its size to $700 million in assets, $37 million in net worth, and 250 employees. It also maintains a mortgage servicing portfolio approaching $2 billion in volume, with 35,000 customers in 46 states, including some 20,000 in Kansas.

In the past two years, Fidelity has risen to become the top residen-tial mortgage lender in Wichita and Sedgwick County.

"Our goal," says President Clark Bastian, "is to develop lifetime cus-tomers. They have placed their trust in us, and we cannot exist

without them. Our mission is to provide exceptional value that ex-ceeds their expectations and earns their respect. We will continue to invest in our team members to improve their awareness of our customers' changing needs."

For decades Fidelity and its em-ployees have provided leadership and dollars to community con-cerns. Annually, more than 40 local charities and cultural organizations benefit from its philanthropy.

"This community has been very good to my family and our com-pany," says Chairman of the Board Marvin Bastian. "In return, we try to give something back that will make a difference in the lives of others."

FIDELITY'S $6-MILLION, FIVE-STORY HEADQUARTERS AT 100 EAST ENGLISH STREET REFLECTS THE COMPANY'S COM-MITMENT TO THE HEART OF THE CITY.

FIDELITY SAVINGS OPERATES NINE AREA OFFICES, INCLUDING THE NORTHROCK OFFICE IN FAR NORTH-EAST WICHITA, WHERE CUSTOMERS CAN OBTAIN BOTH DEPOSIT AND LEND-ING SERVICES.

KG&E, A WESTERN RESOURCES COMPANY

MEMBERS OF KG&E'S GREEN TEAM BUILT A FLIGHT PEN AT THE AUDUBON SOCIETY'S CHAPLIN NATURE CENTER TO AID IN THE REHABILITATION OF INJURED BIRDS OF PREY.

TERRY ATWATER (RIGHT), KG&E CUSTOMER ADVISOR, SPEAKS TO STUDENTS AS PART OF THE COMPANY'S C.O.P.E. (CONSIDER OPPORTUNITIES IN A PROFESSIONAL ENVIRONMENT) PROJECT.

KG&E'S MISSION IS TO PROVIDE THE HIGHEST QUALITY ENERGY SERVICES, TO BE A GOOD EMPLOYER, AND TO MAINTAIN THE PUBLIC TRUST.

IN AN INDUSTRY IN WHICH QUICK RESPONSE TO the market is critical, Wichita-based KG&E, a Western Resources Company, regards change in community needs as the ultimate motivator. "Our mission is to provide the highest quality energy services, to be a good employer, and to maintain the public trust," says Kent Brown, president and chief executive officer.

KG&E provides retail natural gas and electric energy to more than 468,000 industrial, commercial, and residential customers in south-central and southeast Kansas. Whether the challenge is quickly restoring service after a storm, leading local economic development efforts, protecting the environment, demonstrating leadership for community projects such as the March of Dimes' WalkAmerica, or providing educational programs in area schools, KG&E regularly demonstrates its broad-based community commitment.

DECADES OF SERVICE

Founded in 1909, KG&E merged with The Kansas Power and Light Company, with headquarters in Topeka, on March 31, 1992. The merged company was named Western Resources, Inc. and now serves more than 578,000 electric customers throughout central and eastern Kansas and 1.06 million natural gas customers in Kansas, western Missouri, and northern Oklahoma.

Shortly after the merger, the Western Resources Power Technology Center was established in Wichita to help industrial and commercial customers address

power quality issues, thereby enhancing the productivity of their electric equipment. Architects, engineers, and others who rely on computers and other high-tech tools now turn to the center for training and support. In the face of tougher federal and state environmental regulations, KG&E is also helping industrial and municipal customers utilize new electrotechnologies to reduce contaminants in waste and wastewater efficiently, safely, and cost-effectively.

Complementing this commitment to introducing new technologies and providing the highest quality customer service, KG&E's crisis response capabilities have garnered national recognition. The company received an Eagle Award from the American Gas Association and Edison Electric Institute for effectively restoring electric and natural gas service to more than 65,000 Wichita area customers following tornadoes in 1991.

"The award is a tribute to our employees," says Brown. "The responsibility to protect the area' quality of life, whether on a day-day basis or following a disaster, KG&E tradition that no one tak lightly."

CONCERN FOR THE ENVIRONMENT

Another tradition stronger than ever at KG&E is concern for the environment. The Green Team, employee-directed environment task force, identifies and pursues wide range of projects including recycling, wildlife habitat develo ment, and wetlands preservation The company strongly promotes energy conservation and the devel ment and use of alternative-fuel vehicles.

KG&E is equally watchful of environmental impact of its own electric generating stations and other facilities. The company use low-sulfur coal in coal-fired gene ing units, continuously monitors air and water emissions to ensure high standards are maintained, and is a partner in the state's onl nuclear-powered generating cen

"Being an energy company ca ries with it a major responsibility We have to be reliable—and avai ble—24 hours a day," says Brow "But where we work is also wher we live. Therefore, our primary r sponsibility is to remain in the fc front, always changing to help o communities grow and prosper.

MPRISE BANK

HERE'S A SAYING AT EMPRISE BANK: "OUR roots are in Kansas, not just our branches." It's an adage that embodies the spirit of Emprise, a statewide, family-owned banking network with a strong commitment to the future of Kansas. ◆ Its predecessor, United American Bank, was founded in

hita as Stockyards National k in 1910. Since it was pur-ed by the Michaelis family of hita in 1965, the $20-million k has grown into a statewide ncial services system that has s of more than $500 million. Our niche is to fulfill the com-ity banking needs of the peo-f Kansas," says Chairman of Board M.D. Michaelis, who n his career with the bank in 9. "We're here to serve the big-corporations, the small com-ity industries, the ranchers, the ers . . . the people who are d to call Kansas home."

FOCUSED ON PEOPLE
What separates Emprise from other banks is a corporate culture that focuses on people. It's a personal commitment—adopted by each employee—that superior service is the rule, not the exception. The people of Emprise Bank make a service promise to their customers, as well as to their fellow employees, that courtesy, attentiveness, and consideration for others really counts. "We're here to make banking easy and enjoyable," says Michaelis, "because customers don't do business with banks, they do business with people."

Michaelis leads by example, spending about half his time traveling from bank to bank across the state and visiting with customers, employees, and community leaders. "The people of Emprise are more than just members of the communities we serve," Michaelis says. "We believe there's a difference between merely serving the community and actually guiding it toward great achievement through leadership."

He adds, "I travel the state so much because I enjoy interacting with our customers and their communities. Customers prefer to bank with people who can call them by name—people who understand their personal and business needs. That's what Emprise is all about."

A CHIVALRIC ENTERPRISE
From Lawrence to Wichita, from Iola to Hays, Emprise serves the diverse retail, business, and agricultural banking needs of Kansans.

When the organization underwent a name change in 1989, the word "emprise" seemed a logical choice. The dictionary defines "emprise" as an adventurous, daring, or chivalric enterprise. Unquestionably, Emprise Bank exhibits a sense of progress and movement, driven by the desire and aspiration to provide exceptional products and service.

"The advent of interstate banking will have an impact on us, but I view it as positive," says Michaelis. "New competitors will mean customer movement within the marketplace. With our culture, people, service, and philosophy of community leadership, we will be firmly positioned to capture new market share."

He adds, "Emprise reflects the traditions and strong values of Kansas, with a vision toward the future. We are committed to the people of Kansas. As we acquire banks, we will continue to choose each community carefully, knowing that our growth and success are interwoven with that of our state."

"OUR NICHE IS TO FULFILL THE COMMUNITY BANKING NEEDS OF THE PEOPLE OF KANSAS," SAYS CHAIRMAN OF THE BOARD M.D. MICHAELIS (LEFT), WHO BEGAN HIS CAREER WITH THE BANK IN 1969.

HCA WESLEY MEDICAL CENTER

FOUNDED IN 1912 AS WESLEY HOSPITAL AND Nurses' Training School, Wesley is a vital member of Wichita's medical community, a comprehensive medical center, and a leader in serving the health care needs of Kansas and the surrounding states. ◆ An acute care center with a staff of more than

700 physicians and 3,000 employees, Wesley is licensed for 760 beds, making it the largest hospital of the Hospital Corporation of America (HCA), an investor-owned corporation. The hospital's traditions of service and leadership in medical care had long been established when it affiliated with HCA in 1985.

The hospital is also the major source of neonatal research for the state. The Neonatal Research Center is dedicated to constantly improving the care available for critically ill infants. In addition, geneticists and maternal-fetal specialists provide genetic counseling, prenatal diagnosis and treatment, and high-risk obstetric care.

The hospital's Center for Repr[oductive] Medicine, with both laboratories and surgical facilities, provides the most advanced repr[o]ductive technology available. The center's in vitro fertilization program has one of the highest succ[ess] rates in the country.

Wesley's efforts in other medi[cal] specialties are equally impressive. The hospital has a separate rehab[ili]tation facility, located in west Wichita, to help patients recover the highest possible quality of lif[e] in the presence of disease or follo[w]ing an injury.

A board-eligible pediatric criti[cal] care specialist, the only one in K[an]sas, oversees the care of critically children in the Pediatric Intensi[ve] Care Unit. Other specialties in-

WESLEY'S NEONATAL INTENSIVE CARE UNIT SERVES AS THE STATE'S PRIMARY REFERRAL CENTER, PROVIDING NEARLY HALF OF THE HOSPITAL DAYS FOR CRITICALLY ILL INFANTS IN KANSAS (BELOW RIGHT).

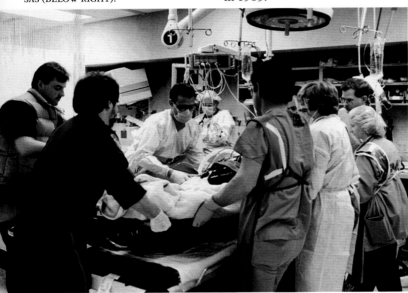

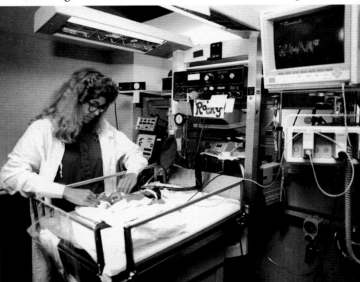

THE SPECIALLY TRAINED STAFF OF WESLEY'S NEWLY EXPANDED EMERGENCY/TRAUMA SERVICES DEPARTMENT CARES FOR A PATIENT IN THE HOSPITAL'S LEVEL I TRAUMA CENTER (ABOVE).

PARENTS ARE AN IMPORTANT PART OF THE TEAM IN THE PEDIATRIC INTENSIVE CARE UNIT (RIGHT), WHICH PROVIDES SPECIALIZED CARE FOR CHILDREN WHO HAVE UNDERGONE SURGERY, ARE CRITICALLY ILL, OR HAVE BEEN INJURED.

IMPRESSIVE LEADERSHIP IN MEDICAL CARE

Wesley justifiably claims leadership in all aspects of prenatal and postnatal care. The hospital delivers more than 5,000 babies each year, more than any other medical center in Kansas. As a Level III Regional Perinatal Center, Wesley provides comprehensive care to mothers and newborns. Wesley's Neonatal Intensive Care Unit serves as the primary referral center for the state of Kansas. Nearly half of the hospital days for critically ill infants statewide are provided at Wesley.

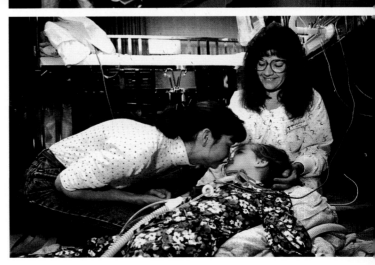

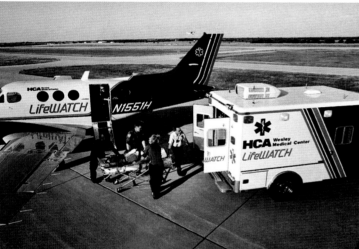

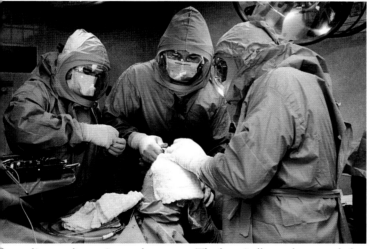

air and ground ambulances provide life-saving treatment and transport for critically injured or ill patients from anywhere in the state.

Also dedicated to disease prevention, the hospital offers Health Strategies, which features programs ranging from sports medicine and physical, pulmonary, and coronary rehabilitation to nutrition and exercise classes. Operating from a completely outfitted $6-million fitness center, Health Strategies also manages employee fitness programs for some of Wichita's largest corporations.

In addition, Wesley has an active physician training program, which provides medical residencies in anesthesia, family practice, internal medicine, obstetrics/gynecology, orthopedics, pediatrics, radiology, and surgery.

Wesley is dedicated to providing the finest in health care services. At a time when the need to manage health care costs is of the highest concern to consumers as well as the medical community, Wesley is committed to long-term quality improvement programs that control health care costs while meeting the needs and expectations of its patients, physicians, and employees; health care insurers; and the communities it serves.

le cardiovascular testing and ment, neuroscience, diabetes ment, orthopedics, cancer ment, lithotripsy, hyperbaric gen therapy, and diagnosis and ment of sleep disorders.

The hospital's newly expanded Emergency/Trauma Services department has been designated a Level I trauma center (the highest classification) by the American College of Surgeons. Wesley's LifeWATCH

BROADWAY MORTUARY

FAMILY, INNOVATION, SENSITIVITY, AND leadership are words that best describe the philosophy of Broadway Mortuary. ◆ Since 1951 the mortuary has been owned and operated by the Cozine family—Jack H., who died in 1976, and his son, William L. (Bill) Cozine. W. Ashley Cozine, Bill's son,

joined the business in 1993 after completing graduate school at Oxford University in England.

crest—a heraldic coat of arms designed by Ashley Cozine—contains the Latin motto, "Virtus Venit Per Ignem," which means "Strength Comes Through Fire."

A TRADITION OF SERVICE

Broadway Mortuary's heritage began in 1913 when two young men, Earl P. Martin and Charles E. Lahey, founded the City Undertaking Co. In 1926 they changed the firm's name to Lahey and Martin Mortuary.

This partnership continued until it was mutually dissolved in 1938. Martin then built a modern building, designed specifically as a mortuary, at 1147 S. Broadway. Through the years, and despite the 1990 fire, the location at Broadway and Lincoln has remained its home.

In 1951 Jack H. Cozine, a prominent Wichita businessman and an executive with The Boeing Company, and Dick A. Morris, a funeral director from Newton, Kansas, bought the mortuary from Martin. Combining Cozine's business knowledge and people skills with Morris' funeral service experience, they brought a new level of service and care to Wichita families.

Through the years, the owners and staff of Broadway Mortuary have been sensitive innovators in modernizing funeral services and bringing change to antiquated funeral practices. They were the first in Wichita to offer adjacent off-street parking and the first to have a uniform fleet of cars that were the same make and color. They developed a modern and efficient ambulance service which was sold to the City of Wichita in 1958 and served as a forerunner to today's county

Emergency Medical Service.

As a result of their leadership, Cozine and Morris rapidly gained reputation for excellence, and the number of families they served increased dramatically. Bill Cozine joined his father as a partner in 1963 after Morris died. Through the years, the Cozine family and staff have carried on the tradition, bringing about creative options for families to consider.

Today, Broadway Mortuary is the recognized service leader in providing educational opportunities on the subjects of dying, death, and grief to ministers, health care professionals, support groups, Hospice, Stephen Ministries, and community and church groups. To accomplish this, the mortuary provides educational seminars featuring nationally known speakers. Likewise, Cozine lectures throughout the community and participates in numerous community service organizations, including the advisory board of the Salvation Army, Rotary, and city governmental boards. He also was a founder of the Wichita River Festival, serving as its ambassador, Admiral Windwagon Smith, in 1981.

Cozine believes the funeral service provides an opportunity not only to express deep sorrow but to celebrate the living of life. "To serve as a funeral director," he said, "is to be involved in the ministry of helping others."

Adds Cozine, "We believe that business principles should conform to biblical standards of fairness, compassion, and integrity. This is our pledge now and for the future."

EASTWOOD STUDIO INC.

BILL AND ASHLEY COZINE REPRESENT THE SECOND AND THIRD GENERATIONS OF FAMILY OWNERSHIP.

BROADWAY'S HERALDIC COAT OF ARMS, DESIGNED BY ASHLEY, BEARS THE MOTTO, "STRENGTH COMES THROUGH FIRE."

TOP RIGHT: TOM IRWIN AND DOUG WATSON HAVE YEARS OF EXPERIENCE IN EXTENDING THE MORTUARY'S MINISTRY.

Broadway's resilient spirit was apparent in its strong comeback from a devastating fire on New Year's Eve, 1990. The mortuary's

CPENNEY

RETAILING BEGINS AND ENDS WITH THE consumer—and the consumer's perception of quality, service, and value. It's a simple philosophy and one that has been the cornerstone of JCPenney, one of America's leading department stores. ◆ Times were simple when Dallas-based JCPenney

landed its operations to Wichita December 1, 1920, just in time the Christmas rush. The origidowntown store was strictly a a-and-carry business, stocking marily clothing, shoes, notions, piece goods.

JCPenney's Towne East location.

"The unique thing about JCPenney is that we're the only national retailer who still buys merchandise at the store level," he explains. "That means our local buyers can tailor merchandise to fit the

method, and we always ask the question, 'Does it square with what is right and just?'"

Doing what is "right and just" is a credo that JCPenney applies to its relationships with customers, suppliers, and the communities in which it operates. The local stores are frequent sponsors of fashion and scholarship pageants, and provide financial support to many other human service, civic, cultural, and sporting programs and activities around the city.

The notions that the customer comes first, that associates share a mutual interest in the success of the business, and that contributions to

More than seven decades later, retail giant anchors both of hita's major shopping centers, pying 160,000 square feet in ne West Square and 200,000 re feet in Towne East Square. ether, the stores employ more 450 full- and part-time associ. In addition to extensive cloth lines, JCPenney stocks jewelry, netics, and home furnishings— the old cash-and-carry policy given way to full lines of credit. oday's JCPenney targets midand upper-middle-income sumers by offering affordable ducts that are comparable in fashion and quality to those by the best-known department specialty stores. The company's chandise is closely aligned to needs of value-conscious shop, with a well-balanced mix of basic items and value-priced ion merchandise, according eorge Scott, manager of

Wichita and south-central Kansas markets. We often have items in our store that you wouldn't find at other JCPenney stores anywhere else in the country. Our buyers know the importance of local tastes and desires."

THE "PENNEY IDEA"
Founder James Cash Penney's "Penney Idea," based on simple applications of the Golden Rule and formally adopted by the company in 1913, remains a guiding philosophy for the national organization and for each local store. Quoting from the "Penney Idea," Scott says that associates still do everything in their power "to pack the customer's dollar full of value, quality, and satisfaction."

"We continue to train ourselves and our associates so that the service we give will be more and more intelligently performed," he explains. "We test every policy and

the community are important have long been a vital part of the company's operating philosophy. These timeless principles have made JCPenney a thriving enterprise in Wichita since the 1920s, and will help it remain a major force in the retail market of the future.

JCPENNY IS CLOSELY ALIGNED TO THE NEEDS OF TODAY'S VALUE-CONSCIOUS SHOPPER, WITH A WELL-BALANCED MIX OF BOTH BASIC ITEMS AND VALUE-PRICED FASHION MERCHANDISE.

WICHITA AREA CHAMBER OF COMMERCE

WICHITA AND THE ENTREPRENEURIAL spirit go together like love and marriage. It seems you can't have one without the other. Wichita's original settlers were Native Americans who found the confluence of the Big Arkansas and Little Arkansas rivers to be an

ideal place for camping and trading. Likewise, the first white men who ventured into the territory came solely to set up trading posts. Thus, it can be said that Wichita was founded by entrepreneurs and business people to promote commerce.

CARRYING ON A LONGTIME TRADITION

For more than half a century, the city's unchallenged leaders were its business people and chief founders—stalwarts like J.R. Mead, William Griffenstein, and William Matthewson. In 1870 these visionaries started the Commercial League—the city's first business organization—which is today considered the ancestor of the Wichita Area Chamber of Commerce. Organized within weeks of Wichita's incorporation as a municipality, the Commercial League worked to improve the city's business climate and economy. Today's Chamber, like its ancestor, carries on in that strong tradition.

Tim Witsman, president of The Chamber, recalls an early reflection on the city's infectious entrepreneurial spirit. "(Wichita) proposed to add to the prairie what the prairie had not; trees where there were no trees, water where there was no water, cereal where there was only grass, fuel where there were no hills, roads and steel rails where there were no navigable rivers, manufacturers where there were no raw materials," wrote Victor Murdock, editor of *The Wichita Eagle.*

"There is no more succinct description of how Wichita came to be and how it grew into a great city," says Witsman. "Success here

has been earned through creativity and hard work. I don't know of another city that has so completely created itself through individual entrepreneurship and community action."

That spirit has nurtured a host of industry giants over the years: men and women like Clyde Cessna, Walter and Olive Ann Beech, William Lear, and Lloyd Stearman, who helped turn Wichita into the "Air Capital of the World." Others include W.C. Coleman, founder of The Coleman Company, and his son, Sheldon Coleman, who built the business into a leading outdoor recreational products manufacturer; brothers Dan and Frank Carney, who gave Pizza Hut to the world; Fred Koch, whose tiny oil and engi-

neering company, Koch Industries, mushroomed into the nation's second largest privately owned conglomerate; Tom Devlin and Frank Barton, who established another international company, Rent-A-

Center; and Ray and Olive Garvey, founders of Garvey Industries, a private grain, farm, ranch, and real estate conglomerate.

The spirit is so alive today that The Wichita State University is considered the nation's hub of entrepreneurial study. Some 20 years ago the university established the Center for Entrepreneurship, and it remains an important part of the city's continuing entrepreneurial spirit.

MORE THAN 120 YEARS OF PROGRESS

The list of economic, social, and cultural accomplishments over Wichita's more than 120-year history is impressive, beginning with the Commercial League's efforts to bring to the young city a U.S. Land Office, a railroad, and a bridge across the Arkansas River on Douglas Avenue.

Several contemporary examples also stand out. When a recession in the early 1980s, The Chamber sought a new way to preserve the economic health of the area. The result was a countywide economic development plan and the creation in 1987 of the Wichita/Sedgwick County Partnership for Growth (WI/SE) to oversee implementation of the plan. This unique partnership between the business and public sectors is financed with pr

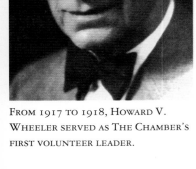

FROM 1917 TO 1918, HOWARD V. WHEELER SERVED AS THE CHAMBER'S FIRST VOLUNTEER LEADER.

COSPONSORED BY THE CHAMBER, THE ANNUAL KANSAS BUSINESS EXPO AT CENTURY II CIVIC CENTER (RIGHT) ALLOWS HUNDREDS OF BUSINESSES TO CAPTURE AN AUDIENCE OF POTENTIAL BUYERS AT A SINGLE LOCATION.

▲ ROGER N. WILSON

▲ FRANK SMITH

▲ JIM EDWARDS

: donations and public monies
geted by the city and county
ernments. The Chamber, under
tract with WI/SE, is the group's
naging partner.

When underground water con-
ination was discovered beneath
ch of downtown and south-
tral Wichita in 1990, liability
ors for property owners and the
eat of federal action to force a
nup promised to bring down-
n redevelopment and business
vity to a halt. The city govern-
at acted swiftly to accept respon-
lity for cleaning up the polluted
undwater.

Originated by the city manager,
proposed solution received
ng support from The Chamber.
rking with local and state offi-
s, The Chamber successfully lob-
d for changes in state law that
uld make the solution work. As a
ult of cooperation between local
ernment and involved landown-
and tenants, the contamination
ow being cleaned up without
eral or state funds. The coali-
's quick action, which received
onal accolades, has rejuvenated
iness activity in the polluted

Perhaps one of the best examples
he city's entrepreneurial spirit is
Wichita River Festival, an an-
l celebration that attracts more
1 200,000 Kansans and visitors
n throughout the United States
r a 10-day period. The event got
to a modest start in 1970 as part
The Chamber's year-long cele-

bration of Wichita's 100th birth-
day. That first year, The Chamber
provided staff support and office
space to ensure the festival's initial
success. A private, nonprofit
corporation—Wichita Festivals,
Inc.—was formed the following
year to produce the event, and it
soon received the enthusiastic support of businesses, individuals,
charitable foundations, local government, and hundreds of volunteers.
The "Riverfest" is now ranked
among the top 100 festivals in
North America according to the
International Festivals Association.

FOUNDED IN 1917

For nearly eight decades, The
Chamber has been a major force in
the local business-community partnership, offering its support and
considerable influence to other important projects and events.

Today's Chamber dates back to
1917, when the Wichita Board of

Commerce was first organized. In
its early years, the organization supported major developments such as
construction of the drainage canal
to divert Chisholm Creek from the
North End industrial area. The
Chamber also played a role in the
city's acquisition of Fairmount College, which has grown from a small
municipal school into The Wichita
State University, a metropolitan
university of national stature.

Over the decades, The Chamber
has continued to push for business
and civic improvements, and its list
of achievements is impressive. In
the 1930s, The Chamber backed
major Works Progress Administration efforts, such as a new airport
terminal. It also helped secure the
Veterans Administration Hospital
and a weather bureau at the airport.

During the 1940s, The Chamber had a hand in numerous war-
related programs, from training
workers to lobbying for higher

IN THE 1950S, THE CHAMBER WAS
INSTRUMENTAL IN BUILDING MID-
CONTINENT AIRPORT (TOP LEFT) AND
STRONGLY SUPPORTED THE WICHITA-
VALLEY CENTER FLOOD CONTROL
PROJECT (THE BIG DITCH), WHICH
HAS AVERTED HUNDREDS OF MILLIONS
OF DOLLARS IN LOSSES OVER THE
YEARS (TOP RIGHT). THE CHAMBER
ALSO HELPED SECURE THE VETERANS
ADMINISTRATION HOSPITAL (LEFT),
WHICH CONTINUES TO SERVE THOSE
WHO SERVED THEIR COUNTRY.

IN 1989 THE WICHITA CONVENTION & VISITORS BUREAU BROUGHT 65,000 AVID BOWLERS AND THEIR FAMILIES TO THE NATIONAL TOURNAMENT AND CONVENTION OF THE AMERICAN BOWLING CONGRESS. THE FIVE-MONTH-LONG EVENT HAD A $28-MILLION ECONOMIC IMPACT ON THE CITY.

THE ANNUAL GOLDEN APPLE AWARDS BANQUET (RIGHT), SPONSORED BY THE BUSINESS EDUCATION SUCCESS TEAM OF WI/SE, RECOGNIZES TEACHERS FOR EXCELLENCE.

allocations of war-related raw materials. Thanks in part to these efforts, industrial employment increased by 800 percent, and the city's population nearly doubled. Wichita produced an astounding 22,000 airplanes for the war effort.

In the 1950s, The Chamber organized the local chapter of the Better Business Bureau, secured construction of Mid-Continent Airport, and lobbied for creation of the Kansas Turnpike. It also strongly supported construction of the Wichita-Valley Center Flood Control Project (The Big Ditch), which has averted hundreds of millions of dollars in losses over the years.

The Chamber went to work in the 1960s and '70s supporting construction of such community projects as Century II civic center, the Sedgwick County Zoo, the Mid-America All-Indian Center, and the Kansas Coliseum. It also supported a new open housing ordinance, created a Convention & Tourism Division, and secured legislative approval for a transient guest tax to support the division's operation.

The division became a separate, nonprofit entity in 1981, operating as the Wichita Convention & Visitors Bureau. Annually, the bureau attracts more than 200 conventions, meetings, and trade shows, as well as over 250,000 delegates and conventioneers who have an economic impact of $15 million. Conventions and tourism have been on the upswing during the 1980s and early 1990s, and sales

efforts have been increasingly successful.

The bureau was the driving force that brought Wichita the MISS USA Pageant from 1990 through 1993. Community support of the pageant amounted to $1.2 million each year in goods and services. In turn, Wichita's annual payoff was a worldwide television audience of 300 million viewers who saw a 12-minute promotion of the city showcasing its quality of life, major industries, and attractions. Most recently, the bureau opened visitor information centers at the Towanda and Belle Plaine service areas on the Kansas Turnpike to promote the city's attractions and facilities.

In early 1987, as deteriorating roads and bridges posed increasing safety hazards, an intense interest developed across Kansas in upgrad-

ing the state's highway system. C[ut]backs in federal funding had forc[ed] reductions in maintenance levels, a situation that adversely affected economic development. With the financial support of WI/SE, The Chamber was instrumental in for[m]ing a coalition of grassroots organizations to work toward passage of [a] major highway program in the leg[is]lature. Through Chamber lobbyi[ng] and a strong effort by the coalitio[n] the 1989 legislature finally passed [a] $2.6-billion comprehensive highway plan. Work is under way, and major improvements in the state['s] road transportation system are being made.

Another recent Chamber effor[t] involved promoting the concept [of] an elected mayor for Wichita. Sin[ce] 1917 the office of mayor had rotated among the elected city commissioners. In the late 1980s it

...ame obvious that a lack of continuity in leadership was having an [adv]erse affect on economic develop[me]nt. The Chamber responded [s]upporting a mayor-council-[ma]nager form of government, an [act]ion that was defeated twice in [city]wide elections. At the same [tim]e, some segments of the commu[nity] proposed that city commission-[ers] be elected by district, instead of [at la]rge as had been the practice. [Th]e Chamber fashioned a compro[mis]e to submit both propositions [to t]he electorate, and voters [app]roved the new form of govern[me]nt in 1990.

[T]he rejuvenation of the Old [Tow]n area of downtown Wichita [has] been a major project for The [Ch]amber and WI/SE for several [yea]rs. As part of an overall down[tow]n plan, city government agreed [to s]pend $17 million over a period

of years on infrastructure improvements. Two local entrepreneurs formed a corporation to push for the construction of a permanent farm and art market in the Old Town area. Working with them, The Chamber and WI/SE helped secure local government funds for the facility and for landscaping, street renovation, and parking in the area. As a result, Old Town has experienced explosive growth and now is one of Wichita's major entertainment and dining districts.

The Chamber also helped facilitate an agreement between local government and the state to renovate the old downtown Dillard's department store building. The goal was to bring most state agencies with offices in Wichita under one roof. In 1991 WI/SE conducted a feasibility study and presented architectural recommen-

dations to state officials. Since legislation was needed, The Chamber lobbied to get the necessary measures passed and, along with WI/SE, helped convince the governor that the proposition was feasible and financially favorable to the state. In order to make the deal work, the city bought the old Wichita Clinic building from the state, and Chamber member banks and savings and loan institutions filled the financial gap with nearly $1 million. Thanks to those efforts, the renovation work is under way, and the state plans to occupy its new offices in 1994.

Through good times and bad, Wichita's business community has worked in partnership with The Chamber for the betterment of the community. Today's challenge is to continue that longtime relationship for a prosperous future.

A NEW FREESTANDING SIGN IDENTIFYING THE CHAMBER BUILDING AND WI/SE PARTNERSHIP OFFICES WAS UNVEILED IN 1988 (ABOVE LEFT).

EACH YEAR FROM 1990 THROUGH 1993, AN ESTIMATED 300 MILLION PEOPLE WORLDWIDE WATCHED AS WICHITA PLAYED HOST TO THE MISS USA PAGEANT. CONTESTANTS IN THE 1993 PAGEANT VISITED THE MID-AMERICA ALL-INDIAN CENTER (TOP), ONE OF THE MANY CULTURAL RESOURCES THAT THE CHAMBER HELPED ESTABLISH. AFTER AN EXCITING WEEK IN WICHITA, KENYA MOORE (BOTTOM), MISS MICHIGAN USA, WAS CROWNED MISS USA 1993.

DONDLINGER & SONS CONSTRUCTION CO., INC.

WICHITA IS STEEPED IN HISTORY AND family tradition, and nowhere is that more evident than with Dondlinger & Sons Construction Co., Inc., a commercial, industrial, and bridge-building contractor celebrating its third generation of family ownership. One of the largest contractors in the state, the company also constructs projects in Colorado, Oklahoma, Texas, Nebraska, and Missouri.

The third-generation Dondlingers—Tom, Nick, Paul, and Marty—took over from their fathers in the 1980s. Their legacy is one of skill, responsibility, and integrity, where a handshake is as binding as a contract.

"We strive to develop partnerships with project owners," says President Tom Dondlinger, who leads the company's management team. "Partnerships are truly important to us, and that's why we give 110 percent to every job we do."

TRADITION SHAPES THE CITY'S SKYLINE

N.L. Dondlinger started his business in 1898 and located in Claflin, Kansas, in the early 1900s. By 1925 he had moved his wife and four sons to Wichita and began building small commercial projects and some of the city's finer residential areas.

The advent of World War II, coupled with Wichita's growth, launched the company into larger commercial projects such as schools and hospitals. In the postwar boom, commercial building exploded, and the company diversified by adding an underground utility division in 1956.

During the '50s, '60s, and '70s, the second generation of Dondlingers began shaping the skylines and infrastructure of Wichita and other Midwestern communities, constructing the Kansas Gas & Electric building, the corporate headquarters of Union National Bank, The Wichita State University's Henry Levitt Arena, Kansas Coliseum, and the Eisenhower Memorial Library in Abilene, Kansas. The company also completed numerous militar[y] projects, including the U.S. Air Force Academy Cadet Dining Ha[ll] in Colorado Springs, Colorado, and projects at Ft. Riley, Kansas, Ft. Leonard Wood, Missouri, and Wichita's McConnell Air Force Base.

"Over the years, we've handled virtually every type of commercia[l] industrial, underground utility, a[nd] bridge construction project," says Vice President Paul Dondlinger. "We've gained a reputation for ou[r] depth of experience, and we work with the region's most respected architectural and engineering firm[s]. Many of these firms work with us on a design/build basis to satisfy t[he] needs of schedule-driven and valu[e]-driven clients."

Schedule-driven and cost-effec[-]tive may be bywords of the construction industry today, but for Dondlinger & Sons, these values never take precedence over safety and quality. During the '80s, for example, the company hired a ful[l]-time safety director who is respon[si]ble for safety training, job-site safety evaluations, and overseeing daily equipment inspections.

"We don't run our safety program merely to be in compliance; we run it to guarantee that we sen[d] workers home safely every night," says Marty Dondlinger, vice president of the underground utility di[vi]sion. "Some of our safety procedures are even more stringent tha[n] OSHA requires, and we're commi[t]ted to keeping it that way. We're extremely proud of our company'[s] safety record, which over the year[s] has remained consistently better than the national average for construction companies."

Such commitment to safety an[d] quality is a lesson well learned by the Dondlingers. "We won't be sa[t]isfied with anything that is less tha[n] perfect," says Tom, who recalls a time in the early '70s when his father, Ray, had a portion of a concrete floor removed because he fel[t] it was less than top quality.

The project owner had ap-
ved the floor, and we were ready
roceed to the next phase. But
d wouldn't hear of it, because it
n't meet his personal standards."
He adds, "Today, we focus a
at deal of attention on continu-
improvement so that mistakes
't happen. In this company, pro-
s are completed to perfection
ry time, on time, and on budget."

CORE PERFORMANCES
at tradition of excellence has
t customers coming back. In the
'50s Dondlinger built the City
Wichita's water and wastewater
tment plants. In the 1990s the
pany completed work on the
's second pair of facilities—a
bined public works project of
re than $38.4 million.
Dondlinger has also done multi-
projects for The Coleman Com-
y, Cessna Aircraft Company,
e Boeing Company, Beech Air-
t Corp., Learjet Inc., Vulcan
emicals, Koch Industries, and
Joseph Medical Center. Among
vork for St. Francis Regional
dical Center is the $35-million
gnostics Center, the largest sin-
construction project in Wichita
late. Additionally, the company
won repeat contracts with
gwick County and the State
Kansas.
Dondlinger & Sons owns one
he largest and best maintained
ts of heavy construction equip-
nt in the Midwest," says Vice
sident Nick Dondlinger, who
ds the company's bridge and
ing division, formed in 1989.
e fact that we own our equip-
nt, rather than rent it, provides a
ificant cost savings for the pro-
owner and helps us maintain
on-time schedules."
That fleet of equipment also
kes it possible for the company
andle projects of literally "epic"
portions. Wichita's 24-story
c Center—the tallest building
Kansas—stands as the beacon of
ndlinger's construction skills.

And, as motorists enjoy the easy
access of the Northeast Expressway,
they drive over 28 bridges and
3 million cubic yards of earthwork
constructed by the company.

Projects built by Dondlinger &
Sons provide offices, churches,
hospitals, work centers, and infrastructure that will be used for generations to come. That seems only
fitting for a company with generations of excellence behind it—and
a new generation committed to
the future.

DONDLINGER & SONS HAS COMPLETED
CONSTRUCTION WORK ON ST. GEORGE
CHRISTIAN ORTHODOX CATHEDRAL.

WICHITA'S 24-STORY EPIC CENTER
(OPPOSITE), THE TALLEST BUILDING IN
KANSAS, STANDS AS THE BEACON OF
DONDLINGER'S CONSTRUCTION SKILLS.

ON THE COMPANY'S LONG LIST OF
HIGH-PROFILE PROJECTS IS THE
KANSAS COLISEUM, A 10,000-SEAT
MULTI-PURPOSE SPORTS ARENA.

CESSNA AIRCRAFT COMPANY

EVERY 20 SECONDS, SOMEWHERE IN THE world, a Cessna aircraft takes off or lands. But that's not surprising, considering that Cessnas make up more than one-half of the world's general aviation aircraft fleet. Since its founding by Clyde Cessna in 1927, Cessna Aircraft Company has rolled off its production lines more than 177,000 piston-engine, turboprop, military trainer, and Citation business jet aircraft. No other aircraft manufacturer comes close to this production record. Cessna sells more light and mid-size business jets annually than all other manufacturers combined, and its sales lead continues to increase annually.

and in 1982 the company celebrated the delivery of its 1,000th Citation. In keeping with its outstanding record of delivering 1,000 Citations in a decade, Cessna's "Celebration 2000" climaxed in 1993 with the delivery of the 2,000th Citation.

Russell W. Meyer Jr., chairman of Cessna Aircraft Company, says,

headquarters in Wichita is the world's largest dedicated business jet service facility.

Also located at Cessna headquarters is the Customer Center, a state-of-the-art facility and showroom that opened in 1992 as another component of Celebration 2000. In a mock-up showroom, customers can compare several Citations side by side, observing floor plans, cabin configurations, and flight-deck options firsthand.

Cessna's interior designers at the facility use a variety of high-tech audio-visual equipment to help customers select cabin colors, fabrics, carpeting, amenities, and cockpit instrumentation. These selections appear on an advanced computerized visualization system that creates

THE 200,000-SQUARE-FOOT CITATION SERVICE CENTER (ABOVE AT REAR) AT CESSNA HEADQUARTERS IN WICHITA IS THE WORLD'S LARGEST DEDICATED BUSINESS JET SERVICE FACILITY.

SINCE ITS FOUNDING IN 1927, CESSNA HAS ROLLED OFF ITS PRODUCTION LINES MORE THAN 177,000 PISTON-ENGINE, TURBOPROP, MILITARY TRAINER, AND CITATION BUSINESS JET AIRCRAFT (ABOVE RIGHT).

Over the years, Cessna's superior research and development capabilities have produced dozens of technological advancements that have propelled the company to the forefront of its industry. For example, Cessna's CitationJet is the first business aircraft to use a natural laminar flow wing—a major breakthrough in aerodynamic efficiency. The first business aircraft ever to operate at a speed of Mach .9 is Cessna's Citation X, the fastest business jet in the world.

CELEBRATION 2000
Cessna delivered its first Citation business jet in 1972. Over the next 10 years, additional Citation models were designed and produced,

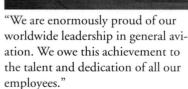

"We are enormously proud of our worldwide leadership in general aviation. We owe this achievement to the talent and dedication of all our employees."

When Cessna introduced the first Citation, it also introduced the industry's only factory-direct service network. That growing network today includes 10 company-owned Citation Service Centers across the United States, plus a network of authorized service centers worldwide. The 200,000-square-foot Citation Service Center at Cessna

color prints of the cabin and cockpit, showing each element "installed," right before customer eyes. In one trip to the Customer Center, prospective owners can totally customize an aircraft to their exact specifications.

AVIATION'S HIGHEST AWARD
In the aviation industry, the Collier Trophy is the highest tribute to aeronautical excellence. Although it was created in 1911, 75 years went by before the award was given to a business aircraft manufacturer.

...t company was Cessna, which ...ived the honor in 1986 in recog-...on of the Citation fleet's extraor-...ry worldwide safety record. ...s safety record is all the more ...arkable considering that the ...tion fleet is exceptionally large ...extremely active. Hundreds of ...panies worldwide today own ...or more Citation business jets. ...essna's turboprop cargo and ...enger plane, the Caravan, also ...sts an impressive safety record ...rugged reliability. Customers ...ude Federal Express Corp., with ...e than 250 Caravans in its serv-...leet, the U.S. Postal Service, ...the Royal Canadian Mounted ...ce, among many others. ...lot only has Cessna given the ...ld the most—and some of the ...st—aircraft, it has taught the ...ld how to fly. Cessna is the ...er in pilot training through its ...ldwide network of Cessna Pilot ...ters, where more than 400,000 ...ts have learned to fly since the ...ram was introduced in 1970. ...Cessna Pilot Center flight ...ing system is in use in 40 ...ntries around the world.

...E 21ST STREET PROGRAM

...ough the general aviation indus-...ed a strong expansion of the ...l economy in the late 1980s, ...everyone in Wichita shared in

that recovery. The economic gap between the employed and the unemployed actually widened, and for company Chairman Russ Meyer, the situation called for a special commitment to help train out-of-work Wichitans.

Cessna selected a vacant building on 21st Street, and with extensive

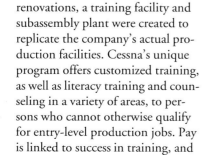

renovations, a training facility and subassembly plant were created to replicate the company's actual production facilities. Cessna's unique program offers customized training, as well as literacy training and counseling in a variety of areas, to persons who cannot otherwise qualify for entry-level production jobs. Pay is linked to success in training, and when trainees complete the pro-

gram, they are guaranteed a job at Cessna.

On a visit to the facility in 1993, U.S. Labor Secretary Robert Reich commented: "The Cessna 21st Street Project is the product of outstanding collaboration among corporate managers, labor unions, local schools, and government agen-cies at the city, county, and state levels. I am enormously encouraged by what I see here."

For Cessna, a longtime Wichita company that has made substantial contributions to the city's reputation as the "Air Capital of the World," the 21st Street Project is another example of great people making great ideas fly.

ABOVE, FROM LEFT: CITATION VII, CITATION V, CITATIONJET, CITATION II, AND CITATION VI.

STATE-OF-THE-ART COMPUTER-AIDED DESIGN TECHNIQUES (ABOVE LEFT) IMPROVE AERODYNAMICS, SAFETY, AND PASSENGER COMFORT.

CESSNA'S TURBOPROP CARGO AND PAS-SENGER PLANE, THE CARAVAN, BOASTS AN IMPRESSIVE SAFETY RECORD AND RUGGED RELIABILITY (ABOVE).

CLOCKWISE FROM TOP LEFT: CITATION V, CITATIONJET, CITATION X, AND CITATION VII.

WICHITA
1928 - 1959

1929	The Boeing Company
1929	Cochran Mortuary
1930	Dillon Food Stores
1932	Beech Aircraft Corporation
1933	Kamen Supply Company, Inc.
1936	M. Bruenger Trucking Company
1938	Allen, Gibbs & Houlik, L.C.
1939	Continental Airlines, Inc.
1939	Star Lumber & Supply Co.
1940	Koch Industries, Inc.
1941	Builders, Inc.
1945	Morris, Laing, Evans, Brock & Kennedy, Chartered
1946	Sheplers Inc.
1946	Wescon Products Co., a division of Latshaw Enterprises, Inc.
1950	Ernst & Young
1950	Vulcan Chemicals Division of Vulcan MaterialsCompany
1951	International Cold Storage Company, Inc.
1953	Bill Bachman & Associates, Brad Bachman Construction and Bachman Enterprises
1953	Rusty Eck Ford
1954	KAKE-TV
1955	Kreonite, Inc.
1958	Pizza Hut, Inc.

THE UNION STATION WAS IN ITS HEYDAY IN THE 1930S AND 1940S WHEN TENS OF THOUSANDS OF WICHITANS DEPENDED ON THE TRAIN AS A PRIMARY MEANS OF OUT-OF-STATE TRANSPORTATION. MANY TRAVELERS FOUND AS A VERY WELCOME SIGN THE WORD WICHITA CARVED INTO THE END OF THE PLATFORM CANOPY.

THE BOEING COMPANY

THE WICHITA DIVISION OF THE BOEING Company is a direct descendant of the Stearman Aircraft Company, which was founded in 1926 by Kansas native Lloyd Stearman, an aircraft designer and barnstorming pilot. The history of Boeing Wichita, which today is Kansas' largest private employer, is a microcosmic reflection of key events in American aviation history, as well as some important world events.

IN 1986 BOEING WICHITA MADE A COMMITMENT TO CONTINUOUS QUALITY IMPROVEMENT. AS A STRATEGIC BUSINESS TOOL, THE PROGRAM IS HELPING THE COMPANY CUT WASTE, SHORTEN TIME BETWEEN PRODUCTION STEPS, BUILD A BETTER PRODUCT, AND INCREASE CUSTOMER SATISFACTION.

COMPANY BEGINNINGS

One of Stearman's first business ventures was a brief partnership with fellow aviation pioneers Walter Beech and Clyde Cessna in the early 1920s. Stearman then moved from Wichita to California in 1926 and founded the Stearman Aircraft Company with two partners.

A year later, Stearman moved back to Wichita, bringing his company with him, and introduced a three-passenger biplane. In 1929 he sold the young business (but remained with the company) to United Aircraft and Transport Corporation in Seattle, previously known as the Boeing Airplane and Transport Company.

That business decision paid off, as the company under new ownership soon landed its first of many government contracts when the

and activity for the company was under way, world events soon ha America preparing for war. Boein and its Wichita operation began playing critical roles early on. In 1941 the government contracted Boeing Wichita to build the B-2 Superfortress that would be the workhorse bomber for the European and Pacific theaters. The go ernment built a special plant for production south of the original Stearman factory, and the first B rolled out in 1943. Once the factory was in full gear, it built 4.2 B-29s per day at peak production During the war, Boeing Wichita also built 44 percent of all two-s primary trainers for the Army Ai Corps and Navy.

POSTWAR ACTIVITY

Following the war, Boeing conti ued to lead the industry in devel ing military aircraft and technol-

Navy selected it to build biplane trainers. Through the '30s, during which time United Aircraft changed its name back to Boeing and renamed the Wichita plant the Stearman Division of Boeing Airplane Company, the Wichita operation built its own designs under its own model designations.

As this early period of prosperity

ogy. It also began applying its ex tise to becoming a major supplie to the commercial aviation industry, which was just taking off

In 1948 Boeing Wichita bega programs to modernize and mod B-29s and begin building its nev medium-range bomber, the B-4 During the next 10 years, Wichi would build nearly 1,400 B-47s

ENGINEERS AT BOEING WICHITA USE COMPUTER-AIDED THREE-DIMENSIONAL INTERACTIVE APPLICATION (CATIA) SOFTWARE TO DESIGN AND DIGITALLY PREASSEMBLE THE PORTIONS WICHITA WILL PRODUCE FOR THE BOEING 777, THE COMPANY'S NEWEST WIDE-BODIED TWINJET.

begin tooling and production he B-52 Stratofortress, the key nber aircraft of the Strategic Air mmand (SAC).

More than 450 B-52s were deliv-d to the SAC by the time the tract was fulfilled in 1962. the end of that year, Boeing chita had produced more than 000 military aircraft since it was rded its first military job in the s. At the close of B-52 produc-n, the company began applying re of its resources to support k on Boeing commercial jetlin-Although military support was the primary mission for the chita operation, the plant began ding parts for commercial jets final assembly in Washington e, where Boeing remains dquartered. Commercial pro-tion in Wichita continued to ease for decades.

MMERCIAL AVIATION DERSHIP

nmercial aviation today ac-nts for about 80 percent of The ing Company's $30.1 billion in

gross sales (1992). Although de-mand for both commercial and mili-tary products has decreased in recent years, Boeing has responded with the flexibility and innovation that continually rank it among *Fortune* magazine's 10 most admired companies, and its continuing suc-cess is impressive.

The nation's leading exporter and the world's number one aero-space company, Boeing boasted 60 percent of the world market for commercial jets at the end of 1992. Its market leadership rests as much on its broad product line as on its product quality. While every Ameri-can air carrier is a Boeing customer, an impressive 80 percent of 1992's $17.8 billion in new orders came from non-U.S. carriers. Indeed, 1992 was a banner year for Boeing: It delivered 441 jetliners, a com-pany record.

Parts production for jetliners is divided among Boeing facilities in Washington state (in Renton, Auburn, Spokane, Everett, and at the corporate headquarters near Seattle), Philadelphia, and Wichita,

with final assembly on all models in Washington.

Wichita produces part of every jetliner made by Boeing, including about 80 percent of the 737, the best-selling passenger jet in aviation history. Wichita also designs and builds engine covers and nose sec-tions for the mid-size 757, the wide-bodied 767 twinjet, and Boeing's 400-passenger flagship aircraft, the 747.

For Boeing's newest model, the 777 twinjet, the Wichita Division designed and is building the air-craft's nose section, engine mounts, and engine covers.

DEFENSE AND SPACE ACTIVITIES

Cutbacks in national defense spend-ing have affected Boeing as well as other major military contractors, but the company's diverse product offerings in military electronics, hel-icopters, and airplane and space products have ensured its position as a primary supplier meeting the defense needs of America and its foreign allies.

THE ADVENT OF RESPONSIBILITY CENTERS AND MANUFACTURING BUSINESS UNITS AT BOEING WICHITA REPRESENTS A NEW WAY OF BUILDING AIRPLANES. FUNCTIONING AS SEPARATE COST CENTERS WITHIN THE COMPANY, THEY ALLOW EMPLOYEES TO SPECIALIZE ON PRODUCT LINES TO REFINE THEIR EXPERTISE, INCREASE QUALITY, AND REDUCE COSTS.

The Wichita Division is responsible for all engineering to enhance the B-52's conventional weapons capabilities.

In 1990 Boeing Wichita delivered to Washington, D.C., two specially modified 747s to serve as Air Force One. The 747s replaced Boeing 707s used by the executive office since 1962. The Wichita operation is responsible for managing all future engineering and support services for the life of the planes.

BOEING COMPUTER SERVICES
Serving the Wichita plant's commercial group and its defense and space group, Boeing Computer

Wichita's Product Support Division, a part of the Boeing Defense & Space Group, is responsible for technical improvements to military products now in use. Current projects include new engines for the KC-135 aerial refueling tanker used by American and French forces, and upgrading avionics for the B1-B strategic bomber. Boeing Wichita recently finished the engineering and production of high-tech, lightweight, composite-material wings for the Navy A-6 Intruder, a carrier-based attack aircraft.

Defense budget cutbacks also have necessitated extending the life of military aircraft such as the B-52.

Services (BCS) supplies advanced computing and telecommunications services for Boeing Wichita.

The computing organization's most recent major responsibility was providing computer-aided design (CAD) and computer-aided manufacturing (CAM) capabilities and systems integration to make Boeing's new 777. These computer software capabilities allow designers and engineers to model in three dimensions and to see how parts fit together in a simulated assembly before actual manufacturing begins. Similarly, how parts of the plane react under the stresses of flying and loads can also be computer-evaluated, speeding up the testing

process and thereby reducing the cost of the airplane.

BCS-Wichita also provides an electronic network that interconnects the Wichita campus with da and voice communications capabities worldwide. This world-class network connects Boeing with its suppliers and manufacturing part ners throughout the world.

CONTINUOUS QUALITY IMPROVEMENT
Boeing will be an entirely different company in the year 2000 as a result of its commitment to and implementation of the Continuous Quality Improvement program. According to Dick Ziegler, commnications manager for Boeing Wichita, the program, begun in 1986, is the key to the company's long-term competitive strength.

"To visualize what the full implementation of this program can do for Boeing," says Ziegler, "ima ine a single thread that winds itsel throughout the entire company, through every employee from the new hire to the chairman. In a ma ner of speaking, with this thread will be able to 'trace' what we do every day towards reaching our quality, production, and custome satisfaction goals. Each person's co tribution to the process can be ide tified, which encourages efficienc creativity, and accountability."

All Boeing employees attend training in CQI. As a strategic bu ness tool, the program is helping Boeing cut waste, shorten time be tween production steps, build a b ter product, and increase custome satisfaction.

Company management believe strongly that by the time the first 777 is delivered in May 1995, Boeing will have proven the value and efficacy of the CQI program.

THE 777—BOEING PARTNERSHIPS TAKE FLIGHT
Boeing's newest jetliner is sized to bridge the passenger-load gap

the awards are already coming. The passenger cabin received the 1992 Industrial Design Excellence award, marking the first time the Industrial Design Society of America had ever honored an airplane interior. But more important is how commercial carriers around the world view the 777. During 1992 alone, Boeing announced 42 new orders for the aircraft from six customers. Since the program was launched in October 1990, the company has announced 130 orders from 13 customers with options for 94 more.

"Our increased emphasis on customer orientation and partnerships has helped us build a jetliner the

ween the company's 767 and
7 airliners. The 777 will carry
5 to 400 passengers in first-class
l coach cabins. Major assembly
he aircraft has begun, with the
t 777 scheduled for delivery in
y 1995.

Ziegler says that the company
worked with its domestic and
eign customers closer than ever
ore throughout the design pro-
s on the 777, which has been
obed the "customer-driven jet-
er." An exhaustive series of meet-
s with airline companies helped
eing define the plane's range,
ight limits, avionics, and passen-
cabin design. Then 777 design-
ld teams, which included airline
npany and supplier represen-
ves as well as Boeing personnel
m a number of departments,
luated design components
m every angle before they were
eased to manufacturing. These
ltidisciplined teams have helped
eing ensure that the 777 will
produced in an efficient, cost-
ective manner, and that the end
oduct has superior quality and
ability.

Because of customer input, the
7 has a wider interior cross-
tion than any competing air-
ft, an open, spacious environ-
nt with extra passenger head
m, and increased volume in over-

head bins that are lower and more accessible when open. The cabin also has greater interior flexibility, allowing airlines to reconfigure the cabin design quickly and easily to adapt to changing market requirements.

After viewing some of the designs for the 777, prospective customers said the plane had to be lighter and fly farther. So the design-build teams are finding ways to trim 16,000 pounds off the aircraft—equal to 80 passengers and their baggage—and are well on their way to reaching that goal.

The result of this innovative approach is a plane that has excited the entire aviation industry, and

market wants," says Ziegler. "Our Continuous Quality Improvement program has helped us build a superior quality, cost-efficient product."

A brief review of the history of Boeing Wichita outlines the important role the division has played in the aviation industry, in world events, and as a Boeing team member. Likewise, its impressive list of current projects and programs reveals a company intent on shaping and creating its own future, challenging itself, and pursuing excellence as its highest goal.

COCHRAN MORTUARY

SINCE ITS FOUNDING IN 1929, COCHRAN Mortuary has remained a family affair. The mortuary that prides itself on following the Golden Rule has served Wichita for more than 60 years and is in its fourth generation of family ownership and operation. Building on that tradition, a fifth-generation family member is preparing to take over in the years ahead.

"We treat others as we would want them to treat us," says Terri

ORDER OF THE GOLDEN RULE
Cochran is the only mortuary in Wichita to have membership in the highly respected International

ducts conferences and educationa programs for its member funeral directors and publishes informati literature on emerging trends in funeral services and business practices.

"In addition to following OGI standards, we believe in the value the funeral service. Thanks to thi business philosophy, our families know they are dealing with local people who care," says Bob Phifer who is an OGR director.

"We respect tradition, but we also honor change," he adds, poi

AS A MEMBER OF THE INTERNATIONAL ORDER OF THE GOLDEN RULE (OGR), COCHRAN MORTUARY AND ITS EMPLOYEES HAVE PLEDGED TO UPHOLD THE HIGHEST STANDARDS OF PROFESSIONAL AND PERSONAL CONDUCT.

TERRI COCHRAN PHIFER (CENTER) AND HER HUSBAND BOB PHIFER (RIGHT) CARRY ON A LONG TRADITION OF FAMILY OWNERSHIP AND OPERATION. THEIR SON TODD (LEFT) IS PREPARING TO TAKE OVER IN THE YEARS AHEAD.

Cochran Phifer, who with her husband, Bob Phifer, has operated the mortuary since 1987. "Our family is here to serve. We have an excellent staff that is trained and caring. We're known by our people."

Cochran's key people include John Rodda, longtime funeral director and embalmer; Jack Webster, personnel manager, funeral director, and embalmer; Shannon Reed, after-care counselor and funeral director; Henry Harvey, pre-arrangement representative; and the Phifers' 21-year-old son Todd, an assistant funeral director who plans to continue the family's ownership and management of the mortuary in the future.

Order of the Golden Rule (OGR). Members of this nonprofit organization pledge to uphold the highest standards of professional and personal conduct. Those standards include having "due regard and respect for the reverent care of the human body, for those bereaved, and for the overall spiritual dignity of man" and serving "any deserving family in time of need, regardless of monetary consideration."

To qualify for membership, a funeral home is evaluated and rated by families it has served. OGR then continues to evaluate each member on a monthly basis by contacting other families that have been served. The association also con-

ing out that many important thin have remained the same. For exam ple, Cochran Mortuary is still housed in the founder's N. Broad way home, which soon will be 10 years old; its 14-member professional staff of funeral directors, counselors, and assistant directors understands the importance of hel ing people deal with death before and long after the funeral; and th company generously donates its services for those in need, regardl of their economic status.

Says Bob Phifer, "We always as our families, 'What else can we do for you?' and they know we mean sincerely."

EECH AIRCRAFT CORPORATION

N THE SPRING OF 1932, IN THE DEPTHS OF THE Great Depression, Walter and Olive Ann Beech launched a new company—Beech Aircraft Corporation. Their goal was to build the finest general aviation aircraft in the world. They started with fewer than 10 employees and a design for a single-engine cabin biplane,

ich they named the Staggerwing. st-year sales totaled less than 7,000. In spite of the difficult nomic times, the company's

including maintenance and support of both civilian and military fleets, and state-of-the-art fabrication of composite parts.

h-performance quality products nd a market, and Beech Aircraft w.

Today, more than 60 years and 000 aircraft later, the company t evolved from this modest bening occupies more than 6 mil- a square feet of manufacturing, s, and support space, has annual s well above $1 billion, and ploys thousands of people ldwide.

One thing hasn't changed over years, though: Beech Aircraft's l continues to be building the st airplanes in the world.

SOLID LEADER

ecent years Beech has solidified reputation as the leading nufacturer of business and spe- ized military aircraft by consis- tly outselling its competitors. It has diversified into other areas,

Beech has the strongest and broadest product line in the general aviation industry. Its products range from high-performance, single-engine piston aircraft designed primarily for the owner-flown market and airline pilot training, to sophisticated business jets for corporate and military customers.

Beech's line of twin-engine King Air jetprops is the world's most successful business aircraft. In fact, there are nearly 5,000 King Airs in service worldwide—more than any other aircraft in service of its type. Beech products are operated by all four U.S. military services, and the name Beechcraft is known around the world as a symbol of quality in aviation products.

In 1980 Beech Aircraft became a wholly owned subsidiary of the Raytheon Company. Headquartered in Lexington, Massachusetts,

Raytheon is a large, diversified technology company with sales in four business segments: electronics, aircraft products, energy and environmental services, and major appliances. Like Beech, Raytheon has established a reputation for producing products of outstanding quality and high performance.

Beech continues to maintain its headquarters in Wichita in the factory complex it has occupied since 1934. Its facilities were the subject of major expansions prior to World War II, again in the early 1950s, and most recently in the 1980s. The company is the second largest private employer in Kansas and provides subcontract work for hundreds of other Kansas businesses.

Since the 1960s Beech also has had a manufacturing facility in

Salina, Kansas, on the site of the former Schilling Air Force Base. The existence of a positive climate for business growth and the availability of a talented labor force with a strong work ethic have been critical factors in maintaining the company's success in America's heartland.

A subsidiary, United Beechcraft Inc., operates a national network of aircraft sales, fueling, and maintenance bases at airports across America. United Beechcraft is one of the largest and most successful fixed-base operation networks in the world.

Another subsidiary, Beech Aerospace Service, Inc., headquartered in Madison, Mississippi, maintains military aircraft in more than 49 states and more than 200 countries throughout the world.

IN RECENT YEARS BEECH HAS SOLIDI-FIED ITS REPUTATION AS THE LEADING MANUFACTURER OF BUSINESS AND SPECIALIZED MILITARY AIRCRAFT BY CONSISTENTLY OUTSELLING ITS COMPETITORS.

ARTHUR E. WEGNER CURRENTLY SERVES AS CHAIRMAN AND CEO OF BEECH AIRCRAFT CORPORATION.

DILLON FOOD STORES

AS THE OLD SAYING GOES, SOME PEOPLE EAT to live while others live to eat. Luckily for both camps, Dillon Food Stores provides the widest variety of food staples, fresh produce and meats, make-your-own salad bars, delicatessens, seafood shops, and bakeries through the company's 65 stores in Kansas.

DILLONS SUPER STORES, EACH TOTALING MORE THAN 60,000 SQUARE FEET AND OFFERING A UNIQUE ARRAY OF FOODS AND SERVICES, HAVE BECOME A FAMILIAR SIGHT THROUGHOUT WICHITA.

A DIFFERENT WAY TO SHOP

Incorporated in 1921, the chain began when J.S. Dillon, who owned and operated a small group of general stores, opened his first cash food market in 1913 in Hutchinson, Kansas. (Dillons entered the Wichita market in 1930.) Until then, customers were required to pay for their groceries using higher-priced charge accounts.

Cash markets meant lower prices and soon proved popular—and profitable—for Dillons. Other innovative marketing techniques in store design and merchandising—open produce displays, self-service counters for sugar, beans, and dried pasta, and displays of related food items, such as mustards and meats—not only made shopping easier for customers but helped the company expand at an impressive pace.

Growing steadily over the years, Dillons has always paid close attention to customers' changing tastes and looked for new ways to offer better service. For example, store-brand products were added in the '30s, as well as in-store bakeries in the early '60s. Yet even as the self-service craze swept through the industry after World War II, the company never wavered from its original philosophy of service, selection, and value.

A NATIONAL LEADER IN FOOD MERCHANDISING

Dillon Companies, Inc., the parent company of Dillon Stores Division, is today an autonomous operating subsidiary of Kroger Company of Cincinnati, Ohio. When purchased by Kroger in 1983, Dillon Companies had 12 operating divisions, including 55 King Sooper super-

markets in Colorado, 57 Fry's Food Stores in Arizona and California, 27 City Markets in western Colorado, its own ice cream company, and more than 300 convenience stores stretching from Louisiana to California. Today, each division, including Dillon Food Stores, continues to operate independently while serving the unique needs of its particular community or region.

Company officials describe the 18 Wichita stores as "neighborhood tailored." Store managers strive to understand their neighborhood's ethnic makeup, the average age of residents, household incomes, and the number of family households versus single households. They can then tailor their

stock to meet those needs.

"Some stores have larger stocks of ethnic foods, or a slightly more upscale variety of specialty foods," says Kenneth A. Keefer, director of advertising and public relations for Dillons. "Managers are the ones who know their customers best, so they have the authority to order what best fits their customers' demands."

Dillons also combines trial and error with new research techniques to monitor what customers want and need. Bar-code scanners, which record a product's name and size at the check-out counter, allow stores to track their best-selling products while personal customer surveys help forecast what will sell tomorrow. Dillons strives to translate this body of information into creative merchandising, an area in which the company "outshines virtually anyone in the business," says Keefer.

ONE-STOP SHOPPING

As the number of dual-wage households grows, researchers are finding that consumers want to spend less time on routine chores, including shopping. That trend has created a wealth of opportunity for savvy merchandisers like Dillons, where creative merchandising—and a fierce dedication to one-stop shopping—

FROM LEFT: THE DILLONS SALAD BAR
FEATURES HOT SOUPS, SLICED FRUIT,
AND DESSERTS.

EACH DILLONS FLOWER SHOP HAS
TRAINED FLORAL DESIGNERS ON DUTY.

CUSTOMERS CAN CARRY OUT AT THE
CHINESE KITCHEN.

full bloom.

n 1983 the company launched
irst Wichita super store. Total-
more than 60,000 square feet,
1 store offers the widest variety
:aple and gourmet foods comple-
ited by such services as bank
iches, dry cleaners, pharmacies,
:o rental departments, and shoe
ir shops. Wichita already has
Dillons Super Stores, with an-
er scheduled to open in 1994 in
central Wichita.

We try to save customers time,"
Keefer. "They know that with
one stop at the grocery store
y can go to the bank, drop off
cleaning, pick up a prescrip-
, rent a movie, and buy their
:eries."

The growth in single- and dual-
wage households, as well as a new
focus on eating healthier, led Dillons to offer a wider selection of
prepared foods for customers who
would rather leave the cooking to
someone else. A unique service
found only in Dillons Super Stores
is a Chinese delicatessen. The
broad appeal and healthful reputation of Chinese cuisine have
proved popular with customers,
who can choose from an extensive
menu prepared on the spot for
take-out. Fresh-cooked meals are
also available from Dillons seafood
shops, delicatessens, or lavish salad
bars stocked regularly to ensure
freshness.

SERVICE, SELECTION, AND VALUE

No matter what the future brings,
Dillons holds fast to a simple philosophy that has served the company
and its customers well for more
than six decades: service, selection,
and value.

"Our responsibility is to provide
a standard of service in every community in which we operate," says
Keefer. "Economics may determine
store size, but it doesn't dictate
that service and value should be
compromised."

KAMEN SUPPLY COMPANY, INC.

KAMEN SUPPLY COMPANY, INC. IS AN old-line family business that has enjoyed success, survived downsizing, and regained its market position with a vigorous spirit of rebirth. ◆ Now celebrating its fourth generation of family leadership in Wichita, the company evolved from Kamen Iron and Metal Company, founded in 1896. Beginning as an offshoot enterprise of the original company, Kamen was established in 1933 as a plumbing supplier with one small warehouse. Over the years it has added warehouses and yard facilities across Kansas and Col-

PRESIDENT HARLAN R. KAMEN (LEFT) AND VICE PRESIDENT KEITH A. ALTER STAND IN FRONT OF A PORTRAIT OF COMPANY FOUNDER SHERMAN KAMEN.

A STATE-OF-THE-ART SHOWER DISPLAY AT KAMEN'S FIRST NATIONAL FIXTURE SHOWROOM IN WICHITA (ABOVE RIGHT).

orado. The company wholesales the full spectrum of plumbing supplies, from 10-cent bibb washers to gold-plated faucets to plumbing components for refineries and other industrial uses.

Kamen's subsidiary, First National Fixture Corporation, is a master distributor of Kohler, Delta, Elkay, and other name-brand plumbing fixtures. Selling to other wholesale distributors in all 50 states, its large inventories allow it to fill 95 percent of orders from stock.

One of approximately 4,000 wholesale distributors in the country, Kamen is ranked as the 56th largest by *Wholesaler Magazine*.

WHEN BETTER IS POSSIBLE
Empowering employees to provide customer satisfaction is a key element of the philosophy and success of Kamen Supply, says Keith Alter, vice president and son-in-law of Harlan Kamen, company president. The firm's credo, "If better is possible, then good is not enough," also expresses Kamen Supply's dedication to excellence.

"Employees have always been treated like family, and the brotherhood and camaraderie have made a significant difference through the good times and bad," Alter says.

During Wichita's real estate slump in the late 1980s, Harlan Kamen was forced to begin closing his local operations, while warehouse locations elsewhere were able to remain open. In a move that would be significant later, every single employee of the Wichita office remained on the payroll until he or she found another job.

When the Wichita office was in its final phase of shutting down, Kamen and Alter found themselv at a crossroads. "We either had to finish selling out, because we wer too small, or we had to get bigger again," Alter says. "We decided w wanted to be one of the survivors the downturn. We had been in operation for almost 100 years, a we wanted to stay in business."

An opportunity presented itsel in the form of First National Fixture Corporation in Wichita, which Kamen Supply purchased 1989. A year later, six of the employees who had left Kamen suggested that the company buy out their current employer, a local co petitor. After completing these tv acquisitions, Kamen Supply had back all but two of its former employees who had stayed in the wo force. Within five years, the company quadrupled its annual sales and repositioned itself as an indu try leader.

"My father said when he starte 'If we can do $75 a week in business, we can live,' " Kamen recall "Fortunately, we've done a lot better than that, and we're aimin for continued growth. With my son-in-law in the business, we ho to continue running it as a family operation for the foreseeable future."

. BRUENGER TRUCKING CO.

FROM ITS 22-ACRE TERMINAL AND OFFICES in north Wichita, M. Bruenger Trucking Co. dispatches its state-of-the-art trucks that traverse the country carrying foods and manufactured products to and from America's heartland. M. Bruenger's operations are a far cry from the company's

tere beginning in 1936 during Great Depression. Back then, urice D. Bruenger would drive one and only truck to the fertile eys of south Texas, purchase ts and produce, and haul the go back to Wichita, where he uld sell it wholesale.

hauls a wide variety of meats, food products, and manufactured goods from companies in Kansas and neighboring states to destinations throughout the continental United States and Canada. Bruenger's trucks return with cargoes of produce, foods, and other merchandise

company and helped our bottom line," Bruenger notes. "It has also allowed us to be more flexible, to add more customers, and to reduce our operating expenses."

That move was concurrent with some rough times the company experienced in the late 1970s and early 1980s. Though M. Bruenger has enjoyed mostly steady growth during its six decades in business, spiraling fuel costs, federal deregulation of the industry, and a recession forced the company to make significant changes in the way it did business. Butch Bruenger had to cut operations in half in order to remain in business: he reduced the fleet to 125 trucks and downsized

WITH A MODERN FLEET OF 110 TRACTORS, 160 REFRIGERATED TRAILERS, AND 25 DRY VAN TRAILERS, M. BRUENGER HAULS GOODS FROM KANSAS AND NEIGHBORING STATES TO DESTINATIONS THROUGHOUT THE CONTINENTAL UNITED STATES AND CANADA.

rom that modest start has rged the largest Wichita-based onal and national trucking com- y. The firm is headed today by late Bruenger's son, President W. "Butch" Bruenger, who took the company when his father in 1975. It has remained a ily-owned business ever since. He taught me that dedicated ice in the trucking business e important thing," says enger of his father. "We are very ice oriented. That's what has t us in business all these years."

SS-COUNTRY
ANSPORTATION

h its modern fleet of 110 trac- , 160 refrigerated trailers, and lry van trailers, M. Bruenger

for delivery to cities across the heartland.

M. Bruenger's customers include such major companies as Boeing, Excel, Iowa Beef, Binney-Smith, Wichita Metal Fabricators, Exide Batteries, Tony's Pizza, John Morrell, Dole, Del Monte, Chiquita, Dillons, Albertson's, Chelsea Milling, General Felt Industries, Ohse Meat Products, Fleming, Elf Atochem, Hy Plains Dressed Beef, and Farmland Foods.

Since the beginning, the firm has been primarily in the food transportation business. Ten years ago, however, M. Bruenger began hauling "dry" loads—non-perishable manufactured products. It was a key decision that has had a positive impact on the company. "It diversified the

personnel—drivers, maintenance workers, and office staff—to about 200.

Although the company's fleet size and number of employees have remained basically the same, M. Bruenger has experienced its strongest economic growth since 1991. A tradition of dedicated on-time service, whether during lean or prosperous times, has paid off for the company, says Bruenger. "We are a state-of-the-art, service-oriented, financially solid regional and national motor carrier," he says, with pride in the company and its employees.

ALLEN, GIBBS & HOULIK, L.C.

WHEN SOLUTIONS ARE NEEDED FOR complex problems, business owners and executives know they can turn to Allen, Gibbs & Houlik, L.C. for timely answers. ◆ With approximately 70 employees, Allen, Gibbs & Houlik is one of the largest independently owned certified public accounting and consulting firms in Kansas. From its founding as Moberly & West in 1938, the firm has built a heritage of serving client needs that spans more than five decades.

"Our people are committed to helping clients obtain success," says Paul S. Allen, chief executive officer and member of AGH. "Our firm is about clients. We focus on small and medium-size businesses, while also performing specialized services for large organizations."

Through its employee benefits division, AGH helps clients by administering 401(k) retirement plans, flexible benefits plans, and employee stock ownership plans and by acting as third-party administrator for health plans.

The firm's computer consulting division provides a range of data processing solutions. AGH employs top computer professionals, including certified Novell Network engineers and state-of-the-art programmers who understand business. Its professionals can design modern microcomputer networks that up-grade existing systems and provide fully integrated information management.

AGH also provides specialists in state and local tax issues, mergers and acquisitions, business start-ups, and public offerings. The firm has expertise in the manufacturing, health care, construction, distribution, commercial printing, and financial industries.

RESPONSIVE TO EVERY NEED
Just ask Dave Anderson, president of Dealers Leasing, what AGH's dedication to service means.

During a Labor Day weekend, a tornado ravaged east Wichita. Dealers Leasing was hit hard, with damages topping $700,000. Water was pouring through the building, electrical lines were damaged, and worst of all, the company's computer system was inoperable. With automobiles on lease in all 50 states and business equipment in several surrounding states, Dealers faced serious problems. Anderson called his AGH partner for assistance.

Within 48 hours, AGH Senior Consultant Joe Moore helped the company re-establish its computer network from an adjacent hotel. Thanks to Moore's effort, Dealers was operating by regular opening time on Tuesday morning. "We're an information systems company, so we were dead in the water without our computers," Anderson says. "Allen, Gibbs & Houlik was a very important factor for us."

John Samples, president of Kan-Build Inc. in Osage City, Kansas, turned to AGH for solutions to sky-rocketing health insurance costs.

Samples had already converted from a fully funded, traditional health insurance plan to a partially self-funded plan. But to make it work, he needed a quality organization to serve as the plan's third-party administrator. Samples called on John McKean, director of the employee benefits services division of AGH.

McKean delivered by designing claims paying and review systems that helped Kan-Build control its medical costs, while giving the company's employees a first-rate health insurance plan. "As a small business, it becomes tougher and tougher to cut dollars on the bottom line," Samples says. "You need the best people to help you. That's where Allen, Gibbs & Houlik comes in."

DAVE ANDERSON (CENTER), PRESIDENT OF DEALERS LEASING, REVIEWS PLANS WITH AGH'S BRIAN JOHNSON (LEFT) AND JOE MOORE.

"WE'RE AN INFORMATION SYSTEMS COMPANY, SO WE WERE DEAD IN THE WATER WITHOUT OUR COMPUTERS," SAYS ANDERSON, RECALLING THE TIME A TORNADO SEVERELY DAMAGED HIS EAST WICHITA BUSINESS. WITHIN 48 HOURS, AGH HELPED THE COMPANY RE-ESTABLISH ITS COMPUTER NETWORK FROM AN ADJACENT HOTEL.

JOHN SAMPLES (LEFT), PRESIDENT OF KAN-BUILD, TALKS WITH AGH'S JOHN MCKEAN ABOUT HIS PARTIALLY SELF-FUNDED HEALTH CARE PLAN.

ONTINENTAL AIRLINES, INC.

BACK IN THE 1930S, COMMERCIAL AIR-lines were speculative businesses at best. Passengers were few and far between, and it was mail service that literally paid the freight. Such was the foundation for Continental Airlines, which began in 1934 serving mail routes throughout

orado, Nevada, Texas, and New ico. By 1939 the company a mail route to Wichita, mak-it one of the first carriers to e the Air Capital.

oday, Continental and its sub-ary, Continental Express, both dquartered in Houston, Texas, e nearly 200 airports world-e, with an average of more than 00 systemwide departures daily. ough global alliances with Air ada, Air France, and SAS, tinental can offer passengers -stop check-in and ticketing for inations throughout Europe, ca, the Middle East, and the fic.

Global alliances are the wave of future," says Leon Becker, gen-manager of the Wichita opera-. "From Wichita—or from any tinental ticket counter—we tag your luggage and make your assignments all the way to yo or Amsterdam. It makes the enger's airport and airline trans-easy and convenient—and 's what airline travel should

Continental currently serves e destinations in Mexico and tral America than any other carrier. All of these Latin erican locales are served from hita's Mid-Continent Airport, ing Continental the carrier of ice for Wichitans heading south e border.

KING CARE OF BUSINESS EDS

ognizing the special needs of international business traveler, 993 Continental launched nessFirst,^{SM} an international ness class offering first-class

comfort and service at regular busi-ness-class fares.

The centerpiece of BusinessFirst is the best first-class sleeper seat in the sky, an electronically controlled

recliner that provides a full 55 inches of pitch and as much as 15 more inches of leg room than most business-class seats. These custom-designed seats include a personal entertainment system built into the armrest console. A high resolution television monitor offers six chan-nels of continuous music, movies, sports, and news programming.

BusinessFirst is now available on Continental's international 747 and DC-10-30 flights between the United States and Europe, the South Pacific, and Japan.

Another popular service for Continental passengers is the OnePass^{SM} program, which has been rated "Best Overall Frequent

Flyer Program" by readers of *Inside Flyer* magazine for five consecutive years.

MAKING A DIFFERENCE
From Mid-Continent Airport, Continental averages five to six daily departures. The nearly 40 employees based in Wichita serve more than 150,000 travelers each year.

"As an aviation town, Wichita has been very supportive of the airline through the years," says Leon Becker, who has been with Continental in Wichita since 1959.

In return, Continental has been sup-portive of the community, partici-pating in numerous charitable and civic fund-raisers each year.

"The airline industry has become so competitive that we have to be innovative in our approach to fares, amenities, and services," says Barb Van Dusen, district sales manager. "Continental's marketing theme maintains that one airline can make a difference—and we truly believe that. From ticket agents to mainte-nance engineers, the employees of Continental know that our fares and our services have to be the abso-lute best if we're to maintain our position as one of America's great-est airlines."

CONTINENTAL AND ITS SUBSIDIARY, CONTINENTAL EXPRESS, SERVE NEARLY 200 AIRPORTS WORLDWIDE, WITH AN AVERAGE OF MORE THAN 2,100 SYSTEMWIDE DEPARTURES DAILY.

THROUGH GLOBAL ALLIANCES WITH AIR CANADA (TOP), AIR FRANCE, AND SAS, CONTINENTAL CAN OFFER PASSENGERS ONE-STOP CHECK-IN AND TICKETING FOR DESTINATIONS THROUGHOUT EUROPE, AFRICA, THE MIDDLE EAST, AND THE PACIFIC.

STAR LUMBER & SUPPLY CO.

IF YOU LIVE IN A HOME OR WORK IN A BUILDING constructed in central Kansas after 1939, chances are at least something in it came from Star Lumber & Supply. From nails to roof trusses to the finest Saxony carpeting, Star Lumber has been the area's leading supplier of quality building and home improvement supplies for more than 50 years.

The family-owned business includes four stores in Wichita and one in Hutchinson, plus a massive warehouse and distribution center in west Wichita. On any given day, Star has enough lumber in stock to build more than 200 homes and enough carpeting to furnish 500 residences.

FROM START TO FINISH
The company provides the weekend do-it-yourselfer and the professional contractor with all the products and service to accomplish any job, plus a number of specialized services for custom projects, including the largest selection of lumber species in popular grades and lengths.

For the remodeler, home builder, and commercial contractor, Star's floor and roof truss plant offers computer-aided design and automated assembly. The company has full millwork capabilities, including the fabrication of pre-hung doors and windows. Custom woodworking services are also available for all lumber products from oak to cedar fencing.

Star's delivery fleet, including specialized flatbed, box, crane, lift, and semi-tractor trailer trucks, is constantly on the road delivering products. Materials can be loaded onto rooftops or other specified locations, which makes it easy for the contractor and consumer.

Star offers installation of cabinetry, carpeting, vinyl and wood flooring, ceramic tile, fencing, and decking, among other products. Since the early 1960s, the company has maintained a strong focus on the home decorating market. Professional designers are on staff to help customers with everything from product and color selection to custom design of a kitchen or deck.

The newest Star store, which will open at 35th and North Rock Road in the spring of 1994, features one of the most impressive displays of floor covering in the Midwest, as well as a unique drive-through lumber and building materials store. A large selection of doors, windows, and millwork is featured in a massive, two-story-tall display.

Star has added landscaping and green goods to its large assortment of quality products for the home. The cornerstone of the company's purchasing prowess and service edge is its long-term relationship with the industry's leading manufacturers and suppliers, and its ongoing product review process ensures that customers receive the highest quality products available.

THE VALUES OF A LIFETIME
Since the beginning, Star has prided itself on helping to build not only buildings but communities. The company has always had a strong sense of corporate commitment and civic responsibility. Each year, Star's 600 employees devote thousands of hours to community organizations and projects. Additionally, the Star Lumber/Goebel Family Charitable Trust supports dozens of community organizations, including Kansas Special Olympics, the Kansas Cosmosphere, public television station KPTS, Heartspring, the Sedgwick County Zoo, and many others.

Star has thrived under the principles of hard work, honesty, fairness and respect for superb craftsmanship. Strength of family has been a key tradition not only among the Goebels, whose third generation management is led today by President Chris Goebel, but also by the employees, who have become part of Star's extended family. Many employees are from families who have worked for the company for two or three generations. Star's continued success can be attributed in large part to the employees' dedication to high service standards and thorough product knowledge.

As customers build new homes or improve the ones they have, they will continue to look to Star Lumber for the quality, service, and knowledgeable staff that will help make their building projects just a little bit better.

STAR LUMBER HAS BEEN THE AREA'S LEADING SUPPLIER OF QUALITY BUILDING AND HOME IMPROVEMENT SUPPLIES FOR MORE THAN 50 YEARS.

UILDERS, INC.

OR MORE THAN FIVE DECADES, BUILDERS, INC. has been synonymous with residential, commercial, and industrial real estate development in Wichita. Founded in 1941 by Ray Garvey and his son Willard, Builders is now enjoying its third generation of family leadership. The firm is a subsidiary of Garvey Industries,

cal company founded in the y 1930s that today has interests rming and livestock, oil and and grain storage and transport. iving up to its motto, "Everyg in Real Estate," Builders curly owns and manages 2,742 rtment units and 1.4 million are feet of commercial and intrial properties. The company holds approximately 500 acres nd for future development.

E POSTWAR BOOM Ɔ BEYOND

owing World War II, Builders red its first period of massive lential development as thouls of Wichitans sought the erican Dream" of home owner-. To meet the need for quality, rdable housing, the firm con-cted 2,400 homes and 1,800 tments, and developed 20 lential subdivisions during the war years.

hat tradition of excellence con-es today. Since 1980 Builders developed more than 900 apart-t units. The company also plat-and developed the 160-acre nee Mesa Addition, with 545 le sites; the Cottonwood Grove pile Home Park, with 92 lots; more than 500,000 square of commercial and industrial perties.

 the early 1950s, Builders loped Wichita's first major pping center, the 300,000-re-foot Parklane Center. Lod at Lincoln and Oliver streets, lane continues to thrive under company's ownership and man-

agement, and houses its corporate headquarters. In 1965 Builders constructed the O.W. Garvey and R.H. Garvey twin office towers to accommodate Garvey Industries' headquarters, as well as other tenants.

Builders' most ambitious commercial project in recent years was the development of Epic Center, the tallest building in Kansas and Wichita's premier office complex. Built in the mid-1980s at a cost of $28 million, the 22-story tower rises an impressive 325 feet. Its distinctive triangular design and gleaming copper roof make the structure a standout on the city's skyline. Located at Second and Main streets, the property recently was sold and is under new management.

BUILDING A SOLID COMMUNITY

While Builders, Inc. and the Garvey family have contributed much to Wichita's real estate development and economic growth for more than 50 years, they also have been active supporters of a wide range of community organizations and activities.

In 1948 the company planned, financed, and built the internationally known Institute of Logopedics. Now known as Heartspring, the institute is the world's leading educational center for children with severe hearing and speech disorders.

Likewise, the Garveys have been strong supporters of such Wichita institutions as The Independent School (including its recent expansion project), Wichita Swim Club,

Garvey Athletic Center at Friends University, and the Center for the Improvement of Human Functioning. The Garvey Family Foundation also has been a major contributor to local arts, social service, and educational organizations and programs.

Since 1941 Builders, Inc. has helped shape the face of Wichita, both as a major real estate developer and as a good corporate citizen. With the third generation of Garvey leadership in place, the company looks forward to another half-century of business success and community involvement.

PARKLANE GARDENS (TOP) AND WILLOWCREEK MANOR (BOTTOM) ARE TWO OF THE APARTMENT COMMUNITIES BUILDERS, INC. HAS DEVELOPED AND STILL OWNS AND MANAGES.

KOCH INDUSTRIES, INC.

KOCH INDUSTRIES, INC., IS A RESPECTED business entity with a heritage that reflects the strength of its people and the integrity of the Midwest. ♦ As the second largest privately held corporation in the United States, Koch is involved in virtually every aspect of the oil and gas industry, as well as chemicals, chemical technology products, agriculture, hard minerals, real estate, and financial investments.

The company attributes its success to its 13,000 employees, who continuously strive to understand and anticipate their customers'

tion, hundreds of employees who make up Koch's skilled labor force are hired in Wichita and in other Kansas communities.

Koch Industries continues to thrive in the community because Wichita provides fertile soil for business roots. Other U.S. locales have

which increased gasoline yield. Later, he founded the Wood River Oil and Refining Company, which built and operated a major refinery east of St. Louis, Missouri. In 19[..] he purchased Rock Island Oil and Refining Company, leading to the company's crude-oil gathering business.

At the time of his father's death in 1967, Charles Koch, who first joined Koch Engineering Company, Inc., in 1961, was president of Rock Island. Charles renamed the company Koch Industries in honor of his father, and was joined in 1970 by his younger brother, David, who is now executive vice president for Koch's Chemical

KOCH'S PINE BEND REFINERY IS LOCATED SOUTH OF MINNEAPOLIS/ ST. PAUL, MINNESOTA.

needs. Two thousand employees work at Koch headquarters in Wichita, quietly contributing their financial and human resources to the city's prosperous economy. In addition, tens of thousands of customers do business with KII and its subsidiaries, both in the United States and around the world. It's easy to see why Koch Industries is a dynamic force in domestic and international business.

To meet its growing need for engineering, accounting, and marketing professionals, KII recruits graduates from every university in Kansas as well as several colleges throughout the Midwest. In addi-

tried to lure away this oil and gas enterprise, but Wichita "has always remained home," says Charles Koch, chairman of the board and chief executive officer. "We're fond of Wichita because of its family values, integrity, and solid work ethic. Kansas and the Midwest are a source of pride; we're pleased to be one of its corporate citizens."

HISTORICAL ROOTS
Koch's spirit of ingenuity is the legacy of Wichita native Fred C. Koch, the company's late founder. While in his 20s, Koch developed a version of the widely used thermal cracking process for refineries,

Technology Group. Charles Koch continues as chairman and chief executive officer; Bill Hanna is president and chief operating officer.

Koch has experienced hundredfold growth under Charles' leadership because of his commitment to the free enterprise system. Koch employees apply market-based theories and principles to meet business needs. "We believe many businesses experience serious problems when they do not apply market-based framework to their everyday practice," says Charles Koch. "Most companies promote excessive decision-making by a central authority, blocking their

ity to fully use the knowledge of
r people."

Koch Industries' philosophy of
rket-based management has cre-
d a flexible, responsive corpora-
n that can marshal its resources
erve customers, preserve its ex-
sive investments in community-
ed operations, or react to
tuations in the world's financial
rkets. This philosophy ensures
aordinary customer service and
forces the firm's fundamental
es, such as humility, intellec-
honesty, and respect for the
que contributions made by
people.

PPLY, TRADING AND
ANSPORTATION

h's Supply, Trading and Trans-
tation Group is responsible for
le oil gathering, refinery supply,
spot sales of products from its
neries in Pine Bend, Minnesota,
Corpus Christi, Texas. It also
es in crude oil, refined prod-
, feedstocks, chemicals, natural
gas liquids, ammonia, petro-
n coke, coal, and other related
ducts and derivatives.

FINING AND CHEMICALS

h's Refining and Chemicals
up is responsible for refinery
rations, wholesale marketing,
exchanges of refined products
chemicals. The company's
ning businesses, located in
Paul, Minnesota, and Corpus
isti, purchase and process
nestic crude delivered by its
nsive pipeline system.
Companies within this group
produce commodity chemicals
are used worldwide in the man-
ture of consumer goods such as
tic soft drink bottles, textiles,
construction materials. Koch
produces specialty chemicals
l in carbonless paper solvents,
trical oils, and agricultural
ents.

DROCARBONS

Koch Hydrocarbon Group pro-
es, purchases, processes, trans-
s, stores, trades, and markets

natural gas, gas liquids, and carbon
dioxide, as well as anhydrous ammonia and its derivatives.

The group's Gas Liquids Division operates more than 1,300
miles of pipeline associated with its
Medford, Oklahoma, fractionator.
The Natural Gas Division gathers
and transports natural gas through
2,600 miles of onshore pipeline to
six gas processing plants where gas
liquids and sulfur are extracted
from natural gas streams.

CHEMICAL TECHNOLOGY

Koch Industries' Chemical Technology Group supports the durable
equipment needs of chemical pro-

cessing/refining and related industries. The John Zink Company, for
example, supplies combustion
equipment and has been an innova-
tor in fuel-efficiency and environmental technology.

MATERIALS

Koch Materials Company produces
and markets asphalt-based products
derived from crude oil for paving,
industrial, recreational, and water-
proofing uses. Koch Materials is
also the major producer and marketer of products for roofing applications and tennis court coatings,
including DecoTurf® II, the surface
for the prestigious U.S. Open.

KOCH INDUSTRIES, INC. FACILITIES
IN WICHITA.

THE COMPANY'S LEADERSHIP
INCLUDES (FROM LEFT) DAVID KOCH,
EXECUTIVE VICE PRESIDENT; CHARLES
KOCH, CHAIRMAN OF THE BOARD AND
CHIEF EXECUTIVE OFFICER; AND
BILL HANNA, PRESIDENT AND CHIEF
OPERATING OFFICER.

THE MATADOR CATTLE DIVISION IS ENGAGED IN QUALITY BEEF PRODUCTION AT RANCHES AND FEEDLOTS.

THE PRESTIGIOUS U.S. OPEN TENNIS TOURNAMENT (BELOW RIGHT) IS PLAYED ON DECOTURF,® ONE OF THE SPECIALTY COATING PRODUCTS OF KOCH MATERIALS.

KOCH ENGINEERING COMPANY, INC. IS THE LEADING SUPPLIER OF STRUCTURED PACKING TO THE NORTH AMERICAN REFINERY AND CHEMICAL PROCESSING MARKETS.

AGRICULTURE

The Koch Agriculture Group includes ranching operations in Kansas, Montana, and Texas, cattle feeding programs and feedlots in Kansas and Texas, and farm/grain retail operations in 10 states. The Matador Cattle Division provides grassland beef production on approximately 450,000 acres, making it one of the top 10 calf producers in the nation.

MINERALS

Iron blast furnace slag, a by-product of steel manufacturing, is the major raw material utilized by Koch Minerals Group to create GranCem® cement, slag aggregate, and other products. GranCem, used in road and building construction, mining, and utilities, provides superior strength to concrete. Slag aggregate is used in concrete, asphalt hot mix, concrete block, and precast products to serve the needs of various industries and customers.

FINANCIAL SERVICES

The Financial Services Group provides worldwide financial products support to other Koch businesses. In addition, the group manages investments in domestic and international financial instruments, trading, and the company's diverse real estate holdings. Koch Financial Corporation provides lease financ-ing for essential-use equipment needed by municipalities, such a police cars, fire engines, street cle ers, ambulances, and computers.

COMMUNITY INVOLVEMENT

The presence of Koch Industries felt around the world, but nowh is it more appreciated than on home soil. Koch's corporate, fou dations, and family contribution have provided millions of dollars human service organizations, as well as educational and cultural groups.

Each year, for example, the co pany is the Prime Partner of Kan Special Olympics and its annual Summer Games. Many employe and their families also volunteer the weekend event to make the games a memorable experience f more than 2,000 special athletes.

Recently, the Fred C. and Ma R. Koch Foundation provided a Challenge Grant to build a full-time faculty at the school of the Wichita Center for the Arts. The foundation's financial gift helpe broaden the base of involvement and support from the communit while continuing to strengthen educational programs and facult Koch Industries is the sponsor o Wichita Symphony's Fall Pops Concert and Young People's Concerts, featuring many of the most distinguished soloists and musicians from the Wichita com munity and around the world.

Koch Industries' support of th Big Brothers/Big Sisters program

udes funding for employee
olvement. As a result, Koch
ployees are matched as Big
thers and Sisters, and some
dren of Koch employees are
ched as "Littles." This level of
mitment ranks Koch first in
capita involvement among
or local employers.

hrough a new Mobile Screen-
Van operated by the Midwest
cer Foundation and funded
XII, thousands of Wichitans are
ning about the early signs of
st and prostate cancer. The van
traveled thousands of miles
nd the Wichita area—to local
ls, businesses, and grocery
es—to provide more people ac-
to affordable cancer screening.
och supports the mission of
local Boys and Girls Club: "To
d good citizens through every-
leadership and guidance in be-
or and attitude." The company
tributes financially to help
vide and maintain community
ers where young people from
bled homes are encouraged
ay in school and avoid gang
vity.
och Industries also has made
ncial contributions to the Cere-
Palsy Research Foundation. By
gning workstations and adap-
devices, the foundation enables
ple with physical disabilities to

make the transition into the
workplace, thus enhancing their
self-sufficiency and pride.

NFTE

Working with young people to
overcome barriers is a high priority,
too. That's why the Koch family's
multimillion-dollar support of the
National Foundation for Teaching
Entrepreneurship is an integral part
of their contributions program.

NFTE introduces at-risk, inner-
city youth to the world of business
and entrepreneurship. Through special training programs, the organization teaches these young people
how to create and maintain their
own small businesses. Founder
Steve Mariotti launched NFTE to
encourage the economic participation of this neglected segment of
the population.

The Charles G. Koch Charitable
Foundation is vitally interested in
teaching young people about the
free enterprise system through

NFTE. In 1991 the foundation
brought the New York-based organization to Wichita. Offered to secondary school students throughout
the community, NFTE provides opportunities for these young people
to use their initiative as entrepreneurs to realize their dreams.

Supporting programs like NFTE
is one way Koch Industries demonstrates its commitment to the communities in which it operates. It's
a commitment that is continually
reinforced.

KOCH INDUSTRIES
AND WICHITA—
A WINNING COMBINATION

With its history of continuous family involvement, commitment to
market-based management, and
community generosity, Koch is a
proud corporate citizen of Wichita.
The employees of Koch Industries
are proud of Wichita as well, for its
rich heritage, positive family environment, and high quality of life.

EVERY PARTICIPANT IS A WINNER TO
KOCH EMPLOYEES, SEEN HERE CHEER-
ING FOR ONE OF THE ATHLETES AT
THE SUMMER GAMES FOR KANSAS
SPECIAL OLYMPICS (ABOVE).

MATT SILVERTHORNE, AN INSTRUCTOR
AT NORTH HIGH, COACHES STUDENTS
TO USE THEIR ENTREPRENEURIAL
SKILLS (INSET).

NUMEROUS BUSINESSES DEPEND ON
KOCH CHEMICAL PRODUCTS IN THE
MANUFACTURE OF A VARIETY OF
GOODS (LEFT).

MORRIS, LAING, EVANS, BROCK & KENNEDY, CHARTERED

THE OIL AND GAS BOOM THAT STRUCK KANSAS in the 1940s created a need for talented legal advisors who understood energy exploration and production. In 1945 Lester L. Morris, one of the preeminent oil and gas attorneys of the time, and Verne M. Laing seized the opportunity and founded a law firm centered on the myriad legal issues surrounding the oil and gas industries.

In the beginning, oil and gas clients comprised the majority of the firm's business. Through the years, the firm has helped independent and major producers and pipeline companies develop and expand the state's energy business. Some of those clients, such as Coastal Refining (formerly Derby Refinery), have continued to retain the firm since the 1940s.

Today, Morris, Laing, Evans, Brock & Kennedy is one of the largest firms in the state. With 29 attorneys on staff and offices in Wichita and Topeka, it serves virtually every type of commercial endeavor. Says Partner Bob Guenthner, "As our energy clients have grown and diversified, so have we."

PRACTICE AREAS AND EXPERIENCE

In addition to its work in oil and gas, the firm now practices in the areas of utility law, environmental law, real estate, tax and tax planning, trusts and estate planning, mergers and acquisitions, and business and commercial law. The firm has an impressive list of clients, including individuals and small to medium-size local businesses such as Huber, Inc., McGinty Machine Co., Emprise Financial Corporation, and Southwest National Bank. Morris, Laing, Evans, Brock & Kennedy also has served clients with regional, national, and multinational operations such as Exxon, Texaco, and Enron, representing these major clients in state and fed-

eral courts around the country.

The firm's litigation department is highly regarded for its expertise in handling complex administrative and regulatory issues for energy companies, utilities, financial institutions, corporations, and individuals. Attorneys from Morris, Laing, Evans, Brock & Kennedy regularly appear before the Kansas Corpora-

tion Commission in proceedings involving oil, gas, pipelines, and other utilities. Firm attorneys have litigated issues before the Federal Energy Regulatory Commission, Department of Energy, Department of Transportation, Federal Home Loan Bank Board, Federal Reserve Board, and Comptroller of

the Currency.

The firm is involved in substantial litigation activity in the areas toxic tort, product liability, and personal injury cases. Morris, Laing, Evans, Brock & Kennedy also has developed one of the largest insolvency practices in the state, offering in-depth knowledge and experience in non-judicial restructurings as well as Chapter 11 reorganizations.

In addition, the firm has had experience as lead trial counsel in complex civil and commercial cases with state, regional, and national ramifications. For example, Joseph W. Kennedy, who heads the firm's litigation department, served as liaison counsel for the oil industry in the Department of Energy Stripper Well Exemption litigation, a landmark case with nationwide impact. The issue, involving price control regulations with over $1 billion at stake, was ultimately settled in 1986 in favor of the refining industry.

In the areas of toxic tort and product liability, the firm was one of the first in the United States to

WITH 29 ATTORNEYS AND OFFICES IN BOTH WICHITA AND TOPEKA, THE FIRM SERVES VIRTUALLY EVERY TYPE OF COMMERCIAL ENDEAVOR.

ate a case involving exposure to
zene and has successfully han-
l radiation exposure claims on
alf of numerous clients.

n 1992 the firm handled his-
c litigation against the State of
isas, representing Wichita's
fied School District 259 in a
essful challenge to the state's
ool finance formula. The results
iis case created a more fair
ribution of funds to school
ricts statewide.

o support the firm's litigation
rts, the Wichita office of
ris, Laing, Evans, Brock &
nedy is equipped with a confer-
e room designed for mock trial
entations. Using state-of-the-
video, computer, and communi-
ons equipment, attorneys and
its can prepare together to
eve successful courtroom
icts.

**TICIPATING AND MEETING
ENT NEEDS**

nded on the philosophy of re-
isiveness to client needs, the
has positioned itself on the
ing edge of computer technol-
utilizing computerized legal
bases for research, evidence,
document tracking and for
iisticated accounting and tax
ulation functions. The firm has
ixtensive in-house research
iry and is a subscriber to a
ety of legal and financial data-
services.

lorris, Laing, Evans, Brock &
nedy opened its Topeka office
990 in response to the firm's
vth in the areas of utility,
inistrative, and regulatory law
to provide representation for
its in northeastern Kansas. The
e, staffed by two attorneys and
oort personnel, is located in the
t of the governmental and fi-
cial district of the state capital.
he Topeka office offers quick,
onal access to government of-
, the Kansas Corporation Com-
ion, Kansas appellate courts,
the many other federal bank-

THE FIRM HAS AN EXTENSIVE IN-
HOUSE RESEARCH LIBRARY AND IS A
SUBSCRIBER TO A VARIETY OF LEGAL
AND FINANCIAL DATABASE SERVICES.

USING STATE-OF-THE-ART EQUIPMENT
AND FACILITIES, ATTORNEYS AND
CLIENTS CAN PREPARE TOGETHER TO
ACHIEVE SUCCESSFUL COURTROOM
VERDICTS.

ruptcy and district courts in which
the firm's attorneys are licensed to
practice. It also serves as a base of
operations for attorneys from the
Wichita office who are trying cases
or appearing before government
agencies in Topeka.

After almost 50 years of growth,
Morris, Laing, Evans, Brock &
Kennedy foresees a continuing

success story. "A measure of our
success is the fact that we have
represented clients in a variety of
businesses, many of whom have
been with us for nearly 50 years,"
Guenthner notes. "We're continually adding new clients and expanding our practice to meet those
clients' needs."

SHEPLERS INC.

IF YOU WANT A CLEAR REMINDER OF WICHITA'S deep roots in the Old West, you need only look as far as Sheplers—the world's largest western wear chain. Located in the city for nearly 50 years, the 60,000-square-foot flagship store on the west edge of town stocks enough boots and jeans to outfit a capacity crowd at the Kansas Coliseum. And with brand names such as Wrangler, Levi, Stetson, Panhandle Slim, Justin, and Dan Post, the store provides clothing, leather goods, belt buckles, hats, Native American jewelry, coats, and accessories for the entire family.

Established by Harry Shepler in 1946 as a harness, tack, and saddlery company, Sheplers gained a loyal clientele by guaranteeing customer satisfaction with an old-fashioned handshake. Retailer Bob Dry bought the company in 1968 and added jeans, boots, and ladies' apparel. Soon, Sheplers began opening branch stores nationwide and introduced a four-color catalog. In 1976 Dry sold the company for $22 million to W.R. Grace & Co., a New York-based, multinational conglomerate.

SUCCESS THROUGH NICHE MARKETING

In 1979 the popular movie *Urban Cowboy* brought two years of unprecedented sales to Sheplers. But when the western wear fashion craze passed, the stores began stocking their shelves with a wider variety of merchandise. In the process, Sheplers lost its niche—and many of its loyal western wear customers.

W.R. Grace looked for ways to return the western wear giant to its former prominence and profitability. In response, the job of managing Sheplers was offered to New York native Lou Cohen, a 25-year veteran of retailing who had gained valuable experience with Bloomingdale's, Bullocks, J.L. Hudson, and Gimbels.

Cohen knew niche marketing well. And a year and a half later,

Sheplers had permanently wiped out its stock of nontraditional western wear, once again focusing solely on its western lifestyle clothing lines. "Our customers wanted the essence of western wear: fit, comfort, quality, and durability," says Cohen. "We stuck to the basics, because that's what our customers want."

Cohen's success returned the company to profitability by 1986 just as W.R. Grace announced it was abandoning the retail busines Undaunted, Cohen was introduc to local entrepreneur Fran Jabara and together they negotiated a su cessful financial partnership with Kansas Public Employees Retirement System (KPERS). With a $10.2-million loan from KPERS Cohen and five other managers— John Mosley, Mike Anop, Greg McDuffie, John Wilcox, and Stan Gall—purchased the chain.

In just two and a half years of local ownership, Cohen and the management group repaid the $10.2-million loan, plus $1.6 mi lion in interest, netting the KPEF fund nearly $17 million in return on its original $600,000 investment. Says Cohen, "This will go down as the most successful transtion that has ever occurred in the state fund."

FOR NEARLY 50 YEARS, SHEPLERS HAS BEEN SYNONYMOUS WITH THE FINEST IN AUTHENTIC WESTERN WEAR AND ACCESSORIES.

SHEPLERS' 60,000-SQUARE-FOOT FLAGSHIP STORE IN WICHITA CONTINUES THE COMPANY'S TRADITION OF PROVIDING FIT, COMFORT, QUALITY, AND DURABILITY.

SHEPLERS IS A LIFESTYLE

ay, as retail stores begin to look re and more alike, Sheplers ntains an ambience and client e that sets it apart. With 20 es in nine states and more than 0 million in annual sales, plers has found success within parameters of the market it ws best—authentic clothing for everyday wearer of boots and s. For the Sheplers customer, ts and jeans are a lifestyle, something to wear only on kends.

Ultimately, the *Urban Cowboy* erience taught us some valuable ns," says Cohen. "We learned to be intimidated by western r fashion trends. And we ned that we want more custom- but never at the expense of los-

ing the customers we have. During the *Urban Cowboy* period, we went on an ego kick and tried to become something we weren't supposed to be. Sheplers began as a country store dedicated to the folks who worked with their hands and built America. We won't change our stores or our business unless our customers want us to."

Under Cohen's leadership, Sheplers has grown by double digits each year, and profits have more than kept pace with that growth. The company's catalog business now accounts for nearly 30 percent of sales, with more than 18 million copies mailed around the world.

On the drawing board are plans to open two to five stores per year in cities across the country. That means Cohen will spend even more

time on the road, learning about his customers and his employees. He personally visits every store at least three times a year and talks to each employee on every visit.

"I think these trips are very important to the company, and I won't consider not doing it," he says. "In 25 years of retailing in department stores, I learned all the things not to do. I've simply reversed everything I learned, and the philosophy is working here. Our company is based on loyalty from our employees and our customers. It's part of the spirit of the Old West that we never intend to lose sight of again."

WESCON PRODUCTS CO.
A DIVISION OF LATSHAW ENTERPRISES, INC.

ANYBODY WHO MOWS A LAWN, USES RATCHET-ing screwdrivers, scrapes ice from a wind-shield, or uses makeup counts on Wescon Products Co. without ever knowing it. In fact, few Americans aren't touched daily by this Wichita-based manufacturer of cable-control systems, custom-molded plastics, and proprietary-brand hand tools.

Founded in 1946 as Western Control Company, Wescon recognized opportunity in the growing

market for small, two-cylinder engines. Then-new products like power lawn mowers used the two-stroke engines, and cables like those made by Wescon were used for the engine throttle controls.

But lawn mower manufacturers had to turn elsewhere for the plastic casings to house Wescon's cable assemblies. In an effort to enhance production and increase business, the company established itself as a single-source supplier by adding plastic-injection molding capabilities to manufacture the casings. As a result, Wescon became the only molder between Kansas City and Denver.

In 1965 Wescon was purchased by Conchemco, a diversified manufacturer based in Kansas City, Missouri. Conchemco became Latshaw Enterprises in 1988, and Wescon Products Co. remains a wholly owned subsidiary of the company.

WESCON TODAY
As a division of Latshaw Enter-prises, Wescon has grown into a volume producer of thermoplastic

consumer products, product components, and cable-control products, including push-pull throttle cables for lawn mowers, brake-cable assemblies for industrial vehicles, golf cart and snowmobile controls, and heavy machinery. At its 160,000-square-foot manufacturing controls facility on S. West

Street, the company's 350 employees also produce a line of proprietary hand tools, including ice scrapers and ratchet and fixed-shank screwdrivers sold nationwide.

Wescon President Michael Bukaty says customers value the company because of its commitment to quality and a thorough understanding of their product applications. "Our customers appreciate the extra value we give them," he says. "We have the same technology—like computer-aided design—that our competition has. The Wescon difference is the special attention we pay to design and engineering, employee training and retention, and quality control."

Bukaty says that while extensive capital investments in design and production equipment have been important to the company's success, they are actually what is required just to be in the game. "We are equipped to provide original designs and engineering or take existing designs and move them into production," he explains. "But if we didn't make additional investments in employees to minimize turnover and maintain quality to keep production costs down, all the technology in the world wouldn't make a difference."

AT ITS 160,000-SQUARE-FOOT MANU-FACTURING CONTROLS FACILITY ON S. WEST STREET, WESCON'S 350 EMPLOYEES PRODUCE THERMOPLASTIC CONSUMER PRODUCTS, PRODUCT COMPONENTS, AND CABLE-CONTROL PRODUCTS, AS WELL AS A LINE OF PROPRIETARY HAND TOOLS.

RNST & YOUNG

AS ONE OF ERNST & YOUNG'S 110 OFFICES across the nation, the Wichita office has been instrumental in assisting, launching, or growing many successful entrepreneurial and public companies. ◆ One of the largest professional services firms in the world, Ernst & Young is the result of the 1989 merger of

prominent international accounting firms: Arthur Young & Company and Ernst & Whinney. The firm today employs more than 000 people in the United States 67,000 worldwide.

Opened in 1950 with the merger Lunsford & Barnes, the Wichita ce has become the firm of reed for many of the city's largest panies. Its clients represent ually all industries, including nufacturing, financial services, il, restaurant, real estate, oil and aviation, and health care.

Ernst & Young Wichita offers a e range of business services, including the traditional accounting auditing services and the munity's largest tax practice, ch provides tax compliance and prehensive planning and sulting. Reflecting Wichita's n-do" spirit, the firm also offers repreneurial services dedicated erving the needs of emerging wth-oriented companies.

Over half of the firm's Wichita nts are local individuals and ll businesses. Office Managing tner Robert R. Crawford bees it is from that pool of grow-enterprises that the future's er businesses will emerge. me of our largest clients are comies or individuals that started a virtually nothing," he says. any people think we concene solely on established busises, but we view ourselves as repreneurs working with other repreneurs to create the kind of

success stories that have made Wichita a world-class leader in many industries."

As a result, Ernst & Young's local client base includes companies that are well known and well respected in the community and the nation. Among them are Fourth Financial Corporation, the state's largest multibank holding company; Excel Corporation, one of the nation's largest meat processors; Cessna Aircraft Company and Learjet Inc., two major aircraft manufacturers headquartered in Wichita; Rent-A-Center, the national leader in rent-to-own electronics and home furnishings; Mueller Industries, a large manufacturer listed on the New York Stock Exchange; and The Coleman Company, a recognized name in outdoor recreational products.

SERVICE INTEGRATION

Drawing on the company's worldwide resources, Ernst & Young Wichita provides integrated professional services that emphasize quality, teamwork, integrity, and objectivity. As a business advisor, the firm places high priority on understanding each client's business or personal financial situation in order to provide sound, proactive advice.

"Our philosophy of service integration brings industry and functional specialists together to address complex client issues," says Crawford. Integrated service teams include, among others, professionals with ac-

counting, tax, computer science, or valuation backgrounds whose specialized expertise is focused on solving client problems. Ernst & Young also provides industry specialists in insurance, financial services, real estate and construction, health care, manufacturing/high technology, and retail/wholesale operations.

Complemented by support from the firm's worldwide operations, the Wichita office provides the most complete accounting, audit, tax, and management consulting services available with a core team that has long called Wichita and Kansas home.

Even for small or emerging businesses, an international resource is critical. "In today's world market, it is essential to have access to worldwide professional resources," says Crawford, "and it is extremely helpful to be able to accomplish this with one call to our Wichita office."

TAX RESEARCH IS AN IMPORTANT ASPECT OF ERNST & YOUNG'S CLIENT SERVICES.

He adds, "Quality worldwide service integration is the hallmark of our firm. We regularly bring clients new ideas in strategic planning, taxes, and opportunities because we take their business and their goals personally."

FROM LEFT: PARTNERS HENRY ZIGTEMA, ROBERT CRAWFORD, RANDY PIERCE, AND JIM GUSTAVSON WORK AS A TEAM TO PROVIDE INTEGRATED SERVICES TO CLIENTS.

VULCAN CHEMICALS DIVISION OF VULCAN MATERIALS COMPANY

THE VULCAN CHEMICALS DIVISION PLANT in southwest Wichita is one of the world's most technologically and environmentally advanced manufacturing facilities in the chloralkali industry. It is a key chemical manufacturing facility operated by Birmingham, Alabama-based Vulcan

Materials Company, the nation's largest producer of construction aggregates and a leading chemical producer. The plant has been in operation as a Vulcan facility since 1957, when it was purchased from Frontier Chemical, a division of Union Chemicals and Materials Company, which opened the facility in 1950 and operated it until the purchase.

LOCATED IN SOUTHWEST WICHITA, THE VULCAN CHEMICALS DIVISION PLANT PRODUCES ORGANIC AND INORGANIC CHEMICALS, PLUS SPECIALTY PRODUCTS AND SOLVENTS USED BY A WIDE VARIETY OF BUSINESSES AND INDUSTRIES.

CHARLES BECK

AREA RAW MATERIALS SUPPORT PLANT OPERATIONS

Large underground salt deposits in the Wichita area provide an exceptional source of raw materials for the plant's chlorine- and alkaline-based products. The plant produces organic and inorganic chemicals, plus specialty products and solvents used by a wide variety of businesses and industries. One of the facility's

primary products is caustic soda, which is used in the food processing industry to peel fruits and vegetables and to refine vegetable oil. In addition, caustic soda is a key element in producing paper pulp, detergents, soap, and bleach.

Another key product of the plant is chlorine for use in the purification of municipal water systems. Other chlorine-based products manufactured by Vulcan are used as agents in pharmaceuticals, plastics, and photographic film; as solvents for the dry cleaning, refrigeration, electronics, manufacturing, and petroleum industries; and as pesticides, fertilizers, disinfectants, and control agents in agricultural water-treatment applications.

AN ENVIRONMENTALLY CONSCIOUS NEIGHBOR

Over the years Vulcan has worked diligently to address local environmental concerns and to make ongoing improvements in employee safety. In 1988 the plant helped establish a Community Involvement Group that is devoted to resolving community environmental concerns. Composed of educators, environmentalists, civic and health leaders, and plant neighbors, the group has worked closely with Vulcan to address key environmental issues.

Vulcan's Chemical Product Responsibility Process® (CPRP) program helps ensure the highest possible environmental protection standards and the health and safety of workers and the public. Vulcan

employees are committed to this corporate program and philosophy, which has earned high marks for both customer satisfaction and public trust. Central to CPRP is the environmentally responsible manufacturing, handling, and disposal of waste materials.

Long before federal law required emergency planning and release notification, Vulcan's plant management worked with community leaders and area emergency services personnel to establish CAER, the Community Awareness Emergency Response program. The program has established open lines of communication between the plant and its neighbors, emergency response agencies, public officials, and hospitals

to ensure public safety in the likely event of a chemical release. Vulcan is also actively involved a variety of pollution prevention asures. Plant scientists and engi-rs are continually designing, nning, and implementing new grams to eliminate, re-use, or stically minimize waste streams. ce 1970 the company has com-ted more than 80 such projects, ich have produced outstanding ults. Between 1988 and 1992, plant reduced its air emissions 75 percent. By 1995 Vulcan will ve reduced the amount of hazard-s waste needing disposal by 90 cent over 1988 levels. A $13-llion calcium chloride manufac-ing facility, which began eration in December 1992, will ount for a majority of that reduc-n as it converts waste hydrochlo-acid to a sellable product—cium chloride.

The company regularly exceeds vernment and industry regula-y standards in the production d transport of chemicals, and it s received recognition for its em-oyee safety record. Likewise, the nsas Motor Carriers Association s recognized Vulcan for its high ndards in the transportation of emicals and hazardous materials. The company also is dedicated new-product development and enhancing existing products. For tance, chemists and engineers in lcan's research and development oratory are involved in the

development of substitutes for CFCs, the chemicals used in refrig-eration and cooling that are linked to ozone layer depletion. Vulcan's R&D and Customer Service labs are also closely involved in meeting strict customer requirements under international quality standards. The Wichita plant recently received ISO certification—the interna-tional quality standard—for key product lines.

CONTRIBUTING TO THE COMMUNITY

For decades the Vulcan Wichita plant has provided leadership and financial support of educational, cultural, and civic activities. The company is especially committed to local and regional educational sci-ence projects and events, including the Kansas Science Olympiad, a statewide high school competition for which the company serves as a major sponsor. Vulcan also pro-vides science education kits to local schools and universities, and spon-sors science education camps and workshops for students and teachers.

Vulcan enriches the area's cul-tural and recreational opportunities through its support of the Wichita Symphony, Wichita Children's Theatre, Music Theatre of Wichita, Haysville City Park, several local sports teams, and citywide festivals in Wichita, Haysville, and Clearwa-ter. Vulcan employees support and hold leadership roles in numerous

civic organizations, including local and state chambers of commerce, United Way, the Urban League, the Sedgwick County Emergency Planning Committee, Junior Achievement, Boy Scouts, and Rainbows United.

Vulcan's plant management says its efforts to live in harmony with and contribute to the Wichita com-munity are both a corporate respon-sibility and a natural response of gratitude. For over 40 years the Wichita area has provided the plant's quality work force, natural resources, and a progressive busi-ness spirit in which to operate. Vulcan Chemicals Division looks forward to a continuing and fruitful partnership with Wichita.

CHEMISTS AND ENGINEERS IN VUL-CAN'S RESEARCH AND DEVELOPMENT LAB (ABOVE) ARE DEDICATED TO NEW-PRODUCT DEVELOPMENT AND TO ENHANCING EXISTING PRODUCTS.

IN 1988 THE PLANT HELPED ESTABLISH A COMMUNITY INVOLVEMENT GROUP THAT IS DEVOTED TO RESOLVING COM-MUNITY ENVIRONMENTAL CONCERNS (ABOVE LEFT).

THE PLANT ATTRIBUTES ITS SUCCESS, IN PART, TO WICHITA'S EXCELLENT POOL OF WORKERS.

INTERNATIONAL COLD STORAGE COMPANY, INC.

THE 1950S BROUGHT A NEW WAVE OF domestic convenience to Americans—particularly in the area of food storage and preparation. Consumers craved the new pre-packaged frozen foods, and Frank Stevens, a Wichita entrepreneur, foresaw that grocers and other businesses could benefit from space-saving cold storage equipment.

Stevens founded International Cold Storage (ICS) on his back porch in 1951 to design and produce space-efficient, walk-in cold storage units to replace the old-style industrial locker plants that were in use at the time. Headquartered

HEADQUARTERED IN ANDOVER, FIVE MILES EAST OF WICHITA, ICS IS THE NATION'S LEADING SUPPLIER OF OUTSIDE WALK-IN COOLERS, FREEZERS, AND INDUSTRIAL COLD STORAGE UNITS. THE COMPANY IS TODAY LED BY CHAIRMAN OF THE BOARD ROBERT O. LARGE (LEFT) AND PRESIDENT JAMES C. McCLURE.

today in Andover, five miles east of Wichita, ICS is the nation's leading supplier of outside walk-in coolers, freezers, and industrial cold storage units.

The company's pre-engineered, factory-assembled, one-piece outdoor walk-ins are used by supermarkets, restaurants, bakeries, food processing and distribution facilities, dairies, meat processing plants, florists, and schools, among others. ICS also supplies refrigerated stor-age units to America's top 10 fast-food chains.

From its earliest years the company has constructed custom units, including explosion-proof walk-in designs for use by the aerospace industry. ICS also designs and manufactures customized industrial sterilization units for use by medi-cal equipment manufacturers.

At its plants in Andover, Kansas, and Covesville, Virginia, the company employs 150 people and has annual sales of approximately $14 million. ICS remained family owned until 1991, when Deane Stevens, chairman of the board, and Frank Stevens Jr., president, created an employee stock ownership plan, selling their interest to the employees and allowing them to become owners of the company.

"We were concerned that prospective buyers might want to move the company out of the Wichita area. ICS is a Wichita area company and will remain so," says Frank Stevens Jr., who is now retired and living in Port Townsend, Washington.

ENVIRONMENTALLY FRIENDLY

Like all manufacturers in the refrigeration industry, ICS has been faced with environmental challenges due to the use of chlorofluorocarbons (CFCs) in manufacturing and operation processes. But, as would be expected of an industry leader, ICS has eliminated the use of CFCs in its polyurethane foam insulation. The company was the first in the industry to produce as standard walk-in coolers that are totally free of CFCs, and has made its CFC-FREE technology the standard for all future production units.

Extending its expertise in storage technology to a new field, ICS has developed specialized units for the containment of hazardous materials. Flammable, combustible, or corrosive chemical compounds, infectious medical waste, or other products requiring constant temperatures can be stored in portable, secure units that protect soil and groundwater from contamination. In 1991 the company created a subsidiary, International Hazmat Storage (IHS), to build these custom, fire-rated units with explosion-proof electrical systems and spill-containment sumps. Every IHS unit meets or exceeds federal, state, and local regulations on the storage of hazardous materials.

As an important area employer, ICS looks forward to continuing its more than 40-year history of innovation, product line expansion, and company growth.

AKE-TV

WHEN KAKE-TV FIRST SIGNED ON THE air in October 1954, television was in its Golden Age. Golden, because the power of television hadn't yet been fully realized; the novelty was still greater than the power and responsibility TV would soon take on.

ided by intuition and years of erience in radio sales, Martin ansky, general manager of the dgling station, piloted KAKE to ional recognition as a premier munity-oriented television sta- n. "We focused on local market ds," recalls Umansky, now re- d from KAKE but not from vision; he's currently busy as an ependent developer of syndi- ed TV programs. "Broadcast dits today say the way for local ions to succeed is to do what we from the beginning."

ocalism has been a consistent us, whether in news, public af- s, or community involvement. KE, which became an ABC work affiliate in 1954, can be dited with stimulating the elopment of a professional ergency medical system when probing series about Wichita's ependent ambulance services overed gross abuses and poor ient care.

Likewise, the station set a na- tional precedent when its news cameras were the first ever to record the proceedings of a juvenile court. The national Muscular Dystrophy Association credits KAKE with raising one percent of all dollars generated in its annual Labor Day telethons, and the station's efforts in promoting adult literacy were the impetus for ABC's national program, Project Literacy: U.S.

"We develop a direct relation- ship between the station and the community," says Jan McDaniel, KAKE's general manager since 1991 and one of the nation's few female station general managers. McDaniel, who heads KAKE's statewide broadcast network for San Francisco-based Chronicle Publishing Co., which purchased the station in 1980, is tackling dif- ferent challenges, such as the growth of multi-channel cable systems that fragment viewing audiences.

"A television station must help a community see itself," says

McDaniel. "CNN or MTV can't generate participation in commu- nity events or stimulate discussion about local issues. Local-market sta- tions should build a relationship with viewers and be the catalyst for action, not just stir the pot."

Today, local programming re- mains an important element of KAKE's strategy. It offers 15.5 hours weekly of local news and pub- lic affairs programming, more than any other local station. KAKE was the first and continues to be the only station to broadcast Wichita State University varsity basketball and baseball games through good

A LEADER IN LIVE PRODUCTION, KAKE HAS TWO COMPLETE PRODUC- TION SUITES, TWO STUDIOS, A SATELLITE UPLINK TRUCK, AND A FULL COMPLEMENT OF PRODUCTION EQUIPMENT.

seasons and bad. And viewers across Kansas rely on KAKE's weather forecasts, which the station continu- ally enhances through regular invest- ments in the latest forecasting technology.

"KAKE-TV's relationship with its viewers and advertisers is one built on mutual trust," says McDaniel. "We don't sell just time like other stations. We emphasize the quality of our audience and programming. It's taken us years to build that kind of trust, but for viewers and advertisers alike it's a satisfying relationship."

OPERATING AT A FURIOUS PACE, JOUR- NALISTS IN THE KAKE NEWSROOM PREPARE FOR ANOTHER SHOW.

SINCE 1954 THE STUDIOS OF KAKE, CHANNEL 10, HAVE BEEN A WEST WICHITA FIXTURE (LEFT).

KREONITE, INC.

WHEN A PICTURE IS WORTH A THOU- sand words, commercial darkrooms and photo laboratories around the world trust Kreonite equipment to bring the images to life. Kreonite photographic processors, which develop color prints up to 85 inches wide, are used in an array of commercial, industrial, military, and governmental photographic applications.

Here's just a sampling: Kreonite processors are used in all photo labs at Disneyland and Disney World. NASA's Kennedy Space Center in Houston and the Jet Propulsion Laboratory in Pasadena process photographs from outer space with the company's equipment. The White House photo lab in Washington, D.C., is a longtime Kreonite user.

addition, Kreonite develops and markets electronic imaging equipment.

CHANGING THE INDUSTRY

Kreonite founder Dwight Krehbiel was chief photographer for The Boeing Company during World War II. In the back of a B-29 at 37,000 feet, armed with a camera, he was the first person to take a color photograph of the curvature of the earth. His famous image

KREONITE EMPLOYS OVER 200 PEOPLE IN PRODUCTION, ENGINEERING, MARKETING, AND MANAGEMENT AT ITS FACILITY IN NORTH CENTRAL WICHITA.

Kreonite employs more than 200 people in production, engineering, marketing, and management at its facility in north central Wichita. More than 25,000 processors have been built by the company over the years. Because of the unique design of the equipment, Kreonite can still provide parts for many of the older generation processors.

The company has long been known for its photo laboratory design services, and it manufactures a complete line of fiberglass sinks, cabinetry, and other lab furniture to complement those services. In

was published in *Look* magazine in 1948.

Also an inventor, Krehbiel saw that fiberglass would serve as durable material for photographic sinks, as it is much stronger and more chemical-resistant than stainless steel. He marketed his first product, a fiberglass sink, in the early 1950s and consequently revolutionized the photo processing industry. This led to the founding of Kreonite in Wichita in 1955.

The company was more than a business to Krehbiel; it was his hobby and passion, according to

Bill Oetting, the founder's son-in law and company president today Krehbiel enjoyed research and lab work, and in 1972 designed automated film and paper processors, which catapulted the company in worldwide markets.

Kreonite's research and development efforts have continued throughout the years. Since 1992 the company has designed and m keted Profile electronic imaging equipment. Each fully integrated workstation includes software for digital photo retouching and compositing, graphic design and illustion, and presentation graphics.

"With the advances in technology and the shift of photo labs an photographers to the use of electronic imaging systems, the time right for this product," Oetting says. "We expect to be the world leader with imaging products, jus as we are with photographic proce ing equipment."

THE WICHITA WORK FORCE

Today, more than 40 percent of Kreonite's sales come from the international market. Yet, as this international market grows, the company's commitment to its employees and to Wichita is stronger than ever. All research a development plus support engine ing is done at the Wichita facility and more than 90 percent of all manufacturing is conducted on-site.

Kreonite is particularly proud its skilled and dedicated employe One indication of the company's stability and team spirit is the fac that almost 40 percent of the wo force has been with Kreonite for over 10 years. The company has received local, regional, and national recognition for its innovati employment programs—particularly its efforts in working with t disabled. Company representativ serve on the President's Committ on Employment of People with Disabilities, and Kreonite actively participates in civic projects and programs such as the United Way

PIZZA HUT, INC.

MAKE A LIST OF AMERICAN BUSINESS success stories most celebrated by the nation's business community, and that list will surely include Wichita-based Pizza Hut, Inc. ◆ And no wonder. Brothers Dan and Frank Carney opened their first Pizza Hut restaurant in 1958

a rented building in Wichita with a $600 loan from their mother. By the time PepsiCo, Inc. purchased the company in 1977, it was the world's largest pizza chain, with 2,000 restaurants.

Today Pizza Hut, which employs approximately 900 people at its Wichita headquarters, has more than 9,400 food-service units in its worldwide system, including more company-owned restaurants than any other restaurant chain. Its 140,000 employees worldwide serve more than 12 million customers each week. Including Taco Bell and KFC—PepsiCo's other food-service companies—Pizza Hut is part of the world's largest restaurant group, with almost twice as many units as McDonald's.

While Pizza Hut can be credited in large part for pizza's worldwide appeal, topping preferences are decidedly regional and showcase the product's versatility. The overwhelming favorites in the United States include pepperoni, beef, and

Italian sausage, but jalapeno peppers are *de rigueur* with pepperoni or beef pizzas in Texas. In the Pacific Rim, curry pizzas are popular, while sauerkraut and onion pizza is big in Germany. And in Moscow—home of one of Pizza Hut's top volume restaurants—*mockba* is a topping favorite with its combination of sardines, tuna, mackerel, salmon, and onion.

AMERICA'S NUMBER ONE PIZZA

No matter what the topping, Americans like Pizza Hut® pizza best: It has been rated number one among pizza chains for nine consecutive years in a survey of 2,500 households by *Restaurants & Institutions* magazine. Food quality, atmosphere, and cleanliness are the primary reasons cited by consumers for the company's appeal, which is why Pizza Hut continues to dominate the industry.

Pizza Hut maintains that dominance through innovation and con-

stant fine-tuning of its products and distribution channels. The company was the first restaurant chain to offer a five-minute lunch guarantee with the Personal Pan Pizza™ in 1983, and it introduced its successful lunch buffet in 1992. Its domestic delivery business, begun in 1986, now delivers more product than any other chain and contributed $1.5 billion to Pizza Hut's $5.7 billion in worldwide sales in 1992. Pizza Hut® pizza also can be found in airports, shopping malls, school cafeterias, and sports arenas.

While the company is proud of its business success, Pizza Hut is

honored by its role in America's elementary classrooms. The company's BOOK IT!® National Reading Incentive Program encourages youngsters to read by awarding free Pizza Hut® pizza to participants who achieve individualized reading goals. The first project of its kind, BOOK IT!® enrolled more than 17 million children in all 50 states and Canada during the 1992-93 school term.

Driving the company's success and its daily efforts is a long-standing commitment to integrity. Pizza Hut is committed to providing customers uncompromising quality, the highest value, and the kind of service that reinforces the Pizza Hut mission: "To be the first choice for every pizza occasion by always providing 100% customer satisfaction."

FOOD QUALITY, ATMOSPHERE, AND CLEANLINESS ARE THE PRIMARY REASONS CITED BY CONSUMERS FOR PIZZA HUT'S APPEAL.

ALLAN HUSTON (TOP) IS PRESIDENT AND CEO OF PIZZA HUT, INC.

PIZZA HUT, WHICH EMPLOYS APPROXIMATELY 900 PEOPLE AT ITS WICHITA HEADQUARTERS (LEFT), HAS MORE THAN 9,400 FOOD-SERVICE UNITS IN ITS WORLDWIDE SYSTEM.

BILL BACHMAN & ASSOCIATES, BRAD BACHMAN CONSTRUCTION AND BACHMAN ENTERPRISES

WELL-PLANNED RESIDENTIAL DEVELOP-ments including Brookhollow, Valley Park, The Moorings on Crystal Lake, River Park, and Kimberly Hills at Crestview are testament to the vision and commitment to quality of Bill Bachman, a longtime builder, realtor, and developer in Wichita. Today, Bachman and his two sons, Brad and Kurt, head up three Bachman companies that offer Wichitans some of the finest homes and neighborhoods in the area.

STARTING AT THE TOP

A native Kansan, Bill Bachman likes to joke that he first entered the business "at the top." Bachman says, "I attended Wichita State University after serving in World War II, and took a part-time job as a roofer to help make ends meet."

While roofing helped pay the bills, Bachman could see that another aspect of the postwar building and real estate boom in Wichita offered more opportunity. He earned his real estate license in 1947 and soon discovered that customers were willing to buy, but weren't happy with what was for sale. "A lot of the homes for sale at the time were older, and the new ones being built after the war just didn't have the quality people were demanding," says Bachman. "I wanted the quality to reflect in the home."

Seeing an opportunity, Bachm[an] launched his own construction co[m]pany in 1953. In the years since, [he] has built nearly 700 homes in an[d] around the Wichita area.

Although Bachman's sons hav[e] been involved in the business sin[ce] they were children, they assumed leadership positions in the mid-1980s. Brad Bachman heads up t[he] construction company, which co[n]centrates primarily in residential custom building and design. Kur[t] is in charge of Bill Bachman & Associates, a real estate company representing Bachman-built hom[es] and other homes for resale. The third company, Bachman Enterprises, is the developing arm of th[e] triad, with several hundred acres [of] lakefront property under develop[-]ment during the next three years. Bill Bachman is involved in all aspects of the three companies bu[t] spearheads development efforts.

RESIDENTS OF THE MOORINGS CAN FISH, SWIM, SAIL, AND BOAT IN BEAUTIFUL NATURAL SURROUNDINGS.

CHMAN EQUALS QUALITY

hman homes have always meant
lity. Shortly after beginning
construction company, Bill
hman decided the only way he
ld ensure quality was to recruit
own people. "Rather than
one company to pour the
ndation and basement, and have
ther group to lay floors, I em-
ved people in every trade and
, including bricklayers, to build
best home," he says.

oday, this tradition of gather-
a team of craftsmen to custom
d homes is alive and well. Brad
hman, Bill's oldest son, is
narily concerned with designing
building lakefront homes lean-
toward the upper end of the
ket. "Customers need to see
ished models to visualize our
duct," Brad explains, "but we
enjoy showing off our homes
er construction. That's where
qualities stand out."

E MOORINGS ON
STAL LAKE

que to Bill Bachman's projects
s attention to creating an over-
mbience for each of his develop-

ments. He enjoys preserving
tranquil settings and building neighborhoods that have character and
are nice to come home to.

Crystal Lake had been a popular
swimming and fishing hole for
Wichitans since the 1950s when
sand and gravel pits were excavated
along the banks of the Big Arkansas
River. By the 1970s, Bachman saw
the possibility to develop a mean-
dering spring-fed lake bordered by
rivers and wildlife. Channels were
dredged from the main lake, and in
1979 houses were built on streets
named Bentbay, Driftwood, and
KeyWest. Now The Moorings is
home to residents who can fish,
swim, sail, and boat in beautiful
natural surroundings. Although the
development is within the city limits of Wichita, wildlife abounds
and residents have the pleasure of
sighting deer and wild turkeys or
listening to the geese come in the
evening.

"The Moorings was intended to
be a Florida-style community," says
Bill Bachman. "I remember showing a home to an executive and
his wife who were relocating to
Wichita. Once she saw the area she

told her husband, 'Unless you want
to move twice, we better buy
here.' "

The Moorings residents are a
close-knit bunch and organize
many community events. A spring
fashion show, a Fourth of July
champagne brunch, a wind-surfing
regatta, the annual Pontoon Boat
Parade, and a yearly fishing derby
are neighborhood rituals. Summer
brings ice cream socials, while winter offers ice skating parties complete with chili and hot chocolate.
It all lends to the small-town atmosphere that is the personality of this
unique lifestyle.

All of Bachman's developments
carefully follow a master plan that
accentuates the best physical charac-
teristics of the land. The next phase
of The Moorings, Harbor Isle, surrounds another large lake with gor-
geous panoramic views of water
and trees. Bachman strives to create
homes that appear to have been
carefully sculpted to fit the environment and still personally approves
exterior elevations, types and uses
of materials, and structures to be
placed on the site before construction begins.

RUSTY ECK FORD

FROM A HUMBLE START AS A FARM BOY IN rural Sedgwick County, Rusty Eck has joined the ranks of Wichita's legendary entrepreneurs. Over a 40-year period, Eck has become one of the area's most successful automobile dealers and a leading community benefactor, proving that the American Dream is alive and well in Wichita.

Operating with the slogan, "Eck Sells for Less," Rusty Eck Ford is the top Ford dealership in the five-state region covering Kansas, Nebraska, Iowa, Missouri, and part

OVER A 40-YEAR PERIOD, RUSTY ECK HAS BECOME ONE OF THE AREA'S MOST SUCCESSFUL AUTOMOBILE DEALERS AND A LEADING COMMUNITY BENEFACTOR, PROVING THAT THE AMERICAN DREAM IS ALIVE AND WELL IN WICHITA.

RUSTY ECK WAS THE MAJOR CONTRIBUTOR TO WICHITA STATE UNIVERSITY'S BASEBALL STADIUM (RIGHT), WHICH WAS NAMED ECK STADIUM IN HIS HONOR.

of Arkansas. In fact, the company is consistently ranked among the top 20 in *Auto Age* magazine's annual listing of the top 500 national dealers in volume of new car sales, financing, insurance, parts and service revenues, body shop sales, and total dollar income. Rusty Eck Ford also has been named an "All-Star" performer three consecutive times, ranking among the top 100 dealerships in each sales category.

A YOUNG ENTREPRENEUR

Prior to entering the automobile industry, Eck served in the U.S. Navy for two years and then attended automotive school for a year to study body work and service shop management. A friend of Eck's parents, who owned a Ford dealership in Haven, Kansas, asked Rusty's father if he knew of anyone who might be interested in becoming a partner in the agency. Eck's father suggested Rusty, who later bought into the business with assis-

AZIM STUDIOS

tance from his dad and his uncle.

With that, Rusty Eck was off and running. Within two years, his strong marketing skills had increased car sales from only four units per month to an impressive 66 units. On the heels of that success, Eck bought out his partner in 1953 and founded Rusty Eck Ford. After expansion moves to Valley Center and north Wichita, he purchased the present 10-acre location in 1970 at 7310 E. Kellogg in Wichita.

Since then, Rusty Eck Ford has grown rapidly in revenues, profits, and employment. The company today has 200 employees—up from 80 in 1970. In 1992, Eck's best year on record, the dealership sold 4,463 new cars and 3,402 used cars.

"Our strategy," says Eck, "is to have a large selection of vehicles, aggressive and consistent advertising, low prices, and to always take care of our customers in order to maintain a large market share."

AN AGGRESSIVE LEADER

Rusty Eck is widely known throughout the industry and the area for colorful "Fordman" television commercials. Dressed in a superhero costume emblazoned with a large "F," Eck has aggressively sought out new customers since the spots first aired in 1972.

Eck is just as aggressive when it comes to making Wichita a better place to live.

He was the major contributor to Wichita State University's baseball stadium, which was named Eck Stadium in his honor. The dealership regularly supports charitable events for such institutions as Heartspring (formerly the Institute of Logopedics), YMCA, Kansas Food Bank, Anthony Family Shelter, Guadalupe Clinic, St. Joseph Medical Center, and the Wichita Children's Home. For over 20 years, Rusty Eck Ford has sponsored the National Championship Trophy for Wichita's National Baseball Congress non-pro baseball tourna-

ment, as well as local professional sports teams.

Celebrating its 40th anniversary in 1993, Rusty Eck Ford is duly proud of its position in Wichita and south-central Kansas. With a solid foundation and entrepreneurial spirit, the company looks forward to a prosperous future for its business and its hometown.

WICHITA
1960-1993

1960	Chance Industries, Inc.
1962	KFDI Radio and Great Empire Broadcasting
1962	Learjet Inc.
1963	Wichita Surgical Group, P.A.
1964	The Foster Companies
1965	Elf Atochem North America, Inc.
1966	Brittain Machine Inc.
1968	Howard's Optical Dispensary, Inc.
1971	John T. Arnold Associates, Inc.
1971	Klenda, Mitchell, Austerman & Zuercher
1972	AT&T in Wichita
1972	Ryan Aviation Corporation and Ryan International Airlines
1973	The First Place
1973	MetLife-Wichita Information Systems Center
1973	THORN Americas, Inc.
1974	Consultants in Laboratory Medicine, P.A.
1975	Cancer Center of Kansas, P.A.
1979	Casco Plastics, Inc.
1979	Latour Management, Inc.
1980	Advanced Orthopaedic Associates P.A.
1980	Multimedia Cablevision, Inc.
1984	Preferred Health Care and Preferred Plus of Kansas
1987	Hinkle, Eberhart & Elkouri, L.L.C.
1989	Typed Letters Corporation
1991	Grene Cornea, P.A.

Preceding page:

INSIDE AND OUT, THE CAREFUL DESIGN AND INTRICATE CRAFTSMANSHIP OF THE BANK IV BUILDING MAKE IT A WICHITA FAVORITE.
RON JONES PHOTO

NEW CONSTRUCTION (OPPOSITE) IS A SYMBOL OF GROWTH AND PROGRESS— CONCEPTS WICHITANS HAVE COME TO ENJOY AND EXPECT.

KFDI Radio and Great Empire Broadcasting

LONGEVITY AND STABILITY ARE ATTRIBUTES that are practically unheard of in the world of radio broadcasting. But in Wichita, KFDI and its parent company, Great Empire Broadcasting, have thrived on the unheard of for more than 30 years. In fact, the station has developed a national reputation in its field of country-and-western music and has become a household name to thousands of listeners in Kansas and Oklahoma.

MEMBERS OF KFDI'S AWARD-WINNING NEWS TEAM OFTEN WORK FROM THE STATION'S FOUR MOBILE NEWS UNITS.

MIKE LYNCH (RIGHT, SEATED), PRESIDENT AND CHAIRMAN OF THE BOARD, AND MICHAEL C. OATMAN, VICE PRESIDENT AND CHIEF EXECUTIVE OFFICER, HAVE HELPED KFDI AND GREAT EMPIRE BROADCASTING GROW FOR MORE THAN THREE DECADES.

KEITH BOSCHER, PRODUCTION MANAGER, AND BOB ALLISON ARE AT WORK IN KFDI'S STATE-OF-THE-ART STUDIOS (OPPOSITE, TOP LEFT).

When folks want to hear real down-home country music, they tune to KFDI AM/FM. When the weather turns severe, residents rely on KFDI's news reporters who broadcast eyewitness "windshield reports" on the storm's progress.

The station also is known for its country-style neighborliness and community contact. That's the kind of listener and community rapport that KFDI, Wichita's "Radio Ranch," and its employee "Ranch Hands" have nurtured in the local market for years. And the same is true for each of Great Empire's eight other stations in Omaha, Nebraska; Tulsa, Oklahoma; Springfield, Missouri; and Shreveport, Louisiana.

"We really haven't changed substantially in 30 years," says President and Chairman of the Board Mike Lynch, commenting on the station's long-standing reputation for stability. "We're still locally owned, with a country music format and a strong news operation."

CHRIS CLARK

GROWTH SINCE 1962
Steadiness, determination, and market savvy have made the company one of the Midwest's and country music's radio giants.

Great Empire was formed in 1962 when Mike Lynch and his father, Frank, bought KIRL AM, a small local radio station owned by silent movie stars Mary Pickford and Buddy Rogers. The Lynches, who came to Wichita from Oklahoma City, changed the station's name to KFDI and began easing away from its emphasis on paid religious programming. But the transition to country music was not easy.

Two years later, KFDI was still struggling. Mike Lynch was running the station but needed a program director. In stepped Mike Oatman, who came to KFDI in 1964 from a radio station in El Paso, Texas. The two hit it off and agreed to redirect the station's hodgepodge of programming.

"In those early years, KFDI wasn't focused," recalls Oatman, who today serves as Great Empire CEO. "Mike and I had the same ideas on how to change it."

Country music, news, and per-
ralities became the format.
nch bought out his father's
ajority ownership in 1965, and
atman became co-owner. Within
ear, the pair had transformed the
tion into a financial success and

t Great Empire on a new course
acquisition, targeting other radio
tions in medium-size markets
e Wichita.

Between 1967 and 1981, the
npany purchased a Wichita FM
tion, which became KFDI FM;
TS AM/FM in Springfield;
VKH AM/FM in Shreveport;
OW AM/FM in Omaha; and
3RQ AM/FM in Denver, which
company sold in 1986. In 1990
eat Empire and First Stuart
rporation of Tulsa, operators of
OO AM/FM, merged the
OO assets into Great Empire.
rold C. Stuart is now a stock-
lder in Great Empire, and
OO AM/FM is a welcome part
the Great Empire Broadcasting
nily. In 1993 the company also
came operating manager of
CT FM in Wichita.

AN IMPORTANT FORCE IN WICHITA

Within the 19-station Wichita market, Great Empire today boasts a 42
percent share of the $16 million in
total annual advertising billings. Of
its 225 employees, 56 are based in
Wichita. These employees share in
company ownership and today are
purchasing 26 percent of Great
Empire's stock through an employee stock ownership program.

Over the years, the company's
stations have garnered numerous
awards, and each has cultivated
strong ties with its community. For
example, KFDI received the 1993
Community Service Award for
medium-size markets from the
Country Radio Seminar Board.
The previous year, its Pony Express
news department received the
Edward R. Murrow Award for
medium-size markets from the
Radio & Television News Directors Association.

In the 1970s and again in the
1980s, KFDI was recognized as
Country Music Station of the Year
by the Academy of Country Music
Awards and *Billboard* magazine.
For his lifelong contributions to
country music, Mike Oatman was
inducted in 1993 into the Country
Music DJ Hall of Fame in Nash-
ville. And in 1990 the Wichita Area
Chamber of Commerce honored
Great Empire Broadcasting with
the Over-the-Years Award, which
recognizes longtime economic and
social impact in the community.

This most recent honor probably
came as no surprise to the many
local organizations and events that
have benefitted from the generosity
of Great Empire and KFDI. Each

June, KFDI sponsors the popular
Charlie Daniels Celebrity Golf
Classic, which is the station's major
local charity event. Proceeds from
the tournament and associated
country music concerts are donated
to Starkey Inc., a community-based
nonprofit organization serving
adults with mental retardation and
developmental disabilities.

Great Empire also is an annual
sponsor of the Kansas Special Olympics, the Cattleman's Ball for the
American Cancer Society, the
Junior Livestock Show, and the
Wichita Police Department's
Christmas gifts program for needy
children. "At KFDI and Great
Empire, we believe it's our responsibility to take part in community
service," says Oatman. "It's the
secret to our longevity in Wichita."

Looking to the future, Great
Empire plans to continue growing
through acquisitions, to consolidate
holdings in its existing markets,
and eventually to go public. "Our
strategy is to acquire, be profitable,
and improve our properties,"
says Oatman. "Wichita is a warm
and vital environment for our business growth, and we look forward
to the next decade with great
anticipation."

MIKE OATMAN (TOP), ALSO KNOWN AS
OL' MIKE, STILL DOES HIS POPULAR
MORNING SHOW. IN 1993 HE WAS
VOTED NUMBER ONE DJ BY LISTENERS
IN WICHITA AND SURROUNDING
AREAS.

JOHNNY WESTERN (BOTTOM),
COUNTRY MUSIC LEGEND AND KFDI
RANCH HAND, BROADCASTS LIVE FROM
THE STUDIO.

IN 1990 GREAT EMPIRE AND FIRST
STUART CORPORATION OF TULSA,
OPERATORS OF KVOO AM/FM,
MERGED THE KVOO ASSETS INTO
GREAT EMPIRE. HAROLD C. STUART
(LEFT) IS NOW A STOCKHOLDER IN
THE WICHITA COMPANY.

LEARJET INC.

AS TWILIGHT APPROACHED ON THE CHILLY evening of October 7, 1963, more than 1,000 spectators—aircraft workers, their families, town fathers, and average citizens—lined Wichita Municipal's Runway 32, their eyes trained on a small, silver airplane accelerating down the runway. As its nose

PRESIDENT AND CEO BRIAN E. BARENTS AND THE LEARJET 31A AIRCRAFT AT THE COMPANY'S WICHITA FACILITY.

THE NEW LEARJET 60 MID-SIZE JET FLIES OVER WILLIAM RANDOLPH HEARST'S SAN SIMEON ESTATE IN NORTHERN CALIFORNIA.

pointed skyward and its wheels broke ground, a company's fortunes—and the very concept of the business jet—were launched.

Thirty years after that famous first flight, a Learjet taking to the air still turns heads. Perhaps because of its sleek lines and dazzling performance, its early adoption by a number of major companies and celebrities, and its lineage as the best known creation of Bill Lear, the very name Learjet has become synonymous in the public mind with business aircraft.

DECADES OF REFINEMENT

Today, the Learjet tradition of building high-performance aircraft for business, government, and others continues. Since the introduction of the Learjet 23, the company has developed 10 major model designations, each incorporating

new refinements, and has built more than 1,700 aircraft. The 35A, in continuous production since 1976, has become a mainstay of corporate flight departments and charter operators, with more than 600 produced.

The Learjet 31A, certified in 1991, provides unparalleled performance and economy of operation within its market segment. No other light jet can take off fully loaded from a 3,000-foot runway and can top thunderstorms at 49,000 feet en route to a destination half a continent away.

The mid-size Learjet 60, certified in 1993, provides passengers with a comfortable, stand-up, walk-around cabin. It also features the most fuel-efficient engines in its class, as well as aerodynamic refinements developed in conjunction with NASA. The Learjet 60 is the

only U.S.-built aircraft in its price category to provide coast-to-coast range.

Learjet has now embarked on the development of an entirely new aircraft, the Learjet 45, intended to fill a market need for an aircraft sized between the light and mid-size jet. The 45 will provide exceptional performance and comfort at very moderate costs of operation and ownership. The first flight is scheduled for March 1995 and certification for July 1996.

LEARJET TODAY

Learjet employs more than 2,800 people at its Wichita facilities, which cover more than 1 million square feet of enclosed space. Total employment is more than 3,500, with employees also located in major service centers in Tuscon, Arizona, and Hartford, Connecticut, and in smaller facilities worldwide.

In June 1990, Learjet was purchased by Bombardier Inc., a Montreal-based, multinational corporation with transportation interests ranging from the railroad cars which will run through the English Channel Tunnel to the Ski-Doo® and Sea-Doo® recreational vehicles.

"Our relationship with Bombardier provides the stability and confidence so necessary to invest in long-term development programs which are critical to our future success," comments Brian E. Barents, company president and CEO since 1989. "Learjet has weathered good times and bad in the business aircraft market. Today, the renaissance continues with a state-of-the-art product line and aggressive plans for expansion. We are poised to recapture the market leadership position this company enjoyed for so many years."

WICHITA SURGICAL GROUP, P.A.

THE WICHITA SURGICAL GROUP, P.A., THE nation's largest private group of surgical specialists, proudly calls Wichita home. Since founder George J. Farha, M.D., began his private surgical practice in 1963, his vision for the future of surgery has instinctively spanned the decades, bringing together a unique group of surgeons specializing in adult and pediatric thoracic and cardiovascular surgery, general surgery, pediatric surgery, peripheral vascular surgery, colon and rectal surgery, organ transplantation, and surgical care of burn, trauma, and critically ill patients.

Dr. Farha's vision and commitment to excellence, which inspire and lead his colleagues, are built on a foundation that the patient comes first, that quality care and service are paramount, and that involvement in teaching, research, and the development of innovative, cost-effective surgical technology is crucial.

As founding chairman and professor of the Department of Surgery at the University of Kansas School of Medicine-Wichita, Dr. Farha has had the privilege to participate in teaching and training many men and women who are well known in his own practice, the community at large, and other states. Dr. Farha also has helped establish departments that are vital to research, teaching, and new technology, such as the first Noninvasive Vascular Laboratory at St. Francis Regional Medical Center, of which he is currently director.

Sharing his brother's vision for excellence in surgery, Dr. Jim Farha joined the practice in 1964, bringing to Wichita and the Midwest what is known today as "modern heart surgery." Dr. Jim Farha pioneered coronary artery bypass surgery locally and performed the first successful heart valve replacement in Wichita. In addition to heart surgery, he specializes in thoracic

and peripheral vascular surgery.

In 1967 the third member, Dr. David Street, an accomplished general surgeon, joined the Farhas in their surgery practice, and from

kidney and heart transplants, the state's first pancreas transplant, and Wichita's first laparoscopic gallbladder surgery. In addition, the developer and current chairman of the St. Francis Trauma Unit is a member of the Wichita Surgical Group, and the group's 25 surgeons hold academic clinical appointments at the University of Kansas School of Medicine-Wichita.

When asked about medicine in the '90s, Dr. George Farha says, "Medicine has been and will continue to be a noble profession, as nothing compares to the preserva-

LARRY FLEMING

that point the group has continued to grow by attracting the nation's finest surgical specialists.

Since its founding, the Wichita Surgical Group has been a key participant in the evolution of medicine and surgery in Wichita. The combined efforts and expertise of these specialists have led to many surgical firsts, such as Wichita's first

tion of human life. It is my hope that many young men and women will be encouraged to consider this wonderful profession, not only as physicians, but to serve as nurses or in other allied-health positions that are needed to carry medicine into the next century."

MEMBERS OF THE WICHITA SURGICAL GROUP'S BOARD OF DIRECTORS ARE (FROM LEFT) DR. DAVID STREET, DR. GEORGE FARHA, AND DR. JIM FARHA.

Elf Atochem North America, Inc.

WHEN THE SUMMERS TURN HOT AND humid, Kansans usually develop a newfound appreciation for cool air. Although most people don't realize it, the R-22 refrigerant used in their air conditioning units is probably produced in Wichita by Elf Atochem North America, Inc.

Located on a 14-acre site in southwest Wichita, the plant can produce more than 7 million pounds of refrigerants per month. It also packages a full line of refrigerants in containers ranging from 30-pound cylinders to 180,000-pound rail cars. Elf Atochem-Wichita is a primary packager of R-134a, a leading alternative to CFC-12 refrigerant. Because it has no known damaging effect on the ozone layer, R-134a was recently selected by General Motors for use in the air conditioning systems of its new automobiles.

Established in Wichita in 1965 as Racon Inc., the company in 1990 became part of Elf Atochem North America, Inc., which is part of the chemicals manufacturing sector of the Elf Group, a French conglomerate. Elf Atochem N.A. specializes in the production of chemicals for such corporations as Xerox, DuPont, and Wichita's own Coleman Company and Evcon Industries. The local plant generates annual sales in excess of $100 million and employs approximately 130 people.

Elf Atochem-Wichita recognizes the value of automation and the advantages it offers customers and the community. A major portion of the facility's manufacturing and packaging operations is automated and computer driven to allow close monitoring by control-room operators and on-site laboratory technicians. This improves both the safety and the efficiency of the production process.

LOCATED ON A 14-ACRE SITE, THE ELF ATOCHEM-WICHITA PLANT CAN PRODUCE MORE THAN 7 MILLION POUNDS OF REFRIGERANTS PER MONTH. THE COMPANY IS A PRIMARY PACKAGER OF R-134A, A LEADING ALTERNATIVE REFRIGERANT THAT HAS NO KNOWN DAMAGING EFFECT ON THE OZONE LAYER.

Working Together in Wichita

The local plant maintains a symbiotic relationship with its neighbor, Vulcan Chemicals. Vulcan shares operations personnel and provides chloroform from which refrigerants are made. In return, Elf Atochem-

Wichita supplies hydrochloric acid, a co-product of refrigerant manufacturing, to Vulcan, which markets the substance for industrial and food processing uses.

The companies also work together to reduce waste production and emissions. Elf Atochem's facility, in cooperation with Vulcan, has made major production process improvements to increase the quality of the hydrochloric acid produced and thus broaden the market into which it is sold. Additional process changes have been made, and new equipment has been in-

stalled to reduce or eliminate emission sources. Other new equipment enables wastes to be neutralized a emissions to be cleaned.

"In recent years, as much as 7 percent of our annual budget and engineering efforts has been directed toward projects that make the manufacturing and packaging of refrigerants safer and more environmentally responsible," says Ji Marsalis, plant manager. "By 19 we'll have reduced our waste streams by 40 percent, and we'll continue this process throughou the decade."

As recycling takes on greater environmental significance, Elf Atochem-Wichita is leading the way with its refrigerant reclamati facility. Designed to convert use refrigerant to its original state for reuse, it is the designated Elf Atochem reclamation facility in North America and one of the fir to be certified by the American Refrigeration Institute.

"As tough new federal regulations take effect, our refrigerant r cycling facility will be ready to he others comply and make the tran tion to CFC alternatives," Marsa says. "It's that kind of commitme to the future that has fueled our success in Wichita for years."

HE FOSTER COMPANIES

OR THREE DECADES, THE CITY'S AIRCRAFT/ aerospace industry, pipeline/petrochemical and chemical plants, and manufacturing and electronics firms have counted on The Foster Companies for unique engineering and computer services on turnkey, custom-tailored projects. ◆ The Foster Companies

an in 1964 as the Foster Design npany, the state's first contract neering firm to provide on-site porary technical professionals. ough one division of The er Companies still provides service, the organization has nded since 1985 to include in-se engineering, petrochemical neering, industrial design, prod-development, and one of the t sophisticated computer-aided gn and manufacturing (CAD/M) service bureaus in the na-. The Foster Companies today loy more than 100 engineers, gners, computer programmers, draftspersons serving 300 une 1000 clients.

Our clients come to us for inno-ve approaches to design because oring a wide scope of experience neir projects," says Gene Foster, ident. "We push our technical ices as far as the envelope allows chieve the best solution."

he Foster Companies' client ncludes many Fortune 1000 s such as The Boeing Com-y, Cessna Aircraft Company, kwell International, Pizza Hut, Products & Chemicals, IFR, el, Conoco Inc., and Vulcan micals. Product development rs a broad spectrum of in-ries: electronics, heavy equip-t, medical products, vehicle transportation products, luction machinery and tooling, avionics, among others. In nt years, the firm has taken on gn projects ranging from Pizza 's drinking glasses and salad bar ks to tool design for sections of ing's 767 commercial aircraft.

lthough over 80 percent of The er Companies' business comes

from repeat clients, the organiza-tion anticipates that programs now under development eventually will attract a significant number of nationwide firms involved in off-shore operations in Europe.

MAPPING THE FUTURE

Artificial intelligence is the wave of the future in computer design, and The Foster Companies are leading the way to apply the technology.

In 1993 the organization was licensed by the Environmental Systems Research Institute (ESRI) of Redlands, California, to write application programs for ESRI software. Under this prestigious licensing agreement, The Foster Companies developed a state-of-the-art geographic mapping pack-age that, when combined with the user's database, provides statistical correlations.

This software is ideal for munici-

palities, utility firms, school dis-tricts, and others who need to combine geographic information with user-definable data. In fact, the program has allowed one school district to significantly increase its operational and fiscal efficiency by correlating the ages and home ad-dresses of its students with school assignments. Using this data, offi-cials calculated teacher assignments and class loads by school and by classroom. They also determined bus routes, arrival and departure schedules, alternate routing sched-ules, and even anticipated gasoline consumption.

"With rapid changes in technol-ogy, it's not economically feasible for many companies or municipali-ties to stay current. We cater to many smaller manufacturers, utility companies, municipalities—even one-person firms—who need specialized technology but don't have the expertise, personnel, or equipment in-house," says Foster.

"Our greatest service is forming a partnership with each of our clients and tailoring our capabilities and talents to fit their needs," he adds. The Foster Companies will con-tinue to direct attention to leading-edge technology for business enterprises in Kansas and beyond.

THE FOSTER COMPANIES OFFER IN-HOUSE ENGINEERING, PETROCHEMI-CAL ENGINEERING, INDUSTRIAL DESIGN, PRODUCT DEVELOPMENT, AND ONE OF THE NATION'S MOST SOPHISTICATED COMPUTER-AIDED DESIGN AND MANUFACTURING (CAD/CAM) SERVICE BUREAUS.

BRITTAIN MACHINE INC.

KNOWN THROUGHOUT THE AEROSPACE industry for five-axis machining and high-quality precision parts, Brittain Machine Inc. boasts a client roster that includes most of the nation's major commercial and military aerospace companies: Boeing, General Dynamics, Lockheed, Cessna, Martin Marietta, Beech, Learjet, and Piaggio, among others. Founded in Wichita in 1966, the company today has operations in Wichita and California employing more than 180 people and is making strides in building international business.

FOUNDER SETS SIGHTS HIGH FOR COMPANY

Company president and CEO Dewey Brittain opened his one-man shop with $500 cash and one used milling machine almost 30 years ago and has never stopped making improvements. The family-owned company has continually upgraded its operations by reinvesting profits to improve on its capabilities to build a wide range of aircraft parts. Today enjoying over $18 million in annual sales, Brittain Machine occupies 140,000 square feet of manufacturing space in Wichita and another 44,000 square feet in Cerritos, California.

Brittain's belief in reinvestment, plus his keen insight into changing market needs, led the company to add computerized numerical control equipment, climate-controlled facilities, computer-aided design and manufacturing (CAD/CAM) capabilities, and five-axis machining far sooner than similarly sized competitors.

Brittain Machine now owns 12 five-axis mills, some with material tables as long as 90 feet. A single five-axis mill, which can cost over $1 million, simultaneously rotates both the part being made and the machine's milling spindle. Computer controlled, some machines have the ability to produce a perfect sphere from even the hardest of steels and to machine the most complex pattern from a single piece of metal.

But producing the actual part is only one aspect of what the company does today. Brittain Machine devotes a significant amount of time to research and development, engineering, and producing scale-model designs. "All manufacturers are cutting down the number of suppliers they want to deal with, and they're asking those that remain to tackle a broader variety of projects," explains Brittain.

DEVELOPING HUMAN RESOURCES

In meeting the demands of today's marketplace, the company has thrived not only by making subs[...]tial investments in high-tech eq[...]ment and broadening its expert[...] but also by concentrating on its human resources. "Our willingn[...] to adopt new production and m[...]agement methods, such as the C[...]tinuous Quality Improvement program, gives our customers th[...] world over an innovative partne[...] with a reputation for cutting wa[...] from production costs," says Bri[...]tain. "Attracting an outstanding and responsive staff of engineers programmers, machinists, and quality control analysts ensures company meets customers' prec[...] guidelines and budgets."

Brittain adds that teamwork makes the biggest difference in [...]viding the highest level of custo[...] service. Open communication b[...]tween management and personn[...] also keeps employee turnover lo[...] and enhances the company's cap[...]bilities in handling even the mo[...] challenging assignments. "The t[...] nology is critical," he says, "but people and their commitment t[...] service are what help us remain [...] prime vendor to our customers around the world."

THIS FIVE-AXIS GANTRY MILL WITH AN 80-FOOT TABLE (BELOW RIGHT) IS ONE OF THE NEWEST ADDITIONS AT BRITTAIN'S 140,000-SQUARE-FOOT WICHITA FACILITY.

COMPANY PRESIDENT AND CEO DEWEY BRITTAIN OPENED A ONE-MAN SHOP WITH $500 CASH AND ONE USED MILLING MACHINE IN 1966. TODAY, THE COMPANY ENJOYS OVER $18 MILLION IN ANNUAL SALES.

HOWARD'S OPTICAL DISPENSARY, INC.

FOUNDED IN 1968 AS A SMALL, FAMILY-OWNED business, Howard's Optical Dispensary, Inc. is today one of the largest retail optical companies in Kansas. ◆ With five stores—four in Wichita and one in Salina—and its own lens-production laboratory, Howard's sells more eyeglasses than any other optical

ler in the state. "We stay current with the latest in the optical ," says Mark Nordyke, com- vice president and son of ard Nordyke, founder and dent. "We set ourselves apart the competition with quality ce and by training our people oduct knowledge and cus- er service. True service in the al business is after the sale. 's what we really strive to hasize."

The company's huge inventory includes sizes and styles for customers of every age. Offering all types of lenses, Howard's also has special expertise in fitting eyeglasses for patients who have had cataract surgery. The company, which has enjoyed an average annual growth of 12 percent in recent years, employs 40 people, many of whom are certified opticians with years of experience.

BUILDING A SUCCESSFUL BUSINESS

Howard Nordyke started in the optical business as a delivery boy for a laboratory in the early 1950s. There he also mastered the craft of making lenses. After serving in the Army, he went to work for a Wichita optometrist, where he learned how to run a retail optical shop and work with the public.

By 1968 he was ready to launch his own business. He and his wife, Lana, borrowed the money and opened the family's first store in the Parklane Shopping Center. Howard also set up a laboratory in the garage at home to make the lenses. The store enjoyed immediate success, and within three years Nordyke moved the lab to that location and had five employees on staff.

In 1972 he opened his second store at Prairie Village Shopping Center; four years later he bought an existing shop in Indian Hills Shopping Center. In 1982 Howard acquired Atlas Optical, now called Howard's Atlas Optical, in the town of Salina, north of Wichita. A year later, the company's main store was moved to 1650 S. Oliver in southeast Wichita, and Howard's opened its fifth store in 1985 at 230 S. Maize Road in west Wichita.

The Nordyke family is heavily involved in the company and the community. In addition to his son, Mark, Howard Nordyke's daughters, Linda Charmchizadeh and Belinda Payne, are office managers, and their husbands are store managers. Howard's serves as a sponsor for the annual Kansas Junior Livestock Show and the annual Charlie Daniels Celebrity Golf Classic, which benefits Starkey Inc., a development center for the mentally retarded. The company also is an enthusiastic backer of Wichita State University's baseball program.

IN 1968 HOWARD AND LANA NORDYKE OPENED THE FAMILY'S FIRST STORE IN WICHITA. TODAY, HOWARD'S SELLS MORE EYEGLASSES THAN ANY OTHER OPTICAL RETAILER IN THE STATE.

CHANCE INDUSTRIES, INC.

A REPUTATION FOR MANUFACTURING QUALITY amusement rides and transportation products for markets worldwide, and a deep commitment to safety and innovation are the hallmarks of Chance Industries, Inc., parent company of Chance Rides, Inc., and Chance Coach, Inc. Chance Rides is America's largest manufacturer of amusement rides, and Chance Coach produces quality transit vehicles.

FROM MINIATURE TRAINS TO CLASSIC CARROUSELS

In 1960, when Harold Chance established Chance Manufacturing, the company had one product—the C.P. Huntington miniature train, a gas-powered, handcrafted, scaled replica of an 1863 Central Pacific Railroad train. Still in production, it is a familiar ride at amusement and theme parks worldwide.

During its first decade in business, the company diversified its offerings and manufactured a number of portable rides for the amusement industry, with such well-known names as the "Trabant," "Sky-diver," and "Zipper." In 1970 Chance Manufacturing began building carrousels and has since become the world's largest manufacturer of this popular ride. Most people would agree that Chance Rides is responsible for reviving America's love affair with carrousels.

With an understanding from the outset that classic styling for carrousels is important, Chance Manufacturing began production of the ride with manufacturing rights from the Allan Herschell Co. of Buffalo, New York, then America's oldest and largest manufacturer of amusement rides. "For many years and up through the '70s, carrousel animal design got away from classic styling," says Richard G. Chance, president and chief executive officer of Chance Industries. "People will accept new looks and technolog[y] in amusement rides, but carrous[e] have a nostalgic appeal that mak[es] it important to uphold the tradi[-] tional 'look.'"

In 1986 Chance Rides, Inc. p[ur-] chased the manufacturing rights and molds to the exclusive Bradl[ey] & Kaye line of carrousel figures. Created at the turn of the centur[y,] Bradley & Kaye animals are carr[ou-] sel classics that reflect Chance's commitment to Old World styli[ng,] precise detailing, and intricate handwork.

In fact, the only major differe[nce] in the method of production tod[ay] is that the traditionally wooden figures are made of more durable fiberglass. Each molded figure is hand-finished for detail, and the[n] sanded, primed, and painted wit[h] as much care as was its wooden predecessor. In addition, no two [fig-] ures are exactly alike. Chance art[ists]

have full rein in painting the carr[ou-] sel menagerie—including horses, sea dragons, rabbits, bears, zebra[s,] and lions—in order to create unique figures and some of the fi[n-] est carrousel animals ever produc[ed.] The figures, in combination wit[h] the elaborately decorated and painted carrousel structure, a col[or-] ful canopy, bright lights, and call[i-] ope music, make for a ride that is hard to resist.

Chance Rides carrousels can b[e] found today in Japan, Taiwan, China, Sweden, Holland, Englan[d,] Hong Kong, Korea, and South America, as well as throughout th[e] United States. "The most popula[r] rides we build are carrousels and the 'Giant Wheel,'" says Chance[.] "Both rides appeal to the whole fa[m-] ily." The "Giant Wheel," which i[s] the largest Ferris wheel made in America today, is 90 feet tall and

CHANCE RIDES' 50-FOOT "GRAND CARROUSEL" (BELOW RIGHT) FEATURES A MAINTENANCE-FRIENDLY SYSTEM AND ELECTRIC, VARIABLE-SPEED DRIVE FOR SMOOTH, QUIET OPERATION.

IN RECENT YEARS, CHANCE COACH HAS INTRODUCED THE AMERICAN HERITAGE STREETCAR, WHICH FEATURES AUTHENTIC TURN-OF-THE-CENTURY STYLING.

gondolas large enough for a family of eight.

Other Chance Rides thrill rides include the "Falling Star," which gives riders a 65-foot accelerated free-fall; the perennially popular "Zipper," with free-spinning passenger cages mounted on a rotating boom; and the "Rotor," which features a floor that drops out while centrifugal force keeps riders in place.

Although every ride is designed to be spectacular, safety is of the utmost concern. Portability also is important since many operators follow regular state and county fair routes. The Chance Rides "Century Wheel," a 64-foot wheel ride, was named Best New Ride at its 1993 debut at the International Independent Showmen's Foundation Extravaganza. It was cited for its ease in passenger loading and because it could be easily transported on one trailer.

CHANCE COACH — PERFECT FOR SMALL TRANSIT MARKET

Although it's likely that amusement park visitors will enjoy a Chance ride during their day of fun, it's also likely that they will be transported from the parking lot to the park entrance on a Chance Coach tram.

Chance Manufacturing introduced its first tram, the Starliner, in the 1960s. Chance Coach, Inc. was formed in 1980 and now sells the Sunliner tram. The company's trams, used for sightseeing tours as well as parking lot transportation, are in service at Sea World Florida, Universal Studios Florida, the Houston Space Center, and some of America's finest zoos, including the Miami Metro Zoo and the Kansas City (Missouri) Zoo.

The Chance Coach subsidiary, representing about one-third of the company's total sales, also manufactures several bus models that are smaller than standard city buses. With demand increasing for compact, efficient mass-transit vehicles, Chance Coach buses are finding a positive reception with city transit systems, airports, and metropolitan park-and-ride systems.

The "Streetcar," part of the company's American Heritage coach series, features authentic turn-of-the-century streetcar styling. Diesel powered, it boasts Philippine mahogany seats in an antiqued finish and shiny brass trim. Numerous cities have purchased the buses for period-look transportation throughout historical districts. "Streetcar" orders continue to grow, with deliveries already made in over two dozen cities including Tokyo, Japan, and Wichita.

Richard Chance says that Chance Industries' success can be attributed in large part to its focus on pleasing its customers by producing the finest amusement rides, trams, and buses. "We define quality as meeting or exceeding customer expectations," he says. "Value means more than price in our business. In the final analysis, our goal is to make our customers more successful."

THE "ZIPPER," WITH ITS FREE-SPINNING PASSENGER CAGES MOUNTED ON A ROTATING BOOM, IS JUST ONE OF CHANCE RIDES' POPULAR THRILL RIDES.

THE "CENTURY WHEEL" (ABOVE LEFT) WAS NAMED BEST NEW RIDE AT ITS 1993 DEBUT AT THE INTERNATIONAL INDEPENDENT SHOWMEN'S FOUNDATION EXTRAVAGANZA.

STILL IN PRODUCTION, THE C.P. HUNTINGTON MINIATURE TRAIN, A GAS-POWERED, HANDCRAFTED, SCALED REPLICA OF AN 1863 CENTRAL PACIFIC RAILROAD TRAIN, WAS CHANCE MANUFACTURING'S FIRST PRODUCT IN 1960.

JOHN T. ARNOLD ASSOCIATES, INC.

WHEN IT COMES TO COMMERCIAL/ industrial real estate in Wichita, you won't find John T. Arnold Associates watching from the sidelines. Instead, look for this team of talented professionals to make things happen. ◆ The company has been at the forefront of the community's development for more than two decades, leading the way to form creative partnerships that have helped Wichita grow.

John T. Arnold left a top marketing position in the oil business to enter commercial, industrial, and investment real estate. While handling the real estate needs of oil companies, he became fascinated with the opportunities he saw in real estate development and learned valuable lessons about the complexities of investment properties. At the same time he discovered a niche where he had an opportunity to put creative, problem-solving talents to work to benefit local businesses and the community. He founded John T. Arnold Associates in 1971.

"For me, this challenging field brought everything into focus," Arnold says. "It was just what I had been searching for—an opportunity to combine creativity with a rewarding business."

A PEOPLE BUSINESS

John T. Arnold Associates was founded on the philosophy that real estate is a people business. People and their needs, which are the driving force behind real estate transactions, are the focus of atten-tion at the firm, says Arnold.

In the early years the going wa[s] tough, but Arnold approached co[m]mercial real estate investment wi[th] an innovative style. In fact, the fi[rm] handled three of the first four lim[]ited partnerships approved and registered in Kansas, including t[he] state's first.

During the mid-1970s, the co[m]pany saw new opportunities in t[he] industrial market. It became in-volved with developing industria[l] and commercial land and began handling the relocation of major national and international firms [in] Wichita.

As a reflection of Arnold's civi[c] interest, he was the catalyst in est[ab]lishing a real estate chair in the business college at Wichita State University. It is the only real esta[te] chair in Kansas and one of only a handful among universities in th[e] Midwest. Every year students fro[m] across the country benefit from t[he] position endowed through Arno[ld's] foresight.

Two decades after its foundin[g] John T. Arnold Associates remai[ns] focused on its original goal. Buil[d]ing on a well-established reputati[on] for outstanding service, the com-pany continues to specialize in b[rok]ering commercial, industrial, an[d] investment properties, utilizing [a] team approach to creatively mee[t] client needs.

The firm's associates are exper[i]enced problem solvers committe[d] to serving people first. Likewise, they exemplify the Midwestern work ethic, with a strong focus o[n] Christian values. The company e[n]courages community involveme[nt] and every associate understands the importance of giving person[al] time and talent to improve the community.

John T. Arnold Associates care[s] about building a better future fo[r] Wichita through quality real esta[te] development. The company has helped make that happen for the city since 1971, and it will con-tinue in its commitment to keep Wichita growing.

THE FIRM'S OFFICERS INCLUDE (FROM LEFT) DON ARNOLD JR., SECRE-TARY-TREASURER; MARLIN PENNER, PRESIDENT; DON ARNOLD SR., VICE PRESIDENT; AND JOHN T. ARNOLD, CHAIRMAN OF THE BOARD.

AZIM STUDIOS

DVANCED ORTHOPAEDIC ASSOCIATES P.A.

ECHNOLOGY IN ORTHOPAEDIC SURGERY and treatment of orthopaedic injuries have taken giant steps in recent years. Patients who only a few years ago remained in the hospital for one or two weeks after surgery now recover so quickly that their hospital stays average only three

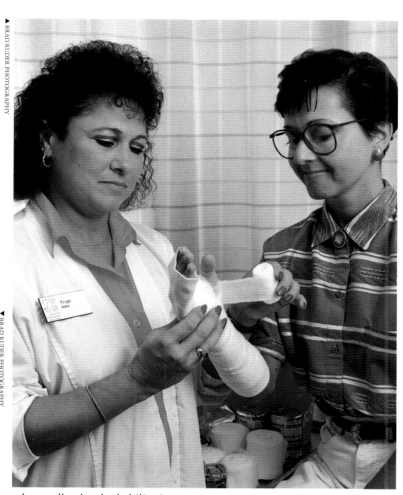

ve days, or they may be treated rely as outpatients. Wichita's anced Orthopaedic Associates . is on the leading edge of new elopments of this type.

dvanced Orthopaedic Associtreats a broad spectrum of opaedic problems and condi-

upper extremity reconstruction and reimplantation. Each of the group's physicians is a surgeon, and each subspecializes in areas such as the hand, shoulder, spine, hip, knee, and foot.

Advanced Orthopaedic Associates over the years has developed a

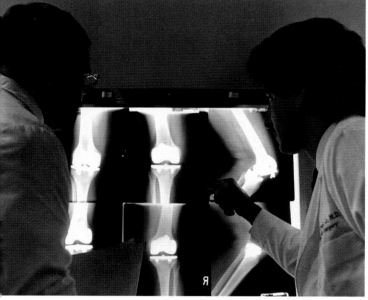

s, from birth anomalies and genital deformities to sports ines and arthritis. "Our medical osophy is patient oriented," a physician spokesman for the p. "We try our best to under- d our patients' needs and rve them in the best way ible."

CIALISTS IN A NUMBER AREAS

physicians in the group care nfants, children, teenagers, and ts, as well as the elderly popula- . They treat sports, industrial, occupational injuries. In addi- the group performs microvas- r surgery, including hand and

strong practice in sports medicine directed not only to treating an injury after it occurs, but also to preventing an injury from occurring. The group works with most of Wichita's professional and amateur athletic teams, including the Wichita Wings professional soccer team, the Wichita Thunder minor league hockey team, Wichita State University sports programs, and several of Wichita's high school athletic teams.

Advanced Orthopaedic Associates' physicians are on the staffs of St. Francis Regional Medical Center, St. Joseph Medical Center, HCA Wesley Medical Center, and the Veterans Administration Hospi-

tal, as well as local rehabilitation hospitals. They devote time to teaching as faculty members of the University of Kansas School of Medicine-Wichita and are involved with the Orthopaedic Research Institute, among other professional activities.

Advanced Orthopaedic Associates extends its expert care beyond the Wichita area. The physicians make monthly visits to clinics in some southwest Kansas communities, caring for patients who are unable to travel to Wichita for routine office visits.

To remain current on new developments in technology, treatment, and surgery, the physicians belong to the Academy of Orthopaedic Surgeons and regularly participate in and attend educational seminars. They also are members of the American Medical Association, the Kansas Medical Society, and the Medical Society of Sedgwick County.

PROVIDING MOST SERVICES ON AN OUTPATIENT BASIS IS A GOAL OF ADVANCED ORTHOPAEDIC ASSOCIATES.

ORTHOPAEDIC SURGERY IS A CONTINUOUS LEARNING PROCESS (LEFT). ONE ADVANTAGE FOR A GROUP PRACTICE IS IMMEDIATE CONSULTATION WITH COLLEAGUES.

COORDINATING PATIENT CARE IS A PRIORITY OF THE PHYSICIANS AND STAFF AT ADVANCED ORTHOPAEDIC ASSOCIATES.

KLENDA, MITCHELL, AUSTERMAN & ZUERCHER

THE LAW FIRM OF KLENDA, MITCHELL, Austerman & Zuercher believes that those who seek its service require personal attention, quality representation, advice grounded in experience, and a cost-effective approach to problem solving. By understanding and responding to these needs,

the firm has, over the years, grown with its clients.

The firm actively seeks new associations with individuals and business enterprises. To effectively achieve the goals of its clients, Klenda, Mitchell, Austerman & Zuercher channels client services through a coordinating attorney who draws upon the pool of talent and expertise available in the firm's practice groups. The coordinating attorney also supervises cost control and billing. This team approach is designed to ensure an immediate

response to the needs of clients and to lower the cost of services.

PERSONAL ATTENTION AND CREATIVITY ACHIEVE CLIENT GOALS (RIGHT).

KLENDA, MITCHELL, AUSTERMAN & ZUERCHER IS DEDICATED TO EXCELLENCE IN PROVIDING PROFESSIONAL LEGAL SERVICES TO MEET THE CHALLENGES OF TODAY.

THE ATTORNEYS

Klenda, Mitchell, Austerman & Zuercher is dedicated to excellen in providing professional legal ser ices to meet the complex challeng of today. The firm takes pride in history of support for the entrepr neurial spirit in both Wichita and the Midwest. Through a multi-faceted practice, it represents individuals, publicly and privatel held companies, government age cies, and financial institutions.

▼ PROCTOR T. RITCHIE

Klenda, Mitchell, Austerman & Zuercher believes that the depth of its talented pool of attorneys and certified legal assistants enables the firm to serve its clients aggressively, creatively, and effectively. It also recognizes that personal attention has been the hallmark of its success. By combining these elements, the firm is able to provide cost-effective solutions to the problems that face all of its clients, regardless of their size.

While the firm's offices are locate in Wichita, the practice is region national, and international in sco

Klenda, Mitchell, Austerman Zuercher believes that today's leg environment dictates collaborati among its attorneys, each of who concentrates in specific areas of t law. As a result, the firm is able t respond efficiently and economi cally to the needs of its clients. B limiting the scope of their indivi ual practices, the firm's attorneys

...e been able to broaden the ...th of their knowledge in their ...sen areas of concentration. In ...ition, their collaboration and ...bined resources enable the firm ...etter attain its clients' ultimate ...s.

...lenda, Mitchell, Austerman & ...rcher maintains a regional, ...onal, and international perspec-

...that is balanced by its attor-...' active participation in the life ...e Wichita community. The ...believes it has a duty to con-...te to and actively support ...itable and cultural organiza-...s. As a result, firm attorneys ...e on the boards of charitable, ..., and educational institutions.

... PRACTICE

...anding theories of liability, com-...and pervasive governmental

regulation, and frequent changes in the law often clutter the path to success for today's businesses. As a result, the successful business person has been compelled to retain law firms in various sections of the nation. Klenda, Mitchell, Austerman & Zuercher, with its concentrated areas of practice and team approach, is able to reverse this trend. Its size enables its attorneys to concentrate their practices in diversified areas of the law. Thus, the firm is able to provide a full range of services to clients, especially when experienced counsel, coupled with swift, decisive action, is crucial.

Clients who might otherwise have been compelled to seek the advice of firms in other cities have come to appreciate the availability of comparable legal services pro-

vided by Klenda, Mitchell, Austerman & Zuercher. The firm's attorneys are available and positioned to assist clients in the strategic planning necessary to identify the legal consequences of proposed business strategies. As a full-service firm, Klenda, Mitchell, Austerman & Zuercher is able to offer the benefit of experience in a broad range of legal services required not only by major corporations but also by start-up companies, mid-size entities, and individuals.

The firm's practice is divided into several areas of concentration: securities, litigation, mergers and acquisitions, franchise, estate planning, environmental, banking and commercial, taxation, health care, labor and employment, aviation, real estate, oil and gas, bankruptcy, and collections, to name a few. All areas of practice are, to a degree, interdependent. For example, when necessary in complex commercial litigation, the firm's trial team works closely with the business team. Thus, by selecting members of the team from its various areas of concentration, the firm is able to bring the full weight of its knowledge and experience to bear in finding solutions to the most difficult problems.

Building on more than two decades of success, Klenda, Mitchell, Austerman & Zuercher is firmly committed to upholding the highest professional standards to meet the challenges of today.

SINCE 1971 THE FIRM HAS ASSISTED THE ENTREPRENEURIAL SPIRIT OF WICHITA AND THE MIDWEST.

TODAY'S LEGAL ENVIRONMENT REQUIRES THE COORDINATION OF ATTORNEY SPECIALTIES WITH OTHER DISCIPLINES (LEFT).

AT&T in Wichita:
NCR Microelectronic Products Division, NCR Component Evaluation and Technology Center, and AT&T Sales and Service

T HE MERGER OF NCR CORP. WITH AT&T was one of 1991's biggest business stories. The bigger story, however, is evolving every day as individuals and businesses worldwide benefit from the added strength in information systems technology that NCR has afforded communications giant AT&T.

NCR is today one of AT&T's five service groups—the others are Communications Services, Communications Products, Network Systems, and AT&T Capital Corporation. Together the groups provide seamless communication, information, and financial services around the world.

global markets. The group is a leader in the development and production of computers, software, networking systems, document management systems, automated teller machines, and point-of-service terminals. Employing 52,000 people worldwide, NCR had 1992 sales of $7.14 billion.

machines. As NCR expanded its operations into the computer and information management busine NCR-Wichita followed suit.

NCR merged its Wichita oper tion into the Microelectronic Pro ucts Division in 1993. The unit's mission today is to design, manuf ture, and market computer perip eral systems which "add on" to a enhance the main computer system. Through the sophisticated peripheral products it produces, including computer chips, specia purpose computer boards, and th industry's broadest line of disk array systems, the division is constantly improving technology for the storage and management of large amounts of information.

NCR MICROELECTRONIC PRODUCTS DIVISION-WICHITA IS A LEADER IN HIGH-TECH SOLUTIONS FOR DATA STORAGE, INCLUDING THE 6298 DISK ARRAY SUBSYSTEM (BELOW).

THANKS TO THE REVOLUTIONARY HOT SWAP™ FEATURE DEVELOPED BY NCR-WICHITA (ABOVE RIGHT), COMPUTER SYSTEMS REMAIN ON-LINE AND DATA INTACT EVEN WHEN A DRIVE IS REPLACED.

ENGINEERS AT NCR-WICHITA DEVELOPED THE INDUSTRY'S FIRST RAID CHIP SET AND CONTROLLER BOARDS (RIGHT).

NCR, for years known primarily for its cash registers and adding machines, today develops, manufactures, markets, supports, and services information systems for

Two company divisions, the Microelectronic Products Division and the Component Evaluation and Technology Center (CETC), are located adjacent to one another in northeast Wichita. Together they employ close to 500 people.

MICROELECTRONIC PRODUCTS DIVISION
NCR Corp. established a division in the city in 1972 when it purchased Standard Precision, Inc. of Wichita and renamed it NCR-Wichita. The local division initially continued doing what its predecessor had done—building print hammer assemblies and accounting

Its disk array systems, which a high-performance data storage devices, are based on technology known as "redundant array of independent disks" (RAID). NC Wichita was the pioneer in bring ing this technology to the marke place. Its engineers developed th industry's first RAID chip set an controller boards. Today, NCR' line of RAID controller boards leads the market in sales to origi equipment manufacturers. Its N branded storage subsystems set t pace for such systems worldwide

The 6298 Disk Array Subsystem, NCR's largest RAID storag system, employs a desk-side mo

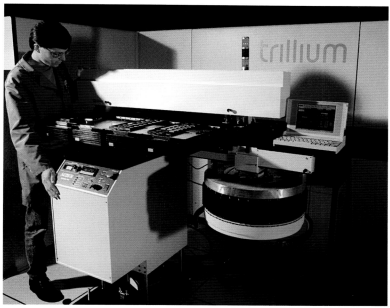

design that can accommodate to 20 individual disk drives thin a single cabinet. Each drive, able of storing up to two gigaes of data, can be replaced while system remains on-line and y functional without loss of ess to any data, including that the failed drive. NCR pioneered Hot Swap™ feature and has ce applied it to every major elent of the subsystem. In addition he division's flagship 6298 sys-, the 335 associates who work he Wichita plant design, build, market a full line of smaller a storage peripherals for personal nputers and workstations, including tape backup systems and optical a storage products.

MPONENT EVALUATION CHNOLOGY CENTER

ablished in 1983 to serve NCR's ldwide development and nufacturing organizations, Component Evaluation Techogy Center is an international oratory for testing, qualifying, evaluating electrical compot devices. In 1985 CETC began rketing its services to companies side NCR and today does a sigcant portion of its business with ernal customers.

At the 30,000-square-foot facil- 150 employees work with the st equipment in environmen-

tally controlled conditions that ensure quality, security, and reliability of testing procedures. CETC provides component testing, processing, engineering, and failure analysis for some of the nation's largest semiconductor manufacturers, distributors, and original equipment manufacturers.

Two programs developed by CETC, the Vendor Management Program (VMP) and the Purchased Component Management System (PCMS), are among the most effective and cost-efficient quality management programs in the industry. They support the engineering and production needs of NCR and other manufacturers by assuring that only the highest quality devices are used and by providing a complete database of supplier information.

Established in 1985, VMP is perhaps the most comprehensive program of its kind in the industry. In developing the program, CETC worked closely with key customers and integrated circuit suppliers to help suppliers establish higher standards for testing, problem resolution, and inspection criteria—with the dual goal of improving part quality and reliability while eliminating the need for extensive inspection of incoming parts by NCR manufacturing divisions. In addition to working with external sup-

pliers, CETC established internal teams to develop methods of streamlining parts procurement in order to eliminate duplication and reduce the number of parts required for various assemblies.

The result is that NCR dramatically reduced the price it paid for electrical components and shortened lead times, while simultaneously increasing quality and reliability levels. The program also brought suppliers into a closer working relationship with NCR. This relationship resulted in savings for the suppliers because they better understood NCR's expectations and had its assistance in solving the problems that generally affected their industry.

The lessons learned from VMP were incorporated in 1989 in the Purchased Component Management System. PCMS is a computerized database that serves as a repository or "reference library" for a broad range of technical and business data on components that have been evaluated by NCR. This information is available worldwide to NCR divisions and other manufacturers as a tool to help them match their parts or contracting needs with appropriate suppliers.

AT&T—EASY ACCESS TO PEOPLE AND INFORMATION

AT&T is dedicated to being the

world's best at bringing people together through easy access to each other and to the information and communications services they need. AT&T continues to build communications and information networks worldwide based on common engineering standards that require unprecedented international cooperation.

Equally unprecedented is AT&T's investment in research and technology. The company that brought the world the transistor, the laser, and the optical computer is developing the networking technology that allows the world to communicate through phones, fax machines, computers, computer databases, and video conferences.

For example, the AT&T Worldwide Intelligent Network is the largest, most technologically advanced communications system of its kind, allowing people worldwide to stay in touch regardless of time zones or weather conditions. This pervasive, high-tech system will actually track down the individual and deliver a phone call or a fax, whether that person is in the office, on a ski lift, or in an airplane. With the network as the hub, AT&T plans a collec-

tion of communications services—including voice and video transmissions and electronic mail—that will make it possible to move and use information in new ways and deliver it to conventional phones, computers, TVs, and cellular handsets, and to a new generation of wireless devices.

Thanks to the network's size and sophisticated software, voices, data, and images can be converted to signals that speed through the air and through glass fibers in fractions of a second. From the United States,

more than 215 countries can be dialed through wire and fiber-op cable circuits that, if stretched ou would circle the earth 80,000 times. In 1992 AT&T activated three major undersea, transocean systems capable of carrying 1 mil lion calls simultaneously.

AT&T is committed to the Wichita area and provides a vast array of premise-based products and leading edge technology. Stephen Adler, general manager f the Wichita Sales and Service Di sion, is excited about how AT&T will bring this new technology to the local business community, th providing customers with a comp itive advantage. For example, AT&T is at the forefront in the development and marketing of video and wireless communicatio technology while continuing to b the leader in the electronic key, PBX, and voice processing marke

AT&T's future is as bright as t ideas it brings to the world. As AT&T continues to build and re fine its networking, telecommuni tions, and other capabilities, the world will become smaller and more accessible through better communications.

THE FIRST PLACE

S HOPPING AT THE FIRST PLACE IS A FEAST for the senses. Customers are treated to samples of fine chocolates, imported cheeses, and other delectables when they enter the store. Gifts of crystal, silver, porcelain, and pewter sparkle on every shelf of the 7,000-square-foot store.

Throughout the day, there is laughter and conversation among customers and owner Helen Galloway and her daughters, Buffy and Kara.

Shoppers at The First Place enjoy the ultimate in customer service. Sales clerks, however, never try to "sell" anything. "I love getting attention when I walk in a store, but I hate having someone hover over me," says Galloway, explaining the no-pressure sales philosophy. "The customer has to want to buy something. We're here to make shopping a fun experience, whether the customer makes a purchase or not."

FINE GIFTS AND MORE

Widely known for its fine gifts, The First Place also carries an extensive line of fine jewelry and offers frequent showings by such noted jewelry designers as David Yurman, Kurt Wayne, and Oscar Heyman. A full-time jeweler is also on staff to craft one-of-a-kind pieces.

"We have customers who can shop all over the world, but they choose to shop here because they know we take great care in selecting our merchandise," says Buffy Hukle, who, along with her mother and sister, visits markets in Dallas, New York, Las Vegas, Kansas City, Atlanta, and Los Angeles. "At market there may be 2,000 designers displaying their pieces. We'll look at every one of them and handpick the jewelry and gifts we want in our store."

The First Place features exquisite crystal from Lalique and Saint Louis, as well as porcelain sculptures by Lladro, Boehm, and Connoisseur (featuring designs by Fleur Cowles). It also has exclusive rights in Wichita to carry silver by Mark Blackman. In addition to offering work by internationally renowned designers, The First Place carries sculpture by Babs Mellor, a Wichita artist. A satellite store two doors down from the original shop, Christmas at The First Place, annually features a unique holiday design by Mellor.

Because of its caliber of fine gifts and jewelry, The First Place is as stylish as any boutique in the country. "We never want to intimidate the customer," emphasizes Kara Haverty. "We have merchandise in all price ranges, and we go to great lengths to ensure that it is all high quality."

DEVOTION TO WICHITA

While managing The First Place takes a great portion of Helen Galloway's time, she still finds countless hours to devote to civic and philanthropic causes. She currently serves on the board of directors of St. Joseph Medical Center, the Wichita Center for the Arts, and Heartspring, and is a former board member of the Sedgwick County Zoo.

Galloway's community activities keep the store constantly buzzing with community leaders, who come in not only to shop but to meet with the owner about projects or corporate sponsorships. Such involvement, coupled with her business and marketing savvy, led to her appointment by former President George Bush to the National Advisory Council of the Small Business Administration.

"I love being involved with this business and the community," says Galloway. "I've lived here all of my adult life, and I have a great love affair with Wichita."

AT THE FIRST PLACE, OWNER HELEN GALLOWAY AND HER DAUGHTERS, BUFFY AND KARA, OFFER THE ULTIMATE IN CUSTOMER SERVICE.

RYAN AVIATION CORPORATION
RYAN INTERNATIONAL AIRLINES

For a poor kid from Iowa who fantasized about becoming a pilot, the idea of living in and flying out of Wichita, the "Air Capital of the World," was certainly intriguing but beyond Ron Ryan's wildest dream. However, in a true Horatio Alger transition, he has become not only a great

pilot but also an aviation leader in Wichita.

Over the years the city has beckoned a number of aviation entrepreneurs to fly planes as well as to build them. And it was Wichita's dynamic aviation industry that drew Ryan to the city in 1968. He accepted a position as chief pilot for Jack P. DeBoer Associates, a real estate development company that built apartment complexes nationwide.

DeBoer, a pilot himself, recognized the efficiency of charter travel as he criss-crossed the country conducting business. In 1972 DeBoer and Ryan founded DeBoer Aviation, a jet charter service specializing in corporate executive travel. The convenience of charter travel caught on with another national developer and Wichita resident, George Ablah. Together, Ablah and Ryan bought out DeBoer and changed the company's name to Ryan Aviation Corporation.

Today, Ron Ryan is sole owner of both Ryan Aviation and Ryan International Airlines. Ryan Aviation provides ground service and maintenance for corporate jets at Wichita's Mid-Continent Airport. Ryan International Airlines provides cargo and passenger flight services worldwide for the U.S. Postal Service, Emery Worldwide, Air Lingus, Apple Vacations, and many others.

THE AVIATOR'S TRUCK STOP

The flagship of Ryan's operations in Wichita is the successful fixed base operation (FBO) at Mid-Continent Airport. An FBO functions like a truck stop for the aviation industry. It is a touch-

down point where pilots can obtain fuel, maintenance, cleaning, hangar services, and catering for their aircraft. Ryan Aviation also offers its customer pilots amenities such as a lounge area, flight-planning assistance, and the services of its weather data center. The Wichita facilities include 45,000 square feet

of hangar space and 38,000 square feet of office space.

At the FBO's 14,000-square-foot hangar, certified technicians perform maintenance on all types of business aircraft. This includes jets as large as the Grumman Gulfstream and the Boeing 727. Ryan Aviation also provides backup services for commercial air carriers at Mid-Continent Airport.

The Ryan Aviation FBO specializes in maintenance of all kinds of turbine powered aircraft, including Learjet, Cessna Citation, and Beechcraft King Air. Ryan has achieved

the highly coveted FAA Certified Repair Station designation for bo[t]h maintenance and avionics, and it [is] an Airwork Service Center for Pra[tt] & Whitney and Garrett engines. The FBO's inventory, representin[g] several million dollars in spare pa[rts] alone, is augmented by inventory stockpiles of the major aircraft ma[n]ufacturers located in Wichita.

"The underlying philosophy of this company is service, and then it's service, and then it's service," states Ron Ryan emphatically. "F[or] every dollar our customers spend with us, I want them to feel that they have received a dollar-plus return for their money. That mea[ns] providing the best on-time servic[e], the best safety record, the best

maintenance, and the best effort v[e] can make every single time." This statement is a true reflection of R[on] Ryan's philosophy, and the company constantly strives to sustain i[ts] reputation.

FLIGHT SERVICES WORLDWID[E]

Ryan International Airlines derive[s] the largest portion of its revenue from transporting mail for the U.[S.] Postal Service under a subcontract with Emery Worldwide. Other cu[s]tomers include Emery Air Freight Corp., Air Lingus, and various commercial concerns. One of the

RON RYAN (ABOVE) FOLLOWED HIS DREAMS TO WICHITA WHERE HE HELPED FOUND RYAN AVIATION CORPORATION IN 1972.

THE MANAGEMENT TEAM OF RYAN INTERNATIONAL AIRLINES INCLUDES (FRONT ROW FROM LEFT) GERALD C. SNYDER, DIRECTOR OF HUMAN RESOURCES, RONALD D. RYAN, PRESIDENT, WILLIAM A. HAYES, VICE PRESIDENT-FLIGHT OPERATIONS, (BACK ROW FROM LEFT) RAYMOND E. THOMAS, VICE PRESIDENT-TECHNICAL SERVICES, JEFFREY C. CRIPPEN, VICE PRESIDENT-FINANCE, AND JACK SCOTT MCINTEER, GENERAL COUNSEL.

...mpany's more unusual contracts ...ludes flying tons of sushimi ...sh tuna) each day from South ...ific islands to Japan where it is ...d on the open market.

...or the mail and parcel charters, ...company operates a fleet of 35 ...ed aircraft—primarily Boeing ...'s and McDonnell Douglas DC- ...Ryan International maintains ...es for aircraft in over 35 cities. ...il and parcels are picked up at ...ous locations and then flown to ...ery's hub in Dayton and to ...U.S. Postal Service hub in ...ianapolis for transfer to their ...l destinations.

...Ryan International's perform- ...e record is legendary in the ...ustry. Phenomenally, it boasts ...er than 99 percent on-time serv- ...annually. For example, the com- ...y's on-time record for Emery ...rldwide, for which it has flown ...e 1979, has been unparalleled ...he history of Emery's opera- ...s. "If our goal is not 100 per- ...t on time, then why are we ...ng?" is a popular challenge from ...Ryan.

...uch performance and commit- ...t to excellence have won Ryan ...ernational numerous contracts ...repeat business. In 1993 the ...Postal Service, through an ...ery subcontract, awarded Ryan ...)-year extension on its govern- ...t contract. "A long-term con-

tract like this gives us a major boost," says Ryan. In that same year, the company purchased the former Air Midwest headquarters building on West Kellogg in Wichita to expand its corporate headquarters. The Postal Service contract will increase the Ryan staff to nearly 600 employees, and approximately 170 of them are currently based in Wichita.

HELPING OUT OTHERS IN THE BUSINESS

Other aspects of the Ryan compa-nies involve passenger flight serv-ices, charter service consultation, and subcontracting. Recently, Ryan International began operating regu-larly scheduled flights for several U.S. tour operators, ferrying passen-gers to tourist destinations through-out the United States and the world.

While Ron Ryan has continued to expand his own successful busi-ness ventures, as a reflection of his service-oriented philosophy, he has been instrumental in helping other charter services get their fleets off the ground. "Several customers— tour operators and travel agents— have asked us to help them start charter services of their own, and we've always been willing to do so," says Ryan. Recently, he helped launch Morris Air, a Salt Lake City-based carrier that flys passengers to

West Coast destinations. "The only way to succeed financially," adds Ryan, "is through efficiently provid-ing a necessary and needed service to others."

During the start-up process, Ryan International offers personnel and procedural support while the fledgling carrier goes through the required steps to earn its Federal Air Carrier Certificate. Once the airline is certified, Ryan Interna-tional frequently continues to work as a subcontractor for the new carrier.

"We don't look at these start-ups

RYAN INTERNATIONAL PROVIDES CARGO AND PASSENGER FLIGHT SERVICES WORLDWIDE FOR THE U.S. POSTAL SERVICE, EMERY WORLDWIDE, AIR LINGUS, APPLE VACATIONS, AND MANY OTHERS.

as helping to create competition. Rather, we view them as assisting our best customers," says Ryan. "Life is very short, and we get nothing more out of it than we put into it. If we can give other airlines a start in the business, so much the better."

THE CAN-DO SPIRIT OF RYAN

The diversity of Ryan's operations—from transporting fresh fish to repairing multimillion-dollar jet engines—exemplifies the true spirit of Ron Ryan. In his view, opportunities are not merely there for the taking—they are situations waiting to be created. "Make your own luck" is another of Ryan's favorite adages.

"Ronald does things that others claim cannot be done," says his wife, Renae, who serves as executive vice president of Ryan Aviation Corporation. "But that's just the way he is. We call it the 'can-do' spirit of Ryan."

As an example of getting the job done and "flying the extra miles," Ron recently received a frantic call late in the afternoon from a customer in Washington state. He desperately needed a part for his grounded plane. Ron chose to secure the part and personally fly it out that same evening. The Ryan philosophy is always to fly above and beyond the expected in order to be of assistance to others.

That spirit permeates the entire organization. It is the key to the company's on-time performance

record, and it has helped the company achieve certain Federal Aviation Administration certification requirements in record time. For instance, the FAA Part 121 certification, which allows carriers to transport freight, normally takes a year to attain. Ryan Aviation did it in just 60 days—an achievement that led to additional contracts from Emery.

"No company can be any better than the people who work for it," says Ron Ryan. "We couldn't achieve and sustain the records we do without the outstanding, consistent commitment of our employees."

A man who speaks openly about his faith in God and Christian principles, Ryan is matter-of-fact about how his faith influences his life and business. "Whether you want to

call it Christianity or simply the values of honesty, integrity, and love for your fellow person," he says, "these are the things that should be part of every business practice because they just make good sense."

Ryan adds, "I grew up in Iowa where a strong work ethic natural became a part of my values." As of seven children in a family whe

money was very scarce, he began working at age 10. He juggled a variety of jobs from newspaper c rier to short-order cook. With a natural aptitude for mechanics a engineering, he entered apprenti ship programs in high school and eventually landed a job at Wester Electric in Kansas City.

"I was promoted to a position the engineering department, wit the stipulation that I'd earn an e

THE FLAGSHIP OF RYAN'S OPERATIONS AT MID-CONTINENT AIRPORT IS THE SUCCESSFUL FIXED BASE OPERATION — A TOUCH-DOWN POINT WHERE PILOTS CAN OBTAIN FUEL, MAINTENANCE, CLEANING, HANGAR SERVICES, AND CATERING FOR THEIR AIRCRAFT.

ering degree. I went to night ool for a couple of years, but I In't like it much. What I really nted to do was to learn how to ," he recalls.

While in Kansas City, Ryan met WA pilot who convinced him follow his love for flying. And, in e can-do spirit, Ryan achieved private, commercial, multi- gine, and instrument ratings in short months. Although he was t hired by TWA, he managed to d a civilian pilot's position at rt Leonard Wood. Later, Ryan ved on to a distributorship for arjet where he flew charters, gave ing lessons, and served as a co- ot for Learjet flights. Eventually, s led to his association with Jack Boer.

"I'm a pilot and type-rated with Boeing 727, as well as the Lears d the Cessna Citations," says an, who has more than 20,000 ght hours to his credit. "There's old saying that once you get rosene in your blood, you don't nt to do anything else."

For a brief period in the mid- 80s, Ryan did, in fact, pursue

other interests when he sold the FBO and the airline to a Maryland- based company for $16.8 million. For two years, he stayed out of the industry as a condition of the sale, but the "kerosene in his veins" fueled the spirit of aviation, keep- ing it alive in his heart.

When officials at the Maryland company decided in 1988 to divest the organization of its aviation- related business, Ron Ryan pur- chased the FBO for less than $500,000. He also bought the Ryan International portion of the business. This company was on the brink of disaster because the Maryland-based owner had lost all of its contracts.

"Over the years, I have been will- ing to take many steps backward in order to move ahead," says Ryan. "There have been times when I have risked a lot of security to fol- low my dreams in aviation. I'd still rather be up front flying than doing anything else."

Adds Ryan, "There have been a lot of entrepreneurial start-ups in Wichita, and for me to be in the aviation business here along with

Beech, Cessna, Lear, and Boeing has been a real pleasure. Ryan Avia- tion and Ryan International have the best team of professionals in the air charter business. We are commit- ted to Wichita even though the ma- jority of our business is elsewhere. This is our home, and this is where we intend to stay."

With that spirit, it is not surpris- ing to find so many who have made their choice—they're "flyin' Ryan!"

RON RYAN AND HIS WIFE, RENAE, RECENTLY TRAVELED TO THE HOLY LAND. MS. RYAN SERVES AS EXECUTIVE VICE PRESIDENT OF RYAN AVIATION CORPORATION.

MetLife - Wichita Information Systems Center

AT SPEEDS FASTER THAN THE BLINK OF AN EYE, MetLife's Wichita Information Systems Center processes more than 3 million transactions daily for policyholders and benefit recipients worldwide. The 86,000-square-foot Wichita complex is one of four regional data centers in the country supporting the $150-billion-plus mutual company. It handles data transactions for all MetLife field offices involving the company's insurance and financial services lines.

METLIFE'S WICHITA INFORMATION SYSTEMS CENTER PROCESSES MORE THAN 3 MILLION TRANSACTIONS DAILY FOR POLICYHOLDERS AND BENEFIT RECIPIENTS WORLDWIDE.

THE 86,000-SQUARE-FOOT WICHITA COMPLEX HANDLES DATA TRANSACTIONS FOR ALL METLIFE FIELD OFFICES INVOLVING THE COMPANY'S INSURANCE AND FINANCIAL SERVICES LINES.

364 days a year—closing only on Christmas. It is one of the largest data processing facilities in the state and enjoys almost zero turnover among its 200 employees. In fact,

QUIGG PHOTOGRAPHIC

PEOPLE MAKE THE DIFFERENCE
From its tornado-resistant building with 12-inch-thick concrete walls, MetLife operates 24 hours a day,

the Wichita office currently boasts close to 100 "veteran" employees with 20 or more years of service.

"That experience base allows us to excel and to provide the best possible support to our agents and sales staff in the field," says Cindy Poulson, staff services manager. "People make the difference here. Their caring attitude is brought to work every day, and it shows in the work they do."

Wichita's community spirit and Midwestern work ethic were key factors in MetLife's decision to locate in the city in 1973. When the company elected to disperse its data processing facilities nationwide—in order to provide better security and backup in case of natural disaster—MetLife sought out stable communities, dedicated workers, and areas where academic support provided a consistent pool of talent. That description aptly fit Wichita.

The MetLife management staff say they are very fortunate to have a partnership with the people of Wichita and surrounding areas. They credit that partnership with providing excellent service to MetLife field offices—and the company's 55,000 employees nationwide.

And it's excellent service indeed. More than 90 percent of the time the Wichita facility provides data response to field inquiries in less than one second, whether the call comes from Toledo or Taipei.

FOSTERING COMMUNITY SPIRIT
While the speed and success rate of the Information Systems Center are impressive, they cannot overshadow the personal accomplishments of the men and women of Team Wichita. These dedicated individuals selflessly give their personal time to many efforts throughout the community.

"Our employees are our greatest asset," says Poulson, "not only in terms of what they do for MetLife on the job, but also for what they reinvest in our community."

Employees volunteer time with more than 50 civic, cultural, youth and educational entities within the community, in addition to providing countless hours of service through church groups, athletic organizations, informal support groups, and auxiliary emergency services. Participation in American Red Cross blood drives consistently reaches 100 percent, while annual United Way contributions rank close to 100 percent. In cooperation with the Metropolitan Life Foundation, the Wichita Information Systems Center also provides contributions of goods and services to a variety of community projects to help implement programs, provide educational assistance, and strengthen local services.

"Our employees come not only from Wichita but also from several of the surrounding communities," says Poulson. "As a result, our volunteer efforts reach out to all these area communities."

CONSULTANTS IN LABORATORY MEDICINE, P.A.

ATTRACTING AND RETAINING PHYSICIANS and medical specialists has for years been a struggle for rural Kansas hospitals. Thanks to Consultants in Laboratory Medicine, P.A., a Wichita-based physicians group specializing in laboratory pathology, hospitals and patients in south-central

Kansas can be serviced on-site with the highest standards of laboratory expertise and analysis without the expense and concerns that come with permanent staffing.

The nine pathologists who comprise the group handle much of the laboratory analysis for Wichita's St. Francis Regional Medical Center, the largest hospital in Kansas. Additionally, on any given day, at least two of the pathologists travel outside of Wichita to serve the needs of physicians and patients at other Kansas hospitals, including Newton Medical Center in Newton, Augusta Medical Center in Augusta, and Susan B. Allen Hospital in El Dorado. The group also assists hospitals in Coffeyville and Winfield when their pathology staffs are on vacation.

At each location, the pathologists provide on-site analysis and diagnosis of tissue and blood samples, thus saving patients the time and expense of traveling to a larger medical center for laboratory tests. The group serves more than 20,000 Kansas patients each year, about 35 percent of whom are from outside Wichita.

NATIONAL AND INTERNATIONAL RECOGNITION

Incorporated in 1983 (doing business since 1974) by Dr. Joe J. Lin, medical director of laboratories at St. Francis Regional Medical Center, Consultants in Laboratory Medicine handles all aspects of laboratory medicine, including cytopathology, cytology, hematology, chemistry, microbiology, and bloodbank services. Members of the group are certified in anatomic, clinical, and dermatopathology, as well as hematopathology and cytopathology.

The group has been recognized twice nationally by the American Society of Clinical Pathologists (ASCP) for its technical excellence in electron microscopy (work done by Deborah Travis), a state-of-the-art technique using electron beams, rather than light, to bombard the specimen and detail the image. The electron microscope used by Consultants in Laboratory Medicine can enhance an image up to 250,000 times. "We were particularly honored since it is highly unusual for a pathology group in a city the size of Wichita to receive such an award not only once, but twice," says Dr. Lin. The group garnered ASCP's first-place honor in 1990 and its second-place honor in 1993.

Dr. Lin is internationally recognized for his expertise in the field of pathology. He has written 28 papers and contributed to six books on various aspects of pathology, and participates in numerous medical research projects at the Wichita branch of the University of Kansas School of Medicine, where he chairs the pathology department.

He and Dr. Tom Harvey were among a handful of pathologists to have the once-in-a-lifetime opportunity to study the brain of Albert Einstein. "We were able to demonstrate that there was no morphological difference between the brain of Einstein and that of the ordinary person. That led us to postulate that it is the chemical reaction—or electrical impulses of the brain—which created his great thinking," says Lin, who occasionally is called by reporters across the country to discuss the topic.

DR. JOE J. LIN, PRESIDENT, INCORPORATED CONSULTANTS IN LABORATORY MEDICINE IN 1983, NINE YEARS AFTER THE GROUP BEGAN OPERATION IN WICHITA.

THORN AMERICAS, INC.

THE RENT-A-CENTER STORY IS A COLORful thread in the rich tapestry of Wichita's entrepreneurial history. That story began in 1973 when Tom Devlin and Frank Barton joined forces to open their first rental-purchase store in Kansas City, Missouri. It was a modest beginning in the fledgling rental-purchase industry, with Devlin and his wife, Myra, setting up the small operation, and Barton providing financial backing and advice.

Devlin, then only 26 years old but with years of rental operations experience, had a clear game plan to create a new kind of rental-purchase store: It would serve a much-expanded customer base. It would feature name-brand merchandise. It would be the first to offer appliances, and then furniture, when others still only offered the traditional fare of TVs and stereos. It would place great emphasis on employee care and customer satisfaction. And, with a little luck, it would one day reach what the partners thought was an admirable goal: a company size of 10 stores.

It didn't take many years before the partners began revising their goal upward . . . and upward . . . and upward. By 1987 Rent-A-Center had grown to 270 company-owned stores and 165 franchise stores in the United States.

In that year, Devlin and Barton decided to pursue other interests and sold the company to THORN EMI plc, a London-based multi-national conglomerate. Before departing, however, Devlin put in place a dynamic management team headed by Walter E. "Bud" Gates, who has led Rent-A-Center through a continued explosion of store expansion and business growth.

AN INDUSTRY LEADER
Since the 1987 acquisition by THORN EMI, Rent-A-Center has evolved from a single business into a multifaceted corporation. In recognition of its expanded structure, the company took the name THORN Americas, Inc. in 1993. Currently, its corporate entities include Rent-A-Center in the United States (1,108 company and franchise stores); Rent-A-Centre Canada (nine stores); Houston, Texas-based Remco America, Inc. (112 stores); and THORN Services International, the company's logistics and service organization with a 300-vehicle fleet, nine distribution centers, and 70 product service centers. Alaska is the only state that does not have a Rent-A-Center or Remco store.

THORN Americas employs more than 7,000 people in its system, including 500 staff members at its headquarters in northeast Wichita. Currently, there are six Rent-A-Center stores in Wichita.

It is estimated that as a whole, THORN Americas represents a 2[?] percent share of the $2.8-billion rental-purchase industry. Parent company THORN EMI is truly a[?] global presence, with its rental group employing 20,000 people i[?] 2,500 stores worldwide.

As the foundation on which THORN Americas was built, Rent-A-Center isn't content simp[?]

SINCE 1987 CHAIRMAN AND CEO WALTER E. "BUD" GATES (ABOVE) HAS LED RENT-A-CENTER THROUGH A CONTINUED EXPLOSION OF STORE EXPANSION AND BUSINESS GROWTH.

THORN AMERICAS EMPLOYS 500 STAFF MEMBERS AT ITS CORPORATE HEADQUARTERS IN NORTHEAST WICHITA (RIGHT).

MORE THAN 1,100 RENT-A-CENTER
STORES IN THE UNITED STATES SERVE
A BROAD RENTAL-PURCHASE MARKET
WITH ELECTRONICS, FURNITURE,
HOME APPLIANCES, AND FINE JEWELRY.

...e "the biggest" in the rental-
...chase industry. It also is known
...the careful attention paid to
...tomers and employees alike,
...h respect as the centerpiece of
...fforts. Ask Rent-A-Center
...loyees what R.E.S.P.E.C.T.
...ans, and they'll explain that the
...nym expresses the company's
...rating philosophy: Responsive,
...pathy, Service orientation,
...mises kept, Environment,
...tomer care, and Trust.

...VING A BROAD MARKET

...porate strategy has Rent-A-
...ter and Remco stores posi-
...ed to serve the broadest
...sible range of rental-purchase
...omers.

...In the past, the rental-purchase
...ustry primarily targeted low-
...ome markets," says THORN

Americas Chairman and CEO
Gates. "We expanded the market
because we realized rental-purchase
is practical for virtually any consumer, and particularly people
whose lives are in transition. That
includes people who are relocating
for a job, marrying or divorcing, or
who are in a temporary situation
such as a job loss or a short-term
job assignment away from home.
That is why you'll find our stores in
so many different locations, serving
a variety of people and a variety of
needs."

Adds Gates, "Electronics and furniture have been our mainstays, but
we added home appliances several
years ago and recently moved into
fine jewelry. Both product lines
have been very successful and have
allowed us to stretch our imagination to see what is possible in the

rental-purchase mix."

As well as being innovative,
THORN Americas is actively
involved as an industry leader
through the Association of Progressive Rental Organizations (APRO),
the industry's national trade association. In particular, the company
has worked through APRO for ben-
eficial consumer laws, and 36 states
currently have rental-purchase
legislation in place.

As a corporate neighbor in hundreds of communities, THORN
Americas supports a host of charities and special events. In Wichita,
the company is a major supporter
of the United Way, Special Olympics, Red Cross blood drives,
Wichita Music Theatre, and the
Wichita River Festival. Throughout the country, Rent-A-Center
and Remco stores have contributed
or lent products to community and
youth groups, disaster victims,
homeless shelters, and crisis centers.

As corporate steward, Gates says
he never lets the company's vision
waver from quality, whether the
subject is products, service, or people: "Our goal is to build on a great
foundation and become a truly
world-class organization. That
doesn't just mean how well we operate, but how satisfied we make both
our customers and our employees."

CANCER CENTER OF KANSAS, P.A.

AS THE NATION'S WAR ON CANCER GOES ON relentlessly, Kansans who suffer from the disease have access to the finest in state-of-the-art treatment and the newest investigative techniques at the Cancer Center of Kansas. Headed by Dr. Harry Hynes, president and founder, the center is one of the state's largest hematology/oncology group practices and a major participant in regional cancer research cooperatives sponsored and financed by the National Cancer Institute.

The group, comprised of five nationally recognized cancer specialists and researchers, plays an important role in the Wichita Community Clinical Oncology Program (W-CCOP) for which Dr. Hynes is the principal investigator. W-CCOP is a citywide effort with over 50 participating investigators linked to major research centers across the nation. No longer is it necessary for patients to travel long distances for treatment at other cancer centers. Member institutions include St. Francis Regional Medical Center, St. Joseph Medical Center, HCA Wesley Medical Center, and the University of Kansas School of Medicine-Wichita.

Regarded as one of the best programs of its kind in the country, W-CCOP is affiliated with Southwest Oncology Group, one of the nation's largest cooperative research groups. Through this affiliation, W-CCOP members participate in clinical research programs approved by the National Cancer Institute, bringing the newest cancer treatments to patients throughout Kansas. Other W-CCOP affiliations include M.D. Anderson Cancer Center in Houston, Texas, the University of Rochester Cancer Center in Rochester, New York, and the National Surgical Adjuvant Breast and Bowel Project in Pittsburgh, Pennsylvania.

In recent years, the Wichita program has placed hundreds of patients on cancer treatment and cancer control protocols. In 1992 W-CCOP was selected as a clinical center for a National Cancer Institute breast cancer prevention trial and as a center for a national prostate cancer prevention trial.

THOROUGH TREATMENT WITHOUT HOSPITALIZATION

The center's main clinic is located at 818 N. Emporia in Wichita. Satellite offices in Winfield, Arkansas City, Marion, Salina, Chanute, and Dodge City are staffed with highly trained health care professionals, and a physician travels once a week from Wichita to each clinic.

Patients undergo thorough examinations and can receive outpatient treatment at Cancer Center offices, thus increasing convenience and reducing costs. In Wichita, for example, patients can receive complete blood workups, X-rays, and chemotherapy treatment without ever stepping into a hospital. Treatment is provided by highly qualified staff trained in oncology.

But the physical aspects of disease are only part of what the Cancer Center addresses for its patients

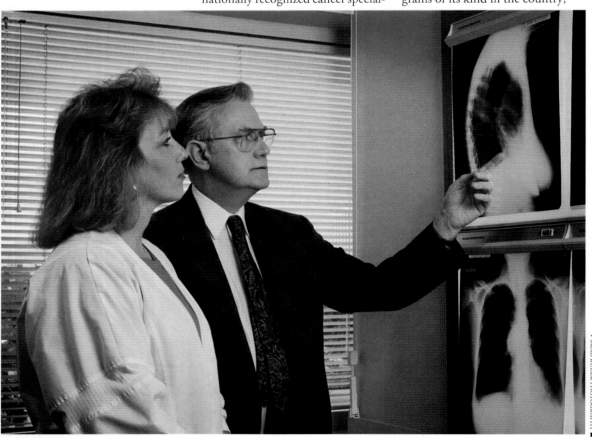

THE TEAM APPROACH IS A VITAL PART OF PATIENT CARE. H.E. HYNES, M.D., DISCUSSES A TREATMENT PLAN WITH A MEMBER OF THE NURSING STAFF (ABOVE).

THE CANCER CENTER OF KANSAS BRINGS THE LATEST ADVANCES AND TREATMENTS TO THE PATIENTS IT SERVES (RIGHT).

and their families. The center provides the services of social workers and works directly with support groups, such as the Leukemia Society of America, the American Cancer Society, Victory in the Valley, and Hospice of Wichita. "We try

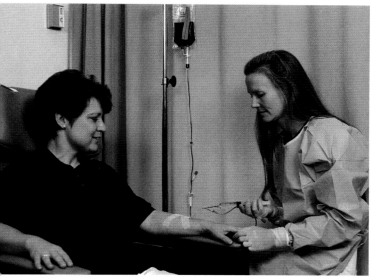

er the latest in scientific care
ile providing strong emotional
port to our patients and their
ilies," says Dr. Hynes, adding
t it's all part of the center's
sion statement: Dedicated to
ality Care.

PTH OF EDUCATION AND PERIENCE

Hynes, a native of Ireland and
ctor of medical education at St.
ncis from 1972 to 1975, estab-
ed the center as the Wichita
matology Oncology Group in
75. Its name was changed in
86 to Cancer Center of Kansas.
Dr. Hynes received his medical
ree in 1958 from the National
iversity of Ireland, Dublin. He
erned at St. Francis and did his
dency and fellowship work in
matology/oncology at the Mayo
nic. Today, he is also medical
ctor of the St. Francis Cancer
iter and a professor of medicine
he University of Kansas School
Medicine-Wichita.

n 1981 **Dr. Shaker Dakhil**, a
ive of Lebanon, became the
up's newest specialist. He served
internal medicine residency at
yne State University in Detroit,
chigan, completed a fellowship
ematology/oncology at the
iversity of Michigan, and today
es as the group's vice president.
Dr. Michael Cannon, a Wichita
ive, completed oncology fellow-
os at M.D. Anderson and the

University of Kansas School of
Medicine in Kansas City, and prac-
ticed in Wichita for four years prior
to joining the group in 1986.
He also received degrees from the
University of Kansas School of
Medicine-Wichita and Wichita
State University.

Dr. David Johnson joined the
group in 1989. A Wyoming native,
he is a graduate of the University of
Colorado School of Medicine. Dr.
Johnson completed his internship,
residency, and fellowship in hema-
tology/oncology at the U.S. Air
Force Medical Center, San Antonio,
and served a visiting fellowship at
the Bone Marrow Transplant Unit
at Fred Hutchinson Cancer Center
in Seattle, Washington. In 1990
Dr. Johnson established the Bone
Marrow Transplant Program at St.
Francis—the first non-university
hospital to receive approval by the
Southwest Oncology Group for
participation in bone marrow
transplant research.

Dr. Dennis Moore Jr. joined
the group in 1994. A graduate of
the University of Kansas School of
Medicine in Wichita, he completed
his internal medicine residency at
Baylor College of Medicine. He
served a fellowship in oncology and
hematology at M.D. Anderson Cancer Center in Houston, Texas, with
special expertise in bone marrow
transplantation.

The five physicians are also on
the staffs of St. Francis, St. Joseph,

and HCA Wesley medical centers.
One is a consultant at Riverside
Hospital, and all are on the University of Kansas School of Medicine
faculty.

With decades of combined experience, impressive credentials, and
an unwavering dedication to quality care, the physicians of Cancer
Center of Kansas will continue to
offer the latest advances in cancer
treatment to patients in Wichita
and throughout Kansas.

PATIENTS CAN REMAIN ACTIVE AND
PROCEED WITH THEIR NORMAL DAILY
ACTIVITIES THROUGH INDIVIDUALIZED
TREATMENT PLANS (ABOVE).

THE CENTER'S HIGHLY TRAINED AND
CARING STAFF OFFER TREATMENT ON
AN OUTPATIENT BASIS (ABOVE LEFT).

LATOUR MANAGEMENT, INC.

WICHITA'S LATOUR MANAGEMENT, INC. is something of a dining oasis for Wichitans and visitors looking for a comfortably familiar menu with a soupçon of sophistication. Its numerous food service operations feature a timeless, casual ambience and moderate prices.

Menus offer everything from wood-roasted chicken with lemon, fresh tarragon, and chili oil to fusilli carbonara—fusilli pasta in a light cream sauce with bacon, mushrooms, and peas.

Antoine Toubia and Randy Adamy are behind every recipe in this food management company that also offers catering, contract food service, vending, and restaurant consulting. Through its full-service and specialty operations, Latour's 600 employees feed 25,000 people every week in Wichita.

Toubia opened his first restaurant, The Olive Tree, in a small strip shopping center in 1979. Despite an understated exterior, the restaurant energized Wichita's palate with a menu of intensely flavored dishes prepared in classic styles. "We never try to follow trends," says Toubia, "but we do stay current, creating dishes that are both familiar and innovative with the finest available ingredients."

A PASSION FOR PERFECTION

Randy Adamy, who has served as the company's president since 1989, says Antoine's obsession for his work doesn't stop at the kitchen. "Antoine is passionate about perfection: the atmosphere, the service, every dish coming from the kitchen, and value," he says. "And he's equally concerned that what Latour offers at each operation has the same quality as our restaurants."

The company's food service operations consist of employee cafeterias at Koch Industries and Cessna Aircraft Company, the stu-

ANTOINE TOUBIA (BACK) AND RANDY ADAMY ARE BEHIND EVERY RECIPE AT LATOUR MANAGEMENT. IN ADDITION TO OPERATING SEVERAL RESTAURANTS, THE COMPANY OFFERS CATERING, CONTRACT FOOD SERVICE, VENDING, AND RESTAURANT CONSULTING.

SINCE IT FIRST OPENED IN 1979, THE OLIVE TREE (RIGHT) HAS ENERGIZED WICHITA'S PALATE WITH A MENU OF INTENSELY FLAVORED DISHES PREPARED IN CLASSIC STYLES.

dent cafeteria at Wichita Collegiate primary and secondary school, and food courts at HCA Wesley Medical Center and St. Francis Regional Medical Center. Hot meals are served, but employees, students, or visitors are as likely to find a morning-fresh smoked turkey sandwich on a croissant in a nearby vending machine operated by Latour.

The firm's catering service can prepare box lunches and serve private dinner parties. Latour can even handle gatherings of up to 2,000 people, as it did when Cessna Aircraft Company hosted an event for owners and operators of Cessna Citation jets. Banquet service for up to 500 is also available in several Latour facilities. The company has even catered internationally at the Paris Air Show.

A separate bakery, Bagatelle, provides fresh-baked breads and desserts for all Latour operations and for restaurants throughout the area. Open to the public with a small deli for breakfast and lunch, Bagatelle offers freshly baked pastries, fresh fruit, and rich coffee for the early riser. Lunch includes a variety of quiches, empanadas, and sandwiches on homemade breads.

"Each of our restaurant menus avoids what we call the 'veto factor,'" says Toubia. "We make sure there is something on every menu for every taste. We believe each meal should be enjoyable, so we take great pleasure in being a part of every guest's day."

CASCO PLASTICS, INC.

FRED SCHILLER IS A STICKLER FOR DETAILS, which is an advantageous way to be for the head of a business that manufactures precision parts. "I once calculated the cost of losing one-half second's production time for each of our 110 machines per day over the course of a year. It came to $750,000," says

Schiller, chairman and CEO of Casco Plastics, Inc.

He adds that the company is committed to producing precision plastic parts right the first time—a goal requiring as much art as science. "We were recently honored by The Coleman Company for having defects in only two-tenths of one percent of all the product we delivered for them in one year," says Schiller. "Our employees make that kind of quality every day."

Producing quality every day builds customer loyalty and new business. In addition to manufacturing plastic shells for Coleman's well-known coolers, Casco does work for NCR, which makes computer systems, Vornado fans, Rubbermaid, and a number of other manufacturers that require molded plastic parts. Casco also serves customers throughout the country and around the world.

BUSINESS LAUNCHED IN 1979
Fred Schiller had spent 10 years learning the craft of tool-and-die making in his native country of Austria before immigrating to the United States in 1965. Finding his way to St. Louis, he landed a job as tool-and-die maker for Sherwood Medical Corporation. Within 10 years he was in charge of opening new Sherwood plants worldwide. Schiller moved to Wichita in 1979 to help establish Casco. The 3,000-square-foot plant, located adjacent to CAC Tool Corporation (Schiller's business partner then), opened two days after his arrival. Casco's business grew steadily: A second plant was opened in Win-

field, Kansas, in 1984, and in 1992 a third production facility was added in New Braunfels, Texas. The company today has more than 275,000 square feet of production space and employs 450 people at the three facilities, including 250 at the Wichita plant.

As production capacity increased, so did Casco's commitment to providing expanded engineering support. Today the company's engineering department provides a wide range of customer services, including preliminary design, material selection, mold design and evaluation, computer-aided design (CAD), and electronic communication with customers' computers.

"We sell more now in three days than we did in our first year of production," Schiller says. "Many of our customers used to be in manufacturing, sales, and marketing, but they discovered they were so much better in sales that it was more efficient to find companies like Casco that could handle prod-

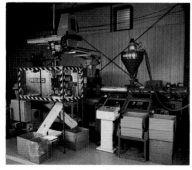

uct manufacturing."

While Schiller is justly proud of how quickly his company has grown to be a key partner with so many customers, he is equally

CASCO MANUFACTURES PRECISION PLASTIC PARTS (ABOVE) FOR NUMEROUS CUSTOMERS, INCLUDING WICHITA-BASED COLEMAN COMPANY.

THE COMPANY RELIES ON STATE-OF-THE-ART EQUIPMENT AND A WICHITA WORK FORCE OF 250 EMPLOYEES TO MAINTAIN A HIGH LEVEL OF QUALITY AND EFFICIENCY (LEFT AND BELOW LEFT).

proud of how employees have adopted the company's "customer first" philosophy. "We spend around $200,000 annually to train employees," he says. "They understand how important they are to the company."

Since its founding over a decade ago, Casco has thrived under stable and strong leadership and by eagerly responding to customers' needs. The company looks forward to continued steady growth and to working with a growing number of satisfied customers around the world.

MULTIMEDIA CABLEVISON, INC.

FROM ITS HEADQUARTERS IN WICHITA'S historic Union Station railroad depot, Multimedia Cablevision, Inc. serves more than 412,000 cable television subscribers in five states and provides residential and commercial security monitoring to customers nationwide.

How the once exclusively rural Kansas and Oklahoma cable enterprise grew to be the flagship cable company for one of the nation's top media organizations is an example of savvy foresight by a homegrown broadcaster.

In addition to cable television services, Multimedia in Wichita provides residential and commercial security monitoring to customers nationwide.

Multimedia Cablevision is headquartered in the historic Union Station railroad depot (right).

In the late 1960s Don Sbarra, then president and chief executive officer of Kansas State Network, a diversified broadcasting company based in Wichita, began developing cable systems in rural areas that the station's broadcast signals couldn't reach. The cable company thus formed was owned jointly by Kansas State Network and a small group of investors. It began serving Wichita in 1978 as Air Capital Cablevision under a franchise agreement from the city.

In 1980 Air Capital was purchased by Multimedia, Inc., a Greenville, South Carolina-based media communications company, and was renamed Multimedia Cablevision, Inc. One of the nation's premier media groups, Multimedia, Inc. has other operating divisions that include newspaper publishing, television and radio broadcast properties, and an entertainment division that produces nationally syndicated television talk shows such as "Donahue," "Sally Jesse Raphael," and "Rush Limbaugh."

ACQUISITIONS AND NEW APPLICATIONS OF TECHNOLOGY

Every year since its purchase, Multimedia Cablevision has grown steadily and is now the 30th largest cable company in the United States, with 450 Wichita employees and 1,100 in the entire division.

"In 1980 we were a $9-million company with $1 million in operating earnings," says Mike Burrus, Cablevision president and a Wichita native. "Today, with subscriber and pay-per-view revenue, advertising revenue, and our security services, our annual revenue is

$155 million, and we generate $53 million in operating earnings."

Multimedia Cablevision's growth has expanded its cable television operations into Illinois, Indiana, and North Carolina. Taking advantage of the fact that hard-

wire cablevision technology also can be used for security monitoring, the company entered that fie[l] in 1982. Multimedia's growth in security monitoring, as in cable, h[as] been steady.

"All of our security monitoring and management activities are based in Wichita," says Burrus. "I[t's] an early example of cable's interactive potential. We've opened security offices in Oklahoma City, Dallas, Miami, Chicago, and Houston, among other cities, and [we] have the capability to handle 500,000 customers."

Community support and involve[ment are top priorities of Multimedia Cablevision in Wichita, as well as in its other markets. For example, Multimedia's annual ProAm golf tournament benefiti[ng] the local chapter of the American Diabetes Association has raised more than $300,000, and the com[pany donates more than $1 milli[on] a year in free broadcast time to lo[cal] nonprofit organizations. The Wichita State University's Elliott School of Communication has re[ceived a major cash grant from M[ultimedia, while the Midwest Canc[er] Research Association, the Cerebr[al] Palsy Research Foundation, and Heartspring (the world's leading [ed]ucational center for children with severe hearing and speech disor-

ders) have all been recipients of th[e] company's philanthropy.

"We're an integral part of ever[y] community in which we operate," Burrus says. "We feel fortunate th[at] our growth has enabled us to contribute in meaningful ways."

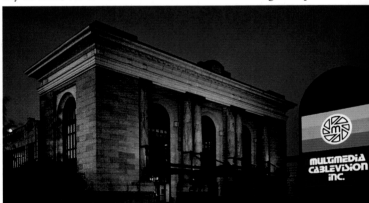

HINKLE, EBERHART & ELKOURI, L.L.C.

NAME JUST ABOUT ANY MAJOR CORPORATE expansion or municipal project in Wichita or south-central Kansas, and you'll find they have one thing in common: Attorneys at Hinkle, Eberhart & Elkouri, L.L.C. helped make the bond financing a reality. "Bond issues are frequently the engine that

drives new growth in a community," says founding member Winton Hinkle. "In issuing bonds, businesses and municipalities are making a major commitment to growth and technology, to the creation of new jobs, and to the health and well-being of our state."

The public and private bond issues handled by Hinkle, Eberhart & Elkouri amount to hundreds of millions of dollars each year. In recent years, the firm has served as bond counsel on issues for St. Francis Regional Medical Center's Diagnostic Center, the Northeast Expressway and Kellogg/U.S. Highway 54 elevated freeway, and plant expansions for both Beech Aircraft Corporation and Cessna Aircraft Company. These projects—and dozens like them across Kansas—account for major improvements in each community's infrastructure and subsequently improve the quality of life for Kansas residents.

The firm was formed in 1987, with attorneys practicing in the areas of tax law and municipal bond financings. While some law firms are diversifying their practices, Hinkle, Eberhart & Elkouri has chosen to continue and expand its business practice. In doing so, it has become one of the state's notable practitioners of municipal bond, business, and commercial law.

GROWING WITH WICHITA

Hinkle, Eberhart & Elkouri has continued to grow, recruiting assertive, dynamic attorneys. In addition to its municipal bond area, the firm practices in the areas of commercial litigation, business, employee benefits, taxation, estate

planning and administration, and real estate. As these areas have expanded and grown more complex, the firm has continued to recruit attorneys to practice in the areas of public administration, environmental law, and civil litigation.

financing and, if necessary, litigation. These clients come to us because of our commercial business knowledge and stay with us because we help their businesses grow."

Wichita's ability to produce talented entrepreneurs and start-up companies has generated some of the most sophisticated business transactions, tax issues, and legal issues in the country.

"Business and legal issues are not always black and white, and it takes courage to make sound judgments," adds founding member Max Eberhart. "In our profession, it's easy to make things difficult. But we emphasize ways to make

THE FIRM'S FOUNDING MEMBERS ARE (FROM LEFT) WINTON M. HINKLE, DAVID S. ELKOURI, AND MAX E. EBERHART.

▶ LARRY FLEMING

"We see ourselves as members of our clients' management teams," says firm member Eric Namee. "A great many of our clients are family-owned businesses and successful entrepreneurs. They look to us for advice and counsel on all areas of their business, including employee benefits, taxation, real estate, public

difficult transactions as easy as possible. The successful completion of a transaction is the name of the game. We're right beside our clients every step of the way, because their success is our success."

PREFERRED HEALTH CARE AND PREFERRED PLUS OF KANSAS

PREFERRED HEALTH CARE, A PREFERRED provider organization (PPO), and Preferred Plus of Kansas, a health maintenance organization (HMO), offer thousands of Kansans quality health care services, coverage, and security with little complexity. ◆ One of the state's largest PPOs today, Preferred

Health Care (PHC) was the state's first such independent managed care plan when it was established in 1984 by a partnership between Wichita's two Catholic medical centers and area physicians. It was formed in response to dramatically rising medical costs and the growing popularity of managed health care programs. The same partnership introduced Preferred Plus

MANAGING COSTS THROUGH PREFERRED HEALTH CARE

Companies such as The Boeing Company, Koch Industries, Pizza Hut, The Coleman Company, and Cessna Aircraft Company count on PHC to control employees' health care costs while providing quality medical care.

PHC is essentially a health provider network, composed of

fered to businesses directly, throug contracting insurance companies, and through third-party administr tors of health benefit plans. The organizations work together with employers to design health insurance plans and structure benefits t meet employers' individual needs. In a PPO plan, individuals pay a greater percentage of the medical costs for services if they are obtained outside the PHC network. The self-funded employer c insurer pays for covered benefits a stipulated in the health benefits plan.

PHC has in place utilization review and quality assurance programs to make certain that partici pating provider services meet quality care standards. All health providers in the network agree to

STATE-OF-THE-ART ADMINISTRATION IS A CRITICAL PART OF MANAGED CARE. KEY MANAGEMENT KEEP ABREAST OF DEVELOPMENTS. FROM LEFT: GREGG DICK, PHC VICE PRESIDENT-FINANCE/CLAIMS/ADMINISTRATION; GARY L. WILLIAMS, PPK EXECUTIVE VICE PRESIDENT AND CHIEF OPERATING OFFICER; MARLON R. DAUNER, PRESIDENT OF PHC AND PPK.

of Kansas (PPK) in January 1992 as an alternative health care program. Through different mechanisms, the two plans provide comprehensive coverage to members, including services provided by individual physicians, hospitals, clinics, pharmacies, and other related health care providers.

1,500 primary and specialty care physicians, 69 hospitals, laboratories, pharmacies, home health care providers, and others across the state that have agreed to highly competitive rates and utilization protocols for their services. PHC's relationship with employers takes several forms; the network is of-

abide by these programs as well as by PHC hospital pre-admission authorization requirements.

"The preferred provider concep allows the individual to choose pr mary care and specialty physician: and other services from a cost-effective network," says Marlon Dauner, PHC president. "Patient

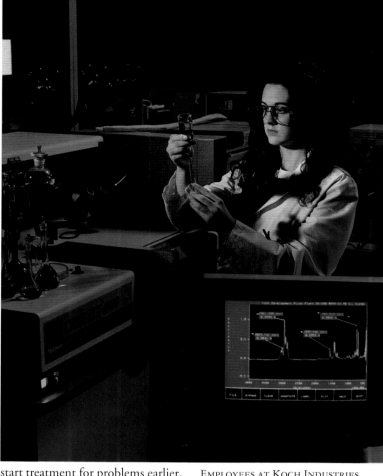

e freedom of choice to a large
ent, but health care quality and
ts are managed. The patient,
ployer, and provider all benefit
en services are obtained within
 PPO network."

The PHC plan, which continues
grow, provides medical services
nore than 160,000 Kansans; it
oday in operation in 75 of the
e's 105 counties through more
n 400 employer groups. In-
ded among its enrollees are
ny employees from both large
 small companies; companies
h as few as two workers can qual-
for a group rate with selected
C contracting insurers. PHC is
 largest managed care plan in
chita.

"Our goal has always been to pro-
e flexibility, maximum coverage,
trolled costs and, above all, un-
npromised care," says Dauner.

EFERRED PLUS OF KANSAS
like its preferred provider
sin, Preferred Plus of Kansas is
 insurer of health benefits sold
ctly to employers as a health
ntenance organization. Enroll-
nt has grown from an initial
00 employees in 1992 to more
n 15,000 employed by more
n 150 businesses in south-
tral Kansas. PPK is marketed

only to companies in state-
approved service areas, which
currently include Sedgwick and
five other counties.

Under an HMO, primary care
physicians manage all facets of
their patients' health care, making
appropriate referrals to specialty
physicians or approving inpatient
or outpatient care at hospitals.
An enrollee in the PPK plan can
choose his or her primary care physician from a list of more than 200
family practice physicians, inter-
nists, and pediatricians. PPK also
contracts with more than 600 physician specialists for referrals.

Out-of-pocket expenses paid by
PPK members are predictable
because flat rates are paid for physician office visits, prescription
drugs, and other services. An
annual premium also is paid.

"Our plan is typically offered to
employers in addition to a preferred provider plan and traditional
indemnity plans," says Gary
Williams, PPK's chief operating
officer. "In contrast to the
more traditional plans, HMO members usually have a broad scope of
benefits and must see their primary
physicians for medical problems.
The goal is not only to prevent
unnecessary visits to specialists or
other health care providers, but to

start treatment for problems earlier,
which, in the long run, is less
costly."

In addition to encouraging members to see their doctors regularly,
PPK places great emphasis on teaching people how to improve their
lifestyles so that some medical
problems may never develop. "One
element of a good HMO is whether
it offers health education," says
Williams. "We have a wide array of
health education materials, including information on diet and nutrition and stopping smoking. We
also offer hearing and vision screen-
ings to employer groups."

Helping doctors work with patients in the managed care environment is another responsibility
PPK gladly undertakes. Beginning
with hospital residency training
programs, PPK offers doctors educational programs on the benefits of
the managed care delivery system
and how best to work within the
system.

Preferred Plus of Kansas and
Preferred Health Care both ensure
quality health care as well as
choice for thousands of Kansans.
Responsive to emerging health care
concerns and issues, the plans
will continue to offer innovative,
cost-efficient, and quality medical
services.

EMPLOYEES AT KOCH INDUSTRIES
(ABOVE) USE THE SERVICES OF PHC TO
OBTAIN THEIR HEALTH CARE.

THE WORLD-FAMOUS COLEMAN
LANTERN IS ONE OF MANY OUTDOOR
PRODUCTS MADE AT THE COLEMAN
COMPANY. COLEMAN'S EMPLOYEES
PARTICIPATE IN A PHC MANAGED
HEALTH CARE PLAN (ABOVE LEFT).

GRENE CORNEA, P.A.

THE OUTDOOR SIGN FOR GRENE CORNEA, P.A., went up in the summer of 1991, but years of training, research, and dedicated patient care preceded the event for Bruce Grene, M.D. ◆ Dr. Grene is an ophthalmologist who specializes in refractive surgery, a form of eye surgery that corrects

vision by changing the shape of the cornea. He performed the first radial keratotomy at Harvard Medical School in 1984, where he received special training in corneal surgery.

A whirlwind of activity surrounds this Kansas native, most noted for his research, teaching, and expertise in the field of refractive eye surgery. Over a span of 10 years, Dr. Grene founded the Wichita Eye Bank and Eye Foundation, pioneered numerous surgical instruments, developed eye medica-

"THE ESSENCE OF OUR WORK IS TO RESPECT NATURE AND TO CARE FOR THOSE WHO TRUST US WITH THEIR HEALTH," SAYS DR. BRUCE GRENE, WHO FOUNDED GRENE CORNEA IN 1991.

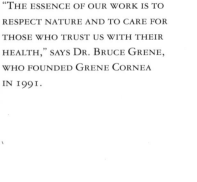

▼ LARRY FLEMING

tions used during and after refractive surgery, and performed over 5,000 refractive surgeries.

As an educator, Dr. Grene has taught refractive surgery to more than 1,500 surgeons in the United States, Japan, Israel, and Europe. In 1991 he founded New Vision Strategies, a company established to train eye surgeons in radial keratotomy.

In the field of research, Dr. Grene's work with dry eye syndrome is widely known. His desire to help dry eye sufferers led to his develop-

ment of Celluvisc,™ an eye medication now manufactured by Allergan Pharmaceuticals. As it turns out, this product helps more than dry eye sufferers: Celluvisc,™ and its cousin, Cellufresh,™ are now commonly used by ophthalmologists and optometrists worldwide to promote healing following eye surgery.

NATIVE SONS
After growing up in LaCrosse and Topeka, Dr. Grene's course of premedical and medical education led him to Lawrence and then Kansas

City, where he graduated from the University of Kansas Medical Center in 1978. Only his fellowship at Harvard Medical School took him outside Kansas to learn from some of the country's finest eye surgeons. Therefore, it is no surprise that Bruce Grene looked to central Kansas to start practicing ophthalmology in 1984.

"Wichita is an important crossroads for people who live in central Kansas. Our presence means that they don't have to travel to Denver, Tulsa, or Kansas City to receive state-of-the-art medical care. My father was a general practitioner, an 'everything-doc,' in western Kansas. So much of medicine has changed since the days when I followed my dad on his hospital rounds. He would be amazed by our technology. Nonetheless, the bigger issues of medicine remain the same. The essence of our work is to respect nature and to care for se who trust us with their lth," says Dr. Grene.

As part of its commitment to vice and accessibility, Grene rnea has provided surgical eye e in numerous Kansas com- nities, including Arkansas y, Winfield, El Dorado, and rden City.

n the summer of 1993 the ene Cornea staff expanded when

rk Wellemeyer, M.D., a native Wichita, joined the team. Like Grene, Dr. Wellemeyer has anced training in corneal and ernal diseases of the eye. He is a come addition to the Wichita dical community: in addition performing cataract surgery, Wellemeyer cares for patients o need corneal transplants and rained to repair some unusual blems that can develop with ucoma and with intraocular s implants.

Grene Cornea also relies on expertise of two doctors of ometry, Cheryl McGuire and bert Moore. Drs. McGuire and ore assist in the post-operative e of corneal transplant, cataract, refractive surgery patients.

"Vision is such a remarkable gift," says Dr. Grene. "The chal- lenge of solving our patients' prob- lems is a complex and rewarding task. Every staff member at Grene Cornea recognizes the special quality of our mission. Our work is much more than a job; it is our purpose."

The team at Grene Cornea treats patients for a variety of ocular prob- lems and conditions and performs refractive, cataract, and intraocular lens surgery.

LOOKING TO THE FUTURE

Early in 1993 Dr. Grene was ap- proved by the Federal Drug Admin- istration (FDA) as a licensed investigator for the use of the ex- cimer laser (investigational device, limited by federal law to investiga- tional use) for correcting vision. The FDA has approved the place- ment of lasers at only 37 centers across the country to test the long- term safety and effectiveness of the procedure.

"In the early 1980s we learned that the excimer laser could etch corneal tissue layer by layer," recalls Dr. Grene. "The first time I experi-

enced excimer laser surgery, I was amazed. I knew I was watching the future unfold right in front of me. Laser technology in eye surgery will help us reach far greater numbers of people."

He adds, "We are very excited to be involved in the study of laser technology. About 10 to 20 percent of patients who are not suited for radial keratotomy are anxiously

THE TEAM AT GRENE CORNEA TREATS PATIENTS FOR A VARIETY OF OCULAR PROBLEMS AND CONDITIONS AND PER- FORMS REFRACTIVE, CATARACT, AND INTRAOCULAR LENS SURGERY.

awaiting this laser technology, which promises to be a more effec- tive treatment for them.

"Working with refractive surgery from the time of its introduction in the United States has been very rewarding. This experience has ena- bled me to do some of the things I enjoy most: teaching and product development. As a result, we've been able to extend our work be- yond Grene Cornea and Wichita. It is incredible that our efforts have had a worldwide impact. It's been particularly rewarding for me to work with this group of doctors and the Team Grene staff. I'm sure the coming years will be just as fun and just as challenging."

TYPED LETTERS CORPORATION

TYPED LETTERS CORPORATION IS ONE of Wichita's "little big" companies. It's relatively small in size and employment, but big in typing, printing, and moving mountains of direct mail letters and collateral documents every day for national and international organizations and universi-

ties. As the biggest consumer of postage in Wichita, the company helps keep the post office very busy.

Founded in 1989, Typed Letters is today the largest company in the United States producing typewritten direct mail packages for clients involved in marketing products and services or raising funds. It averages 50,000 to 150,000 pieces of mail a day and has the know-how and capacity to handle up to 3.5 million pieces a month. Among its clients are American Express, Oracle Corp., Amnesty International, Epilepsy Foundation of America, Habitat for Humanity, Covenant House, the University of Chicago, and Penn State, Emory, Western Kentucky, and Golden Gate universities.

Once clients provide their mailing lists, text, and art, the company types, prints, posts, and mails the

pieces on time. Typed Letters can produce each piece to look like it has been individually written and addressed by utilizing computer-driven typewriters programmed with specially designed software, coordinated electronic pre-press operations, and one-color to six-color presses. Other sophisticated techniques such as identifying gender in the text, custom salutations, and signatures enhance the mailings and increase client response rates often by 30 percent or more.

SPECIALIZING IN PERSONALIZED MAILINGS
"Personalized, quality mailings have been our tradition," says Vice President Randal A. Johnson, who cofounded the company with his wife, President Shirley A. Johnson. "We don't have any direct competitors in our niche."

The company recently began doing non-personalized, mass direct mailings. The move has increased revenues, but more importantly, the owners say, it has given Typed Letters the capability to meet all the direct mail needs of its customers.

"If we take care of our customer needs, they will take care of our needs," says Randal Johnson. "We have a close relationship with our clients. We're very mom-and-pop ish, and people like to work direct with the owners."

The company also manufactur its own envelopes (up to 7 million month), uses mostly recycled pap and vegetable-based inks, and rec cles 15 tons of paper a month.

Though Typed Letters is young it has enjoyed an impressive 25 p cent annual growth rate. Likewise employment has climbed to 57 p ple, most of whom work in produ tion and undergo job training at the company's 22,000-square-foo plant at 7601 West University.

While future growth seems ine table, Randal Johnson says, "We don't want to expand too rapidly take on more business than we ca manage ourselves and assure qual work." But, he adds, a plant expa sion is likely in the near future.

TYPED LETTERS CAN PRODUCE EACH PIECE TO LOOK LIKE IT HAS BEEN INDIVIDUALLY WRITTEN AND ADDRESSED BY UTILIZING COMPUTER-DRIVEN TYPEWRITERS, COORDINATED ELECTRONIC PRE-PRESS OPERATIONS, AND ONE-COLOR TO SIX-COLOR PRESSES.

PHOTOGRAPHERS

VIC BILSON is a photographer and computer network administrator for Douglas Black & White, Inc. A specialist in commercial photography and audio/visual productions, Bilson graduated from and worked as a photographer for Wichita State University. His work has been published in national, regional, and local magazines.

ROBERT BROOKS, a lifelong Wichitan, is employed by the Wichita Public Schools and specializes in black-and-white photography of students.

ALLEN BROWN, a native Wichitan and graduate of Wichita State University, is owner of Allen Brown Photography, specializing in editorial and fashion photography.

WALTER DEPTULA, a Chicago native, has photographed on a free-lance basis since 1988. Major projects have included job-progress photography for clients such as INTEL and IBM. His images have appeared in *Chicago: Second to None* and *Des Moines Visions.* Deptula co-publishes the Chicago Scenes and Events calendar with photographer Jeff Voelz.

DAVID DINELL has pursued a career in photography since his high school days, when he worked on school yearbooks and newspapers. He is currently a photographer and reporter for the *Wichita Business Journal.* Dinell also works free-lance and as a part-time photographer for Wichita State University.

KIRK ECK, a photographer with Douglas Black & White, Inc., attended Wichita State University and the Art Institute of Houston. A specialist in commercial, still-life, studio, and architectural photography, Eck has been published in *Houston* magazine. He was awarded the Best of Show by the Art Institute of Houston and the first and second place in the annual Wichita State University photography show.

LARRY FLEMING is owner of Larry Fleming Photographer, an editorial, corporate, advertising, and portrait photography firm. He is a native of Wichita and a graduate of Wichita State University.

KEVIN C. FOX, a native of Wichita, is owner of Studio 151, commercial and fashion photographers. A graduate of Wichita State University, Fox was named to Outstanding Young Men of America in 1988 and has appeared in Who's Who in the Midwest since 1983. His clients include Pioneer Balloon Company, The Coleman Company, the City of Wichita, and various industry magazines. Fox was the official photographer for the Wichita River Festival in 1993.

JACK L. JACOBS is owner of Jack L. Jacobs Photography, specializing in commercial and advertising photography. His company's clients include Pizza Hut, Cessna Aircraft, Learjet, and The Coleman Company. Originally from Garden City, Kansas, Jacobs graduated from the Brooks Institute in Santa Barbara, California.

TOM JENKINS, a native Wichitan, is employed as a photographer and darkroom technician at Paul Bowen Photography.

RON JONES, an associate of Douglas Black & White, Inc., is employed as a custom color and mural printer. A graduate of the Longstreet Academy of Commercial Art and Photography, Jones also works free-lance, photographing weddings, portraits, and landscapes. His images have been marketed through local arts and crafts shows and at the Crown Center Arts Show in Kansas City.

JIM MARLETT is the assistant director of the Sedgwick County Zoo. A lifelong Wichitan, Marlett specializes in nature images, including numerous photographs of the Amazon jungles of Peru. His work has appeared in zoo publications, flyers, and brochures, as well as in interpretive graphics at the Sedgwick County Zoo.

MADELINE MCCULLOUGH is owner of Madeline McCullough Photography, specializing in black-and-white environmental portraits. A graduate of Wichita State University, McCullough served as staff photographer for *City Life*, assistant editor for *Rural Missouri*, and photographer for KSNW-TV. Her work has been published by the Associated Press and in *The Wichitan*, the *Wichita Eagle-Beacon*, *City Life*, and *Photographer's Forum.*

⋅1 MEYER, a native Wichitan, ⋅mployed by Wichita State ⋅iversity and is owner of Jim ⋅yer Photography, a commercial ⋅tography firm which has ⋅rated in the city for 20 years. ⋅yer produces images for the ⋅eral market, including architec-⋅l and aerial photography. In ⋅course of his career, he has ⋅ived several local Gold and ⋅er Addy awards, and in 1992 ⋅von the Presidents Publication ⋅ard for the University Photog-⋅iers Association of America.

⋅NRY NELSON is co-owner ⋅Nelson & Nelson Creative, ⋅imercial and fine art photogra-⋅rs. A graduate of Wichita State ⋅versity, Nelson worked for 10 ⋅rs with the Wichita Art ⋅seum. His work has been ⋅lished in *Art in America,* ⋅onial Homes,* and various ⋅ndars by Abbeville Press. ⋅son received the United Way ⋅he Plains Outstanding Achieve-⋅it in Photography award in ⋅9. His images have been ⋅ured in a solo exhibit at the ⋅hita Museum of Art and in ⋅ierous group exhibits.

⋅CKY J. NICKEL is an ⋅ciate of Douglas Black & ⋅ite, Inc., and a free-lance ⋅tographer who specializes in ⋅rait, wedding, architectural, ⋅still-life photography. Origi-⋅y from Walton, Kansas, Nickel ⋅graduate of Bethel College in ⋅th Newton, Kansas.

JAMES L. POWELL, originally from St. Louis, Missouri, is employed by the Sedgwick County appraiser's office. A specialist in civic and fine art photography, Powell has exhibited his images in Wichita and Seattle. His photography has also appeared in many government publications and in brochures for Old Cowtown Museum.

RICARDO REITMEYER, originally of Ellis, Kansas, is a staff photographer for St. Joseph Medical Center responsible for photography of medical/surgical procedures, advertising, public relations, portraits, and educa-tional programs. A graduate of Fort Hays State University, Reitmeyer completed several local fine art exhibits in 1989 and was featured in the *Wichita Eagle.* He has received awards in numerous regional and national photography competitions.

LINDA K. ROBINSON is a fine art photographer who specializes in landscapes and nature images. A native Wichitan and graduate of Wichita State Univer-sity, Robinson has exhibited her limited edition photographs at the McFarland Gallery, Clayton Staples Gallery, Watermark Books, Larkspur, Botanica, Impressions of the Mind, Springcreek Gallery, and the Wichita River Festival Art Fair.

JAMES C. SIEBERT is owner of Canyon Film and Video, producers of videos, motion pictures, and still photography. A native Wichitan and a graduate of Wichita State University, Siebert previously was the principal producer of the Air Force One program at Boeing Video Services. He also was a television photojour-nalist for 10 years. Siebert served for two years as the president of Wichita's Old Town Association.

VADA SNIDER teaches photojournalism at Wichita Sate University, where she received a master's degree in communica-tions. She also works as a free-lance photographer, a reporter, and a professional flutist. Her photo-graphs have won several awards, including a national award from the National Newspaper Associa-tion and a regional award from the Society of Professional Journalists.

RIC A. WOLFORD, a professional photographer for more than 20 years, is president of Douglas Black & White, Inc., commercial, advertising, architec-tural, and public relations photog-raphers. His work has appeared in *Time, Adweek, Travelers,* and many corporate brochures and maga-zines. During his career Wolford has received numerous awards from the Wichita Ad Club.

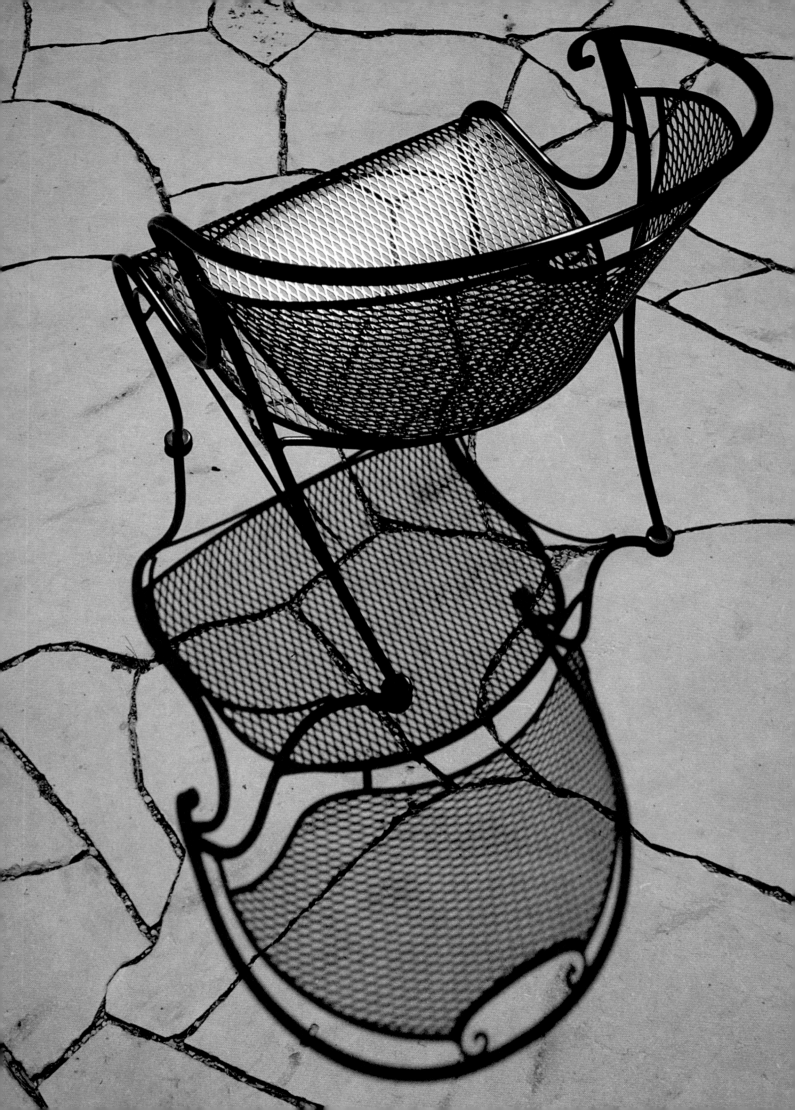

THE GEOMETRY OF WELL-PLANNED
DESIGN IS A TALENT OF MAN AND A
BLESSING OF NATURE.